The New Principal's Fieldbook

Strategies for Success

Pam Robbins • Harvey Alvy

Association for Supervision and Curriculum Development
Alexandria, Virginia USA

Association for Supervision and Curriculum Development
1703 N. Beauregard St. • Alexandria, VA 22311-1714 USA
Telephone: 800-933-2723 or 703-578-9600 • Fax: 703-575-5400
Web site: http://www.ascd.org • E-mail: member@ascd.org

Gene R. Carter, *Executive Director;* Nancy Modrak, *Director of Publishing;*
Julie Houtz, *Director of Book Editing & Production;* Tim Sniffin,
Project Manager; Darcie Russell, *Project Manager;* Shelley Young,
Senior Graphic Designer; Valerie Sprague, *Desktop Publishing Specialist;*
Vivian Coss, *Production Specialist*

Printed in the United States of America. Cover art copyright © 2004 by
ASCD.

ASCD publications present a variety of viewpoints. The views expressed
or implied in this book should not be interpreted as official positions of the
Association.

All Web links in this book are correct as of the publication date below but
may have become inactive or otherwise modified since that time. If you
notice a deactivated or changed link, please e-mail books@ascd.org with the
words "Link Update" in the subject line. In your message, please specify the
Web link, the book title, and the page number on which the link appears.

Paperback ISBN: 0-87120-858-X • ASCD product #103019 • List Price: $29.95
($23.95 ASCD member price, direct from ASCD only)   s4/04
E-books ($29.95): netLibrary ISBN 0-87120-984-5 • ebrary 0-87120-985-3

Library of Congress Cataloging-in-Publication Data
Robbins, Pamela.
   The new principal's fieldbook : strategies for success / Pam Robbins and
Harvey Alvy.
      p. cm.
   Includes bibliographical references and index.
   ISBN 0-87120-858-X (alk. paper) — ISBN 0-87120-984-5 (netLibrary) —
ISBN 0-87120-985-3 (ebrary)
   1. First year school principals—United States—Handbooks, manuals, etc.
2. School management and organization—United States—Handbooks,
manuals, etc. I. Alvy, Harvey B. II. Association for Supervision and
Curriculum Development. III. Title.
   LB2831.93.R63 2004
   371.2'012—dc22
                                                           2003027331

11 10 09 08 07 06 05 04   12 11 10 9 8 7 6 5 4 3 2 1

The New Principal's Fieldbook
—— Strategies for Success ——

Acknowledgments

The New Principal's Fieldbook: Strategies for Success was inspired by the questions, challenges, and triumphs of new, aspiring, and veteran principals from around the world. Their dedication, commitment, and inquiries sent us on a quest to mine the most significant research on leadership and examples of best practice. Together with these resources we combined the sage advice and vivid stories of successful practitioners to create this interactive fieldbook. It is designed as both a guide and a repository for new ideas, inspiration, hopes, and dreams. We are deeply grateful to the many professionals who shared their expertise and friendship and contributed their experiences in the field. We believe their gift of knowledge, seasoned with reality, will allow others who wish to follow in their footsteps to add tools to blaze the leadership path in a relentless pursuit of excellence.

Harvey Alvy is particularly grateful to the school leaders, administrators, teachers, and support staff who have guided his journey as a teacher, elementary and secondary principal, and university professor. Their guidance and sage advice enabled Harvey to weather the storms of his rookie year as a school principal and to define his work as a practitioner and student of the principalship. Ray Cubbage deserves special thanks for his friendship, insights, and manuscript editing. Dan Alvy, Harvey's father, still working at the age of 89, continues to be a role model of tenacity and dedication. Harvey's mother, the late Rebecca Pearl Alvy, inspires us to remember that children come first. Finally, the greatest debt is to Bonnie and Rebecca for their love, support of the journey, and their presence at the finish line, which is always sustaining.

Pam Robbins also would like to thank Ray Cubbage, her husband, for his companionship, support, rich ideas, feedback, and incredible patience as this book became a reality. A special thank you is due to D.D. Dawson for her many hours of word processing, keen insights, and critical eye. Her perspectives enhanced both content and format. The pages of this book are more substantial thanks to the principal stories of Betsy Dunnenberger of Harrisonburg City Schools, Virginia; Mahri Asti of Fairfax County Schools, Virginia; and Virginia Connelly of PS/IS 123 in the Bronx, New York—these principals make a difference daily in the lives of students. Thanks are also due to David Robbins, Pam's dad, for his reflective leadership perspectives as a former principal and central office administrator, and to Pam's mom, Muriel Robbins, who reminded us about the importance of linking heart and mind in order to soar.

We extend our thanks to Anne Meek, an early advisor in this endeavor, and to Shelley Young for her dedication to designing the book cover. Tim Sniffin, Darcie Russell, and Julie Houtz deserve special recognition for countless hours of editorial assistance. Finally, we would like to especially thank Nancy Modrak, a visionary leader in her own right, as well as the ASCD staff for their confidence in us and valuable assistance with the manuscript.

Preface

A Moment Remembered . . .

On my first day of school as a new principal, I arrived early only to discover that the bells, which had been turned off all summer, weren't calibrated. And the custodian was absent! I realized that in all my years of preparation for the principalship, nothing had prepared me for this. Fortunately, the secretary knew how to program the bells. Right away I realized I would have to depend on others, as well as myself.

Despite having read dozens of books on leadership, having spent hundreds of hours in the classroom, and having been selected as the most qualified candidate for the position, often principals find themselves unprepared for the twists and turns on the leadership path. While calibrating bells may not seem a significant piece of content for an administrative class, bells ringing intermittently in the schoolhouse and interrupting precious instructional time can become a significant obstacle in realizing a vision of student learning.

This situation also reminds one of the subtle complexities of the principalship in action. A seemingly managerial task, programming bells, ultimately is intertwined with an instructional leadership responsibility: protecting quality learning time.

Day in and day out the principal faces surprises—some obstacles—and some opportunities. You can never predict each challenge that will occur on the leadership journey. Decisions made on the spot and the strategies employed to solve problems will determine success or failure. Reflective principals come to realize that they do not have all the answers. In the previous scenario, the act of reaching out to tap the talents of others helped foster uninterrupted instructional time for students.

Why This Fieldbook?

The purpose of *The New Principal's Fieldbook: Strategies for Success* is to provide newcomers to the principalship with research-based practical strategies and sage advice from practitioners designed to help them succeed—right from the start. The fieldbook concept is intended to provide a guide for newcomers by offering a comprehensive view of the opportunities and challenges that beginning principals experience. The book will help to assure that principals develop capabilities that will enable them to proactively respond to the day-to-day responsibilities of the principalship and to the surprises that can throw leaders off center. Additionally, a critical concern of the authors is that patterns or habits developed in one's initial years of service tend to influence success in the remaining years of one's career (Parkay & Hall, 1992). Thus, it is vital that new and aspiring principals be provided with clear, concise, and practical information, along with effective strategies to help them become visionary leaders, skilled in promoting the success of students and teachers, facilitating a positive and learning-focused collaborative culture, and building strong home–school–community bonds.

In each chapter the reader will find (1) content based on research and practice, (2) short stories and scenarios about successful practice, (3) activities designed to invite the reader to interact with content through personal application, and (4) a section to record field notes that reflect one's perceptions of the chapter's content and its implications for practice.

An Invitation

The principalship is an adventure. It requires traversing familiar terrain but in a new role. Recently a new principal commented, "I walked into the teachers' workroom and everyone became quiet. This never happened when I was a teacher." Familiar territory has become surprisingly strange. The newcomer continued, "I never realized how *alone* this role can be. I still feel like the same person, 'a teacher.' I still act the same . . . but the reaction of my colleagues is now different. I am no longer one of *them*, but rather I am now the administrator."

Another new administrator spoke of the rapid pace of the work: "I don't know where the time goes—I arrive at work before the sun rises. The next thing I know, I look at the clock and it is 3:30 p.m. Although I've not always completed my to-do list, I'm amazed at all that transpired during the day."

A new principal in an international school wrote: "I *love* my job. Being a school administrator at a school of 992 kids sure keeps me on my toes. It is kind of a paradox: Some days, the spontaneity of the job is the thing I like the most, but on other days it is the source of my frustration. I like the problem solving and interacting with folks, but the small petty stuff gets me down. However, when I walk down the hall and get hugs and 'high fives' it makes it worthwhile."

Surprises, unexpected obstacles, and opportunities characterize the leadership path. As you make the journey, often alone, in a leadership role, you will traverse uncharted territory while simultaneously helping others along the way. There are no detailed maps. As noted earlier, this book provides a much needed field guide, grounded in the practical experiences of successful principals and supported by solid research. This guide offers tips, tools, and tricks of the trade to help newcomers succeed.

Research on learning (Marzano, Pickering, & Pollock, 2001) has identified the use of metaphor as a powerful tool for fostering understanding. The fieldbook metaphor helps to crystallize the complexities of the principalship and provides a vehicle to illuminate opportunities for effective leadership in action.

Critical Themes

Nine critical themes or threads run through the book's 15 chapters. These themes represent a vision of essential concepts linked to the success of principals in the 21st century. The themes include

- *Committing to a belief that keeps all students at the heart of organizational actions.* This commitment means that in decision making, problem solving, and planning the guiding light should be what is best for all students. Maintaining this commitment influences the nature of conversations within the building as well as the daily, routine interactions. The very culture of the schoolhouse should resonate this theme in its celebrations, rituals, values, norms, reward systems, crisis management, and communications. The physical environment portrays the notion that, above all, kids matter.

- *Being a learning leader.* Learning leaders model the pursuit of knowledge regarding effective practice. They strive to learn from experience and mistakes. Asking questions is a way of life and yields information as well as a way of communicating interest. Learning leaders inspire organizational members to create a workplace where risk taking and experimentation are valued. They set a personal example for the organization.

- *Building trust and quality relationships.* There is tremendous power in forging relationships and networks to garner both skills and the motivation to make a difference. In schools where trust prevails and individuals join hands and hearts in pursuit of a vision to make a difference for students, learning soars (Gordon, 2002). Leaders affect change by shaping conversations in their organizations (Sparks, 2002). By engaging in robust conversations with ourselves, colleagues, the community, students, and their families, school outcomes are created to reflect our collective values. In the wake of September 11th, we are reminded forever that in the final analysis, it is relationships that matter.

• *Acting with integrity and in an ethical manner.* A leader who commits to these virtuous principles possesses an unwavering moral commitment to student success, teacher growth, and quality school communities. Ethical behavior must include a commitment to all students regardless of race, religion, gender, and ethnicity. This also entails heralding the value of ethnic diversity and intentionally taking action to assure that regardless of socioeconomic status every child is guaranteed meaningful, challenging learning experiences. This commitment represents a relentless quest to do what is fair—to do the right thing.

• *Developing a vibrant, healthy, learning-centered culture.* Creating such cultures engages the leader in motivating staff and community members to coalesce around a common core of values including a safe, learning-focused environment, high expectations for student success and staff learning, a climate of joyfulness, a recognition of teaching as a calling, norms that encourage and celebrate the deprivatization of practice, and routine that is focused on making a difference for all students.

• *Recognizing the stages of socialization (and surprise) for the newcomer.* Research and experience document the presence of three evolutionary stages that newcomers to an organization encounter. These include the anticipation phase, when you look anxiously at becoming the new principal; the encounter phase, when you enter the organization; and the insider phase, when you become part and parcel of the organization (Louis, 1980; Schein, 1974). Surprises—in all areas of one's encounters—abound. Thankfully, there comes a point in one's career when a newcomer awakens to a feeling of competence and personal satisfaction!

- *Dedicating oneself to being an instructional leader—by choice—not because it's mandated by the job description.* Instructional leaders are governed by an inner commitment to foster teaching and learning for all within and outside the schoolhouse. Despite the temptation to wallow solely in management functions that may offer immediate gratification upon completion, instructional leaders are able to manage bifocally (Deal & Peterson, 1994). That is, they recognize and operate on the belief that leadership and management *can* go hand in hand and that management functions—such as checking on buses—can offer an important leverage point for the instructional leader by building relationships with those who drive and ride those vehicles.

Paramount to all this, instructional leaders must recognize that they are directly accountable for learning and can influence this outcome in the organization through their actions, for example, by visiting classrooms, analyzing data and making data-driven decisions, facilitating job-embedded learning, and championing teacher excellence.

- *Managing as an essential instructional leadership tool.* As noted previously in the instructional leadership theme, one can get completely tied up in management aspects of the principalship. Remember, however, that management tasks support instructional leadership responsibilities. As a principal has noted, "To facilitate learning, the instructional leader also makes sure the classroom lights are working" (Robbins & Alvy, 2003). Managing the master schedule to allow teachers to meet during the school day combines a very important management function (that of building the master schedule) with an important instructional responsibility (that of providing time for teachers to plan).

What is implied here is that management tasks need to be embraced within the context of the broader system. That is, when the leader effectively and efficiently uses management tools, this action frequently has a positive effect on the instructional program. For instance, when a principal personally calls a supplier or textbook company to ensure that essential instructional resources arrive on time, so that teachers and students will have them at the beginning of the school year, the instructional program benefits.

• *Orchestrating school–community partnerships.* Today, schools cannot succeed alone. When a leader formulates partnerships, a vast support network is created involving essential stakeholders, such as parents, the business community, social services, emergency and medical service personnel, and security personnel, senior citizens, and the media. School leaders must systematically reach out to these stakeholders to maxi mize resources to foster student success socially, emotionally, physically, psychologically, and academically. In times of crisis, community personnel and resources are indispensable.

School leaders should also ask: What are we doing for the community? Full-service schools, which give back to the community by providing evening classes, recreational activities, and medical assistance, illustrate one approach that can emerge from a school–community partnership.

Final Thoughts

Collectively, these themes and related sections of the fieldbook mirror key content areas addressed by the recently merged ISLLC/ NCATE Standards for school leaders (Jackson & Kelley, 2002), and provide needed resources to support new leaders as they embark upon and travel the leadership path. With this preview of what is to come, readers are invited to explore the pages and linger with the ideas that resonate for them. Best wishes for success in the journey to make a difference.

1

Vision as the Compass

It was her very first faculty meeting as a principal. Christine knew this first meeting with the staff would be a pivotal one. She decided she must share her vision in a way that would invite the staff to follow so that, as a consequence, daily life in the building would be guided by a shared vision that places serving students well at the heart of the school and every classroom. After welcoming staff members, Christine explained:

> I have a vision that at this school we will create a culture of care. While this is currently my personal vision, I hope it becomes a vision every one of us will come to embrace. I believe that such a shared vision will become a beacon that guides our efforts to make a positive difference in every student's life at this school.
>
> To understand what a culture of care would entail, I'd like us to begin thinking about a time in our own lives when we felt cared for, and I'd like us to share these experiences. I'll take a risk and begin. As a child, I spent a lot of time with my grandmother. She always spoke softly to me, listened carefully, made me laugh, and took time for me. She had raspberry bushes in her yard. Together, we plucked raspberries from the bushes and talked about what we would make with

1

them. She allowed me to eat as many as I wished! To this day, raspberries remind me of what it feels like to be cared for.

Some staff members looked down, some squirmed in their chairs, others looked up and dabbed tears from their eyes, and still others looked around. Silence fell over the group. Christine's heart was pounding. She wondered if anyone would break the silence.

After what seemed like eternity, a senior member of the staff spoke up and shared her experience with care. Taking her lead, others described their memories.

In the days that followed the staff meeting, Christine began to find small, anonymous gifts in her mailbox—a basket of raspberries, raspberry soap, raspberry-scented candles. She thought, with a smile, "Perhaps creating a culture of care is beginning to emerge as a centerpiece of the schoolhouse."

Two weeks later, it was kindergarten orientation. Traditionally, a bus went around the neighborhood, picked up parents and kindergartners, and brought them to school. Prior to this day, one parent contacted the school and spoke to the assistant principal about pick-up times. The assistant principal mistakenly indicated a time later than the actual pick up. Hence, on kindergarten orientation day the parent and child missed the bus, and the mother called the school. The assistant principal took her call and said, "Sorry, we're not a transportation service; you'll have to find another means of transportation." The resourceful parent, angered by what had transpired, contacted the district superintendent. He heard the parent's story and responded empathetically, "Madam, I realize that you've probably looked forward to this day for five years. If you give me your address, I will personally drive you to the orientation."

Unaware that any of this had transpired, Christine spotted the superintendent walking down the hall with parent and child in tow. Interpreting his presence as a special visit to orientation, she approached him and thanked him for coming to the school for this important occasion. He quietly took Christine aside and told her what had transpired, adding, "I have the car seat in my vehicle;

call me when orientation is over, and I'll take them home." Christine responded, "No, give me the car seat, and I'll personally take them home. I want to talk with the mother about what happened. This is not the way we are going to do business around here."

After orientation, Christine invited the mother and child into her office for a chat. She asked the secretary to take her calls so that she could devote undivided attention to the mother and child. She spoke about her vision of a "culture of care" and expressed dismay that the mother's initial experience with the school didn't convey a caring act. She explained that developing a culture of care takes time and would require great commitment on the part of those who serve children at the school. "But," she added, "I believe this vision will become a reality here."

Christine concluded the conversation and walked the mother and child to her car. After everyone was buckled up in their seatbelts, she turned to the mother and said, "I hope you'll give us another chance." The mother nodded and remarked, "I know new ways take time."

The next morning Christine called the assistant principal into her office. Christine told her about the mother's experience on orientation day. And then, she simply asked the assistant, "Is this something that would happen in a culture of care?" The assistant principal looked down and said, "No," and continued, "I need to write that mother a note of apology."

Vision Defined

Webster's New Collegiate Dictionary defines *vision* as "something seen otherwise than by ordinary sight; something beheld as in a dream." A school vision is a descriptive statement of what the school will be like at a specified time in the future. In schools where all organizational members genuinely share a vision, the vision serves as a compass, lending direction to organizational members' behavior. When the vision is the principal's, but is not embraced by organizational members, individuals may go through the motions or act on *shoulds* rather than as a result of deep commitment. At the heart of any vision is a set of core values and beliefs. Principals new to a school sometimes experience a conflict between their own values, beliefs, and vision for the organization and the existing organizational values, beliefs, and vision. These existing beliefs and values are reflected in the culture of the organization or, as some people say, "the way we do things around here" (Peterson & Deal, 2002). These beliefs play out in individuals' patterns of behavior, mental maps, and unwritten rules or norms for behavior. Many new principals describe what it feels like to encounter a culture where values and beliefs do not align with theirs as "being out of alignment." A high school principal shared an example wherein his personal vision was connected with making a difference—cognitively, affectively, socially, and physically—for every student. Student success was at the heart of his vision. He entered a school where patterns of behavior and unwritten rules protected seniority in the organization as a core value. Veteran teachers were assigned advanced placement classes and the best schedules, whereas newcomers were frequently assigned struggling students with learning challenges and less desirable schedules. He reflected, "I knew I had to work hard to remove this misalignment. I knew what I encountered was what I didn't want. But this situation made me aware that I had to come up with a detailed vision of what I wanted if I was to be successful. I had to make this picture so attractive that it would generate followers—so I wouldn't be the only one sharing this vision!"

Multiple Visions

The situation faced by this high school principal points to the notion that there are often multiple *visions* in an organization:

- *A vision of self as a leader* entails one's beliefs about the leadership role, how one should act, things one should and should not do, and one's code of ethics.

- *A personal leadership vision* represents one's dreams, aspirations, and hopes for the organization and its members. It is also based on a code of ethics and deeply rooted values and beliefs about what is important.

- *A shared vision focused on teaching, learning, and assessment* engages organizational members in forming a collective vision that everyone can buy into, because it is reflective of the shared values and beliefs that place student learning at the center of all practices and actions within the schoolhouse.

- *A shared vision for the school community* embraces the notion that schools cannot operate effectively without an important partnership with the larger community. This partnership affords enriched, augmented resources for members of both school and community.

When these visions are out of alignment or not shared by all organizational members, individuals often perceive a lack of focus and the organization doesn't run smoothly. Prioritizing becomes difficult. Although visions serve to guide people and direct action, competition for attention often exists. For example, administrative newcomers in Louisville, Kentucky, put it this way, "It's hard to stay focused on your vision and take a broad view of things when immediate demands such as bursting pipes, a fight in the hallway, or a possible child abuse situation are facing you." One administrative mentor, in response to this, asked the newcomers to imagine, when competing priorities like these arise, that they are wearing bifocal contact lenses. One lens is for close vision; and the other, designed for distance. The mentor explained,

> It is the nature of the principalship that, at times, you have to go back and forth between your distance and close-up lenses, and, at other times, you try to use them simultaneously. For instance, how you work with students involved in the fight in the hallway (close-up lens) might become a lesson on the value of collaboration and successful conflict resolution (distance perspective). How you work with what may turn out to be a child abuse situation (close-up lens) may be an opportunity to demonstrate a concern for the child's physical,

psychological, and emotional well-being, as well as an opportunity to build trust and become a significant positive adult connection and advocate (distance lens).

"Temptation is all around you," one middle school principal remarked. "It may be part of my personal leadership vision that I protect valuable instructional time. Every minute counts. And then, a vision challenge emerges when a situation arises, and I find myself thinking that the simplest thing to do would be to use the intercom and interrupt classes! Having a vision for teaching and learning makes you stop and think: What is important? What is the best choice?"

Creating a Personal Leadership Vision

Roland Barth defines leadership as "making happen what you believe in" (2001, p. 446). This is accomplished through symbolic and expressive leadership behaviors. From the symbolic perspective, a principal models and focuses individual attention on what is important. From the expressive side of leadership, principals talk with teachers, help to crystallize and communicate the rationale for a vision, and generate shared discussions about what is important in the school. This focus on the meaning of a school leads to the development of a mission statement grounded in the collective beliefs of the staff. The process creates a commitment to a common direction and generates energy to pursue it. But it begins with a personal leadership vision (see Figure 1.1).

Getting clear about the answers to these questions will be reflected in how the principal interacts with others in the school and community, that is, setting priorities and making decisions. To develop a vision consistent with one's values and beliefs, a statement of an envisioned future state is then drafted (see Figure 1.1). Going through this process develops an "inner compass" within the school leader that will point the way on the leadership path. Leaders who develop a personal vision, communicate this vision to others, and act consistently with this vision are perceived with respect and integrity, two vital ingredients for trust.

Figure 1.1

Developing a Personal Leadership Vision

Values and Beliefs

What do I deeply value?

What are my beliefs?

About leadership?

About students?

About staff members?

About community building?

About curriculum, instruction, and assessment?

About learning?

About professional development?

About supervision?

About communication?

About change?

Vision

My vision—a desired future state—entails:

Creating a Shared Vision

While a personal leadership vision is essential for the leader, members of the staff are not involved in its development. Hence, a process is needed so that the staff can articulate a shared, core ideology and an "envisioned future" for the school. Although it would take less time to copy or borrow a vision from another organization, great benefits are derived from engaging with staff in a vision-building process. It generates ownership, commitment, and energy toward making the vision become reality (see Figure 1.2, p. 9). As Stephanie Hirsh, associate executive director of the National Staff Development Council, writes:

> A school vision should be a descriptive statement of what the school will be like at a specified time in the future. It uses descriptive words or phrases and sometimes pictures to illustrate what one would expect to see, hear, and experience in the school at that time. It engages all stakeholders in answering such questions as:
> - What kind of school do we want for our children and staff?
> - What will students learn? How will they learn?
> - How will students benefit from attendance at our school?
> - How will their success be measured or demonstrated?
> - Of all the educational innovations and research, which strategies should we seek to employ in our school?
> - If parents had a choice, on what basis would they choose to send their children to our school? (Hirsh, 1996)

There are several approaches to developing a vision. Certainly, one approach is to invite all stakeholders to come to consensus on the answers to the preceding questions. Then, a vision statement would be drafted, encapsulating their responses.

Another method of vision building involves a "Post-it strategy" (see Figure 1.3, pp. 10–11). This approach has been used successfully in schools throughout the United States, Canada, Europe, Great Britain, and Asia.

The vision derived from this process serves as a beacon, lighting the way for organizational members to collaborate on behalf of students.

——————————— **Figure 1.2** ———————————
Creating a Shared Vision

A shared vision considers
- Quality teaching and learning.
- Who a school serves.
- Characteristics of the students and their families.
- A broad array of schoolwide data (not just test scores).
- Current and past change efforts.
- Desired cognitive, affective, psychological, social, and physical goals.
- Special programs and services.
- Hopes and aspirations.
- Dreams for students' futures.
- High expectations.

Closely related to the vision statement is the mission for the school. As Hirsh says,

> A mission statement is a succinct, powerful statement on how the school will achieve its vision. The mission answers:
> - What is our purpose?
> - What do we care most about?
> - What must we accomplish?
> - What are the cornerstones of our operations? (Hirsh, 1996)

A mission statement serves as a galvanizing force for staff, students, and community. Goals identify how the mission and vision will be achieved. Some schools summarize the vision and mission in a bumper sticker to keep them in the forefront of everyone's mind. Seeing the school you want is the first step in the journey to making the vision become reality.

If the vision is truly shared, it will be evident in both the climate (how a school "feels") and the culture (how "business" is transacted) of the school.

——————————————— **Figure 1.3** ———————————————

Post-it Strategy

Materials Needed
- Chart paper
- Tape
- Markers
- Large Post-it notes
- Index cards

Steps

1. Explain what a vision statement is. For example, "A vision statement communicates what the organization stands for, what its members believe, and what ends will be accomplished in keeping with the purpose and beliefs. It serves as a galvanizing force for action."

2. Build a rationale for the vision statement. This step might include explaining why vision statements are helpful (shared sense of purpose, common direction, energizer) and examining vision statements from other organizations. During this examination, the staff could be asked to analyze the values that seem to be implicit in the vision statement. Identify how a vision statement influences a staff member's life.

3. Invite the staff to take part in the development of the vision statement. Explain that this will allow
the opportunity to synthesize individual staff members' dreams or visions into a statement reached through consensus. This statement will represent the ends to which all within the organization will strive.

4. Ask staff members to think for a moment about the place where they would like to send their own very special child to school. How would the child be treated? What would his or her experiences be like? How would he or she feel? Ask staff members to describe their thoughts on Post-it notes.

5. Now ask the staff members to think about the place where they would like to go to work every day. What would it be like? How would they feel? How would people interact? Write this on Post-it notes.

6. Ask staff members to each take their two Post-it notes and fuse them into one. Tell them to write their thoughts on an index card.

(continued)

─────────────── **Figure 1.3** ───────────────

Post-it Strategy *(continued)*

7. Individuals then meet as table groups of four to six people and share their index cards. After they have all read their index cards, the table group creates a composite representing a group consensus of the individual cards. This is written with markers on chart paper.

8. Pairs of table groups meet and share their charts. They synthesize their two charts into one.

9. The groups continue the process until they create one chart that represents the shared visions of all in the room.

10. If parents and representative students have not been involved in this process, this same procedure may be repeated with them, and the products of their work brought to the faculty. At this point, the staff could incorporate these charts with the faculty work.

11. At another time, a contest could be held or the group could work together to create a slogan that would encapsulate the vision statement.

In large schools, Steps 1 through 7 might be conducted within departments. Departments would then share their completed charts and eventually synthesize their work, cross-departmentally, into one charted vision statement on which all can agree.

Source: The Principal's Companion (2nd ed.), by P. Robbins and H. Alvy, 2003. Copyright 2003 by Corwin Press. Used by permission of the authors.

 **Activity** ─────────────────────

Communicating a Personal Leadership Vision

Although it is essential that the vision of the school be a shared one among organizational members, it must also be one that is compatible with the principal's personal leadership vision. Take a moment to list or graphically depict the ways in which you communicate your personal leadership vision (e.g., writing newsletters, what you pay attention to in visiting classrooms, or prioritizing agenda items for meetings).

Reflective Field Notes ───────

Please use this space to jot down notes that are important for your personal leadership journey. You may do this in a structured way—by responding to questions—or in an unstructured way. Use whatever approach works for you!

- How does vision serve as a compass?

- In what way might vision function as a leadership tool?

- What would you craft as a personal leadership vision? What has influenced your thinking?

- Draft a sample vision statement for staff to analyze for core values and beliefs.

- Which approach to vision building do you prefer?

- Create a graphic organizer to encapsulate key aspects of this chapter.

2

Navigating in "Hidden History"

Culture is a powerful force in any organization in which people share history. It influences the way people think, what they value, how they feel, and how they act. Some cultures are nurturing, but some are toxic. A critical leadership competency is the ability to understand, *read*, and shape school culture. Culture is crucial to promoting staff and student learning, and it can enhance or deter reform and innovation. Roland Barth (2002) emphasized the power of culture when he wrote, "Probably the most important and most difficult job of an instructional leader is to change the prevailing culture of the school. A school's culture has far more influence on life and learning in the schoolhouse than the president of the country, the state department of education, the superintendent, the school board, or even the principal, teachers, and parents can ever have." Every culture is a reflection of "hidden history"—what has come before. "School culture is built up over time as people work together, play together, fight together, cry together, laugh together. The most profound values and relationships come into being as staff members face crises, deal with tragedy, make mistakes, enjoy success and recognize accomplishments—problems solved and conflicts resolved. . . . The past is truly never far away. People remember (and are reminded in the stories that are told) the past and the feelings it produces" (Peterson & Deal, 2002, p. 49).

The newcomer quickly learns about this "hidden history" of the school, as noted author Kent Peterson refers to it, when people respond to suggestions the newcomer makes with comments like, "Oh, we tried something like that five years ago—didn't work then—won't work now!" Stories about things that have happened in the past—legends, now reality—are passed on to the newcomer and inform him or her about why things are the way they seem to be. The newcomer quickly learns about sacred cows, land mines, and traditions as he or she begins to interact with the network of organizational members.

One new principal came face to face with this reality as she navigated her school's hidden history and treaded on sacred ground. Marie was assigned as principal to West Middle School. During late summer, she came into the school and noticed a dingy teachers' room with faded curtains, a dusty wreath on the door, and a hodgepodge of furniture from several garage sales. "I'll surprise the staff and make this an inviting, professional space," she thought. She solicited donations of paint and mini blinds from a local home-improvement store and a sofa and chairs from a furniture mart. Then, one weekend, she and several friends painted the teachers' room, hung mini blinds in place of the faded curtains, threw the dusty wreath in a closet, and replaced it with a Norman Rockwell print. They tossed out the old furniture and brought in the attractive new pieces. They filled an empty bookcase with professional books, journals, videos, and audiotapes and created a lending library. The day before staff came back, she brought in a CD player and classical music CDs. She placed fresh flowers on every table. A cookie jar, filled to the brim, and a new beverage center were placed on the counter. "They'll love it," she thought to herself. "They will work hard this year, and this will be a great beginning-of-the-year perk!" But when staff returned and visited the teachers' room, they left quickly, shaking their heads. They refused to make eye contact with Marie. Their faces appeared disgruntled. "That's a lot of gratitude," she thought. Yet she puzzled over the staff's reaction.

Fortunately, Marie soon encountered a teacher she had known from another school who had transferred to West. "What's this all about?" Marie asked. "Well," the teacher responded, "for several years a paraprofessional named Nancy worked at this school. She put in hours beyond her duty responsibilities. The staff loved her. Last year, she was diagnosed with cancer and passed away a few months later. She made the staff the wreath that was hung on the door. She created it in her hospital bed as a gift to all of us. And you unceremoniously threw it away!" The teacher's eyes welled with tears. "I'm so sorry," Marie responded empathetically. "And fortunately, I didn't throw the wreath away. It's in the closet. Thank you for telling me what was going on. I learned an important lesson from this!" Marie rushed to the closet, retrieved and dusted off the wreath, and placed it back on the door. Although no one ever said a word about this incident, after the wreath reappeared, staff members' reactions warmed toward Marie. The reemergence of the wreath was pivotal in turning the feelings of the staff toward the principal in the culture of the school. It also reminds us of the rich trappings and traditions that are created over time and held dearly in the hearts of organizational members. Whereas a wreath may seem a rather insignificant artifact to a newcomer to the school, its meaning looms larger than life in those who have worked in the building over time. In a very real sense, culture is created as organizational members create meaning within the walls where they spend their lives. It affects how people feel, think, and act. It influences how they interact, do their work, make decisions, solve problems, cope with tragedies, and celebrate successes. Culture has been referred to as a "school's unique personality." Culture influences

- What people wear.

- What people talk about. What people don't talk about.

- Where "business" is conducted.
- How people act and interact
  - privately.
  - publicly.
  - in the halls.
  - in the classroom.
  - in faculty meetings.
  - during inservice days.
  - with guests or visitors.
- Where people park.
- How people acknowledge one another—or don't.
- How resources are generated, sought after, and used.
- How new ideas are viewed.
- How people view their roles (job versus calling, responsibilities).
- Whether people value school improvement.
- Whether they are motivated to "go the extra mile."
- Whether they believe they can influence student learning, school improvement, or one another.
- How responsible they feel for student results.
- Whether they value state standards.
- How individuals view curriculum, assessment, instruction, and climate.
- Whether people believe all students can learn.
- Whether they value adult learning as an integral part of fostering student learning.
- Whether individuals support risk taking and experimentation as vital ingredients of the learning and improvement process.

- Whether individuals value collaborative work and team building.

- How planning time is used.

- How "working hours" are viewed.

- How individuals embrace diversity.

- How supportive individuals are of one another.

- Whether reflection is valued.

- How success is defined.

- How change is viewed.

- What is considered valuable; how appreciation is shown.

- How people spend time.

Peterson and Deal (2002) note that "the unwritten tablet of social expectations found in a culture influences almost everything that happens." For the newcomer, it is important to understand the culture before trying to shape it. When a newcomer moves too quickly in trying to change culture, the culture can well up and "bite you in the act!"

Elements of Culture

Understanding culture involves recognizing its elements (see Figure 2.1). At the heart of every culture is a set of *values* and *beliefs*. In cohesive cultures, common values and beliefs are held by all organizational members. In fragmented cultures, each subculture's members may have their own set of beliefs and values. These values can be detected in the elements of culture. For instance, in a culture that highly values sports, the largest *ritual* may be the sports banquet. The newcomer who wants to change the core value to fostering student learning faces an implicit dilemma. Doing away with the banquet would raise the ire of cultural members. Hence, to begin to shape new values, new traditions must be blended with the old. A new high school principal took this challenge on by introducing special awards at the sports banquet. These included awards for academic improvement, citizenship, attendance, and community service. The next year, there were sports banquets, academic banquets, and community service banquets.

The principal also introduced a new *tradition*. Every week, he asked teachers to submit names of students who had come to class, completed assignments, and returned homework. Each student's name was written on a slip of paper and placed in a large, locked box. Every Thursday afternoon, eight names were drawn from the box. These individuals were invited to sit on a large sofa that was placed behind the goal posts during football season; and during basketball season, along the basketball court. The principal or assistant principal, dressed in formal attire—such as a tuxedo—served the students popcorn, hotdogs, and soft drinks from silver trays! Although, at first, staff members raised their eyebrows, they

Figure 2.1

Elements of Culture

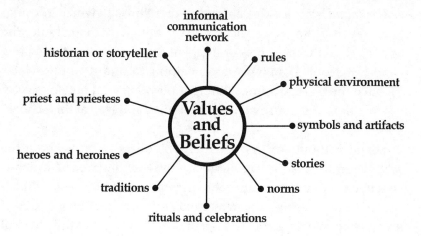

soon changed their attitudes when completed assignments and homework returns increased. Needless to say, students loved the new tradition! Hence, through strategic planning, that is, marrying old traditions with new, the principal introduced new values into the culture of the school. Because of this planning, the new values were not perceived to be in fierce competition with those that existed prior to the new principal's arrival.

Within the culture of the school, a *web of relationships* and roles connects a variety of players. It is as if these players have "cultural job titles." The *hero* or *heroine* exemplifies the values of the culture. The *priests* or *priestesses* in the organization are those that others look to "to bless things" and determine whether "they will fly." The *storyteller* passes on tradition by telling stories. In positive cultures, they are powerful stories of teacher dedication, commitment, and effort on behalf of students. They are stories of students who "made it" because of teachers and because of the environment of the school. In negative cultures, they are stories of anguish, disillusionment, and neglect. The *historian* interprets and passes along history. This person is quick to interpret current events against a backdrop of history and convey that understanding to organizational members.

An elementary school principal recently interpreted the *informal communication network* as "the method through which information travels faster than the speed of any written memo." She added, "I don't know how it happens, but I do know there are a couple of people I can whisper something to, and 10 minutes later I'll have three e-mails from different players and a note or two in my mailbox! The informal network is alive and well at this school" (Dyer, 1991).

Even without any verbal clues, one quickly learns about the school culture. As the saying goes, "the building talks." Much is conveyed about the culture of an organization by the *physical environment*. Are the grounds manicured and cared for? Or, is garbage strewn over what patches are left of the lawn? Care of the physical environment is often a predictor of the care that will be taken of students and staff. What's on the front door of the school? Is it a sign that proclaims "No Trespassing. Report to the Office."? Or is it a sign that reads, "Welcome to Our School. Because students are our most precious resource, we care deeply about their safety. Come and visit the office so we can greet you and serve you well."? What's in the trophy cases? Do they contain sports paraphernalia only or a broader array of artifacts—sports, academics, citizenship, art, music, and peer support? What's on display speaks to any onlooker about what is valued. What's on the bulletin boards in the halls? Are they changed regularly? Do they celebrate all students' work or a selected few? What's on the classroom walls? Much can be learned from displays about what is deemed important—what is held up as vestiges of the culture.

In one culture that heralds values of collaboration, professionalism, sharing, and experimentation, the teachers' room has a bulletin board entitled "Help Wanted." Open lunch bags with a classroom problem described on the face of the bag are stapled to the bulletin board. Containers of index cards and pencils are on a shelf just below the board. Whenever staff members want to share ideas about how to solve a particular problem, they write an idea on an index card and drop it into one of the bags. Conversely, anytime teachers face a similar problem, they are invited to reach into the bag and read the idea cards. This helps solidify a belief system that if only we reach out, perhaps the answer to the problem we're grappling with exists just two or three yards down the corridor! And, it is a profound reminder of the benefits to be derived from collaboration.

In one school in Israel, a huge quilt hangs on the wall of an entry hall. The quilt depicts a vineyard, and interspersed among the vines are all the students' names. This symbolically communicates the importance of every student, as well as their connection to one another and to the learning community.

Newcomers to a culture quickly learn about its *norms*— unwritten rules that govern daily actions and interactions. On the first day of school, a new teacher went to sit in a chair in the teachers' room and was told, "You can't sit there; that's Elinor's chair, and she's sat there for 22 years! By the way—where did you park?"

Of course, Elinor had the unmarked space closest to the building. This culture revered veteran staff members who "had put in their time."

In the Claremont, California, Unified School District, if you are in a meeting with colleagues and you appreciate something they have said, you write them a note on a blue index card. Blue index cards are a regular *artifact* that can be spotted during any meeting. They reflect a culture that values the expertise that each colleague brings to the district and deep respect for one another as professional colleagues.

Jon Saphier and Matthew King (1985) identified 12 norms of school culture that need to be strong to create a healthy school culture:

1. Collegiality

2. Experimentation

3. High expectations

4. Trust and confidence

5. Tangible support

6. Reaching out to the knowledge base

7. Appreciation and recognition

8. Caring, celebration, and humor

9. Involvement in decision making

10. Protection of what's important

11. Traditions

12. Honest, open communication

"If these norms are strong, improvements in instruction, for example, will be significant, continuous, and widespread," note Saphier and King. "However, if these norms are weak, improvements will be infrequent, random, and slow." Though the article addressing these norms was written two decades ago, Saphier comments that the same set still applies. Further, he has discovered that "three of the norms—collegiality, experimentation, and reaching out to the knowledge base—have the strongest correlation between changing the school environment and improving student achievement" (1996).

It should be noted that school culture has a profound impact on students as well as adults. That is, students behave according to what they see modeled by the adults in the building. A new leader has the unique ability to see with "beginner's clarity the cultural patterns" of a school (Barth, 2002). The newcomer can keenly observe students and staff to ascertain whether collaboration or competition thrives within the organization, whether learning is obligatory or viewed as opportunity, whether goodness or evil prevails, whether optimists or naysayers inhabit the schoolhouse, and whether the status quo rules or there are norms of continuous improvement. Taking stock of the student and adult culture is an important first step in identifying productive versus unproductive business practices within the organization. This becomes the foundation in charting where the culture is, how it works, and the leader's vision—shared with staff—about how it might come to be.

One principal described taking stock of a culture as going on an archaeological dig. What are the artifacts of the culture? What do they stand for? How are they used? Are they positive or negative? What types of tradition or ceremony surround them? For example, a new principal assigned to a high school noticed that there was a tradition in place: Whenever a staff member made a mistake, a colleague would scribble "OHB" on a Post-it note and stick it on that person. Curious about the OHB *symbol*, the new principal asked a faculty member, "What's that stand for?"

"Oh," he laughed in response, "it means *only human being*! We recognize and celebrate risk taking, experimentation, and mistakes at this school—as long as people learn from them." Several months later, the principal sent out a meeting notice, and while he specified the time, location, and agenda, he neglected to indicate the date. A staff member quickly noticed the mistake and stuck an OHB award on his lapel. The principal smiled and interpreted this gesture as a symbol that he had finally been accepted into the culture of the school!

Types of Culture

Cultures can be positive, negative, toxic, or fragmented. Artifacts are not always positive. Sometimes an archeological dig can yield negative findings. For instance, a new principal found out that there was a private tradition in the high school in which members of one academically acclaimed department took part in a ritual at the end of each school year: Members of the department wrote the names of students they didn't care for on a large sheet of butcher paper and then stomped on them! The new principal was angered by this practice and wanted to immediately confront the staff members for engaging in this unprofessional behavior. Yet he reflected that he had become aware of this negative tradition only because a disapproving staff member confided in him. He did not want to break trust and betray this confidence. He anguished about what to do and decided instead to address the issue indirectly, but powerfully, in a faculty meeting. He began by asking staff members to think of a person who had a significant impact on their lives. He asked them to write down words that described why these individuals made an impact, that is, what they did. He then said to the staff, "Let's take a look at a teacher who made an impact on individual lives." He played a clip from the movie *Mr. Holland's Opus*, in which former students remembered and celebrated their music teacher. As the video clip ended, the staff sat silently in anticipation of what the principal would do next. Though his heart was pounding in his throat, he continued, "I want you to imagine you are 80 years old. A former student approaches you. What do you want him to remember about you? What he learned? How he was treated by you? Take a moment and write down your answers to these questions on a piece of paper." The principal then distributed envelopes and asked staff members to self-address the envelopes and seal their responses to the questions inside. He collected these and two months later sent the sealed envelopes back to staff members with a note taped to the outside inquiring, "What are you doing today to create memorable moments that will live on in students' hearts and minds? A random deed of kindness may touch a life forever."

POSITIVE CULTURES

Positive cultures reflect an "underlying set of norms and values, history and stories, hopes and dreams that are productive, encouraging, and optimistic. Positive relationships abound around a strong sense of connection to the core mission" (Deal & Peterson, 1999). The characteristics of positive cultures include:

• Core values of professionalism, collegiality, continuous improvement, all focused on staff and student learning.

• A mission to make a difference for students in school and in life.

• A sense of shared responsibility for students.

• A belief that collectively and individually staff and students can grow socially, emotionally, and cognitively.

• The presence of a professional learning community committed to sharing expertise, knowledge about practice, and research to enhance their craft—ultimately to serve students so that no child will be left behind.

• Leadership that builds bridges from old to new, and fosters collaboration and a sense of efficacy with a focus on continuous improvement.

• The presence of trust among colleagues characterized by respect, a belief in one another, caring, and integrity.

• Rituals, ceremonies, stories, and other communications that celebrate staff members' efforts to grow professionally and to serve students well.

• A physical environment that portrays a focus on learning for all members of the school community.

- An established forum or process in place for problem solving, decision making, and conflict resolution.

NEGATIVE CULTURES

Although most schools are characterized by positive cultures, some have negative or toxic cultures. In negative cultures, typically, pockets of negativity exist in which organizational members express cynicism, tell stories that remind staff of past failures, share pessimistic beliefs about one's power to make a difference, and convey a sense of hopelessness. These cultures drain energy from those within the organization. It is important for the newcomer to identify negative group members and seek to understand why they possess negative values and beliefs, what happened to make them that way, and how they are currently reinforced for their negativity. Understanding these aspects of negativity can yield important leverage points for bringing about change. The leader will gain ground in working with these naysayers by listening carefully and devoting attention to understanding why they disapprove of specific practices and presenting alternative positive pictures and scenarios.

TOXIC CULTURES

Unlike negative cultures, toxic cultures can poison those in its midst. Deal and Peterson (1999) write that toxic cultures possess the following characteristics:

- A lack of shared purpose or a splintered mission based on self-interest.
- Staff members who find most of their meaning in activities outside work, negativity, or antistudent sentiments.
- The past viewed as a story of defeat and failure.
- Norms of radical individualism, the acceptance of mediocrity, and an avoidance of innovation.
- Little sense of community, but negative beliefs about colleagues and students abound.

- Few positive traditions or ceremonies to develop a sense of community.
- A cultural network of naysayers, saboteurs, rumormongers, and antiheroes, where communication is primarily negative.
- A dearth of leadership in the principal's office and among staff.
- Positive role models unrecognized in the school and community.
- Social connections that have become fragmented and openly antagonist.
- Rather than hopes, dreams, and a clear vision, a sense of hopelessness, discouragement, and despair. (pp. 88–89)

Toxic cultures have a debilitating influence on old-timers and an intimidating influence on newcomers—teachers, paraprofessionals, community members, and administrators alike. A new teacher described her experience in a toxic culture this way:

> On the first day of school, I went into the teachers' room and was about to share my morning's success with students. But the conversation was so clogged with kid bashing, parent bashing, and gloom and doom that I just grabbed my lunch and went back to my room. It made me sick to my stomach to be in their presence. It was nothing like the optimism that permeated the teachers' room at the school where I did my student teaching.
>
> And the first faculty meeting—I'll just never forget it. The new principal shared Roland Barth's story about "a study conducted at Dartmouth medical school in which surgeons observed one another in the operating room to get better at what they do. The study found that 74 patients of those doctors who were expected to die did not die. The only intervening variable was the presence of the colleagues in the operating room. [Barth, in Sparks, 2002, pp. 49–50]
>
> The principal then proposed the notion that when teachers collaborate and share otherwise well-kept secrets of craft knowledge, students will benefit and thrive. He asked us to share something we had done this week in the classroom that helped students learn. To this request, veteran teachers on the staff clucked their tongues, others shook their heads and laughed, still others put their heads on the table. I felt so bad for the principal, but I was too intimidated to do anything. If it doesn't get better, I'm going to put in for a transfer. I feel so lonely here.

As this testimony suggests, toxic cultures have the capacity to quiet, intimidate, or drive out insiders who may be positive. They drain energy from organizational members and divert the focus from the core mission of a school—to serve students. Working diligently, positive members of a culture will need a minimum of three to five years to transform the toxicity within an organization. For the leader, it is essential to search for positive players who may lurk in the shadows, afraid to confront their "negaholic" colleagues or "keepers of the nightmare," as Peterson and Deal refer to them. Once identified, the leader needs to allocate resources to support positive staff members' efforts. And while it may not serve these individuals well to be publicly acknowledged for their diligence, quiet recognition (in the form of material resources and staff development opportunities) is essential. Word will begin to travel through the grapevine that one needs to be positive to get ahead in the organization.

FRAGMENTED CULTURES

Another difficult type of culture to work with is the fragmented culture, in which several subcultures exist—each with its own values, beliefs, norms, rituals, traditions, and symbols. Some may be positive; some, negative; and some, toxic. An elementary principal described her experience of working with a fragmented culture as "the challenge of trying to unify individual fiefdoms, each with their own exalted rulers and ways of operating that have coexisted for years." Her approach was to search for and identify common ground and unite staff members around common goals. Her mission was to transform the elements of each subculture to support rather than subvert the school's central purpose: serving children. Reflecting on her first-year experiences with transforming the fragmented culture into a cohesive, positive one, the newcomer said, "This is probably one of the most difficult things I've ever had to do. Looking back, I realize I had to keep my focus on consciously transforming the culture; it's so easy to become victimized by the toxic forces. I kept reminding myself why I was doing this. I kept pictures of students all around me as a vestige of that." Change always threatens a culture, particularly because people form strong attachments to the rituals of daily life in the schoolhouse. A fear of the unknown—the new culture—often makes organizational members dig in their heels and resist changes in the culture. In a very real sense, change represents loss—loss of familiar ways of operating. The difficulty of changing a culture is intensified when the individual or individuals who are bringing about the change have little history with organizational members and lack their trust.

Reading a Culture

It is important to read a culture carefully before strategically trying to change it. This may be done informally or formally. One informal method is simply to observe and watch for the following:

- When people arrive at school, where do they congregate? Or, do they go off to their individual classrooms to work as sole proprietors?

- What are the patterns of communication? Who speaks to whom?

- What are conversations among colleagues about? Teaching and learning? Recipes, sports, social gatherings? Are they positive or negative?

- Who do people look to "to bless things" so that they fly?

- Do individuals view their work as a calling or as a job?

- What are the stories that are told? Did they occur in reality?

- What do organizational members value?

- How is time used?

- What is displayed in the physical environment?

- What is celebrated?

- What rituals or traditions exist? What is their focus?

- What's considered right to do?

- What is the history that's related by the historian to the newcomers?

- What is considered a priority?

- How do outsiders view the school?

- What are faculty meetings like?

  - Who sits with whom?

  - What's first on the agenda? What's last?

  - What other activities take place? (Side conversations, leisure reading, paper grading.)

  - How are new ideas viewed or received?

  - Is there a second "meeting" in the parking lot after the faculty meeting?

Of course, this informal method will yield only one person's view of the culture. It is important to validate your data by obtaining others' perceptions as well. There are many formal approaches to reading a culture; some are more structured than others:

- *Time lines.* Creating a time line is a strategy that enables history to be reconstructed by organizational members (see Figure 2.2). It provides a retrospective assessment of what has transpired in the past, constructed by those who have lived through those times. It provides a newcomer with an understanding about how the culture came to be, and it furnishes veterans with a nostalgic glance at the past interpreted in the present tense.

- *A wellness check on the "12 Norms."* This less structured approach invites staff members to reexamine Saphier and King's "12 Norms of Healthy Cultures" in the context of a specific school (see Figure 2.3, on p. 32). As each norm is considered, individuals write down their perceptions of its *wellness* in the culture. These individual responses are collectively summarized by a facilitator and presented back to staff.

• *A "feeling walk."* Professor Maurice Elias from Rutgers University shared this assessment idea. Ask colleagues to take a walk through the school. Notice what's on the walls, what is spoken and in what tone, and how people are treated; contemplate how the space of the school "feels" as you walk through the building and its grounds; and consider: Are there some places that feel good? Better than other places? Why?

The next three assessments are a bit more playful but can be extremely revealing. People often find it less threatening to use a

---

Figure 2.2

Time Line Strategy

Materials Needed
• Butcher paper
• Colored markers
• Masking tape

Directions
• Prepare for the activity by papering the walls with butcher paper that will serve as the medium for the time line that is to be created.
• Explain that the purpose of this activity is to enable all staff members to gain a sense of the history of the school.
• Invite staff members who have been at the school the longest to think about key events that transpired during their first years in the building and jot down dates, events, people, and any emotions they recall ("highs" and "lows"). Suggest that they can use words or graphics to express their emotions.
• Ask other staff members to add to the time line according to the year that they entered the building.
• When the time line is finished, provide time for dialogue, questions, and answers. Invite staff to ponder, "Are there trends or patterns that emerge as you look at the time line?"
• If possible, leave the time line up for a while so that it can continue to serve as a basis for conversation.

---

metaphor or analogy to talk about something close to the bone. All these activities can be conducted within a faculty meeting.

- *"Name That Tune."* Ask staff members to generate a list of song titles that best depict the culture of the school. This approach

―――――――――――――― **Figure 2.3** ――――――――――――――

Wellness Check: 12 Norms of Healthy Cultures

12 Norms	Wellness Data: Presence/Absence/Needs Treatment
1. Collegiality	
2. Experimentation	
3. High expectations	
4. Trust and confidence	
5. Tangible support	
6. Reaching out to the knowledge base	
7. Appreciation and recognition	
8. Caring, celebration, and humor	
9. Involvement in decision making	
10. Protection of what's important	
11. Traditions	
12. Honest, open communication	

Source: Adapted from Saphier and King, 1985.

causes staff members to think analytically about the culture of the school. Some examples that have been derived from this exercise include "We Are Family," "Only the Lonely," "Raindrops Keep Falling on My Head," "Sixteen Tons," and "Whistle While You Work." Peterson and Deal (2002) talk about the importance of doing this activity to assess how the staff members of the school are coping during major reform efforts.

- *Create an advertisement for the school.* Invite staff members to work as self-selected table groups and develop an advertisement for the school. Ask them to imagine that they are recruiting pupils or potential faculty members. What would their advertisement say? What are some key features or unique characteristics that would attract individuals to the school?

- *"Picture This!"* Collect five or six different pictures and post them around the room. They can be abstract or concrete images. Make sure there is variety. For example, some pictures may convey a spirit of collaboration; others, rugged individualism. Some might suggest a positive workplace; others, a negative place to spend time. Ask individual faculty members to walk to the posted picture that communicates their perception of the culture of the school. Once individuals select a picture, ask each group to discuss why they selected that picture. Each group then is asked to report out.

Culture and Working Relationships Among Colleagues

According to Roland Barth (2001), "The relationship among the adults in the schoolhouse has more impact on the quality and the character of the school—and on the accomplishment of youngsters— than any other factor." Given this notion, consider the continuum in Figure 2.4 (p. 34), based on the work of Hargreaves and Dawe (1989) illustrating the variety of ways adults may interact with one another within the schoolhouse.

—————————————— **Figure 2.4** ——————————————

Working Relationships Among Colleagues

| Fragmented Individualism | Balkanization | Contrived Collegiality | True Collaborative Cultures |

- *Fragmented Individualism* represents the traditional form of teacher isolation.

- *Balkanization* consists of subgroups and cliques operating as separate subentities.

- *Contrived Collegiality* leads to a proliferation of unwanted contacts among teachers that consume already scarce time with little to show for it.

- *True Collaborative Cultures* represent "deep personal enduring cultures central to teachers' daily work" (Hargreaves and Dawe, 1989, p. 14).

One may use this helpful typology to reflect on working relationships among colleagues in a culture and identify where staff members are functioning versus where they might be ideally. Obviously, when individuals in schools operate in a collaborative manner, the resources for staff and students are maximized, and learning soars. Chapter 4 addresses methods to help individuals move toward greater collaboration.

Shaping School Culture

One of the most powerful leverage points a leader can use to make a difference in the school is the opportunity to shape culture. This involves strengthening or enhancing culture in some contexts, when it is positive but may be weak; it involves "culture busting" when unhealthy practices need to be eradicated. Culture building may take place when new practices need to be created. Any of these acts involve courage, skill, commitment, energy, foresight, challenge, dedication, and creativity. For example, a new principal was well aware that he had the support of a small pocket of positive staff members, who also objected to what was known in their inner, positive circle as the "Table of Doom." The Table of Doom was a group of negative staff members who always came late to meetings and always sat at the same back table, closest to the door. When anyone voiced a new idea, they rolled their eyes and emoted deep sighs. To openly confront the Table of Doom would surely cause a scene, so the positive staff members invented an alternative, creative plan to begin quietly eroding the negative presence. Before a faculty meeting, they removed all the chairs from the Table of Doom's familiar spot. The chairs were scattered among the other tables in the room. Then, refreshments were served at the table where the Table of Doom usually sat! Table members arrived—late—only to discover they had to disperse and sit at different tables! Their negative influence was significantly dissipated during that meeting. The next meeting, the Table of Doom arrived early but did not demonstrate their previous negative behavior. This was the beginning of the end of their negative presence in the culture. The culture-busting actions had made an impact!

In another school, the new principal was disturbed that faculty members rarely collaborated or celebrated one another. She decided upon a plan of action. She brought a silver tub into the faculty meeting and filled it with crushed ice and six Coke bottles. She said, "I'd like us to consider a new tradition in our school called 'A Coke and a Compliment.' The way it will work is that anyone who would like to compliment colleagues for something they did to make a difference for students may do so by presenting them with a Coke from this tub and publicly acknowledging their efforts." After this invitation, the staff sat silently for several minutes. Finally a senior member of the staff plucked a Coke from the tub and presented it to a new teacher for the way she worked with a hostile parent, by overcoming the parent's concerns and generating her support. The remaining five bottles were quickly presented after the first person took the risk. Although nobody voiced their endorsement of the practice during the meeting, the principal reported that she received a flood of positive e-mail messages after the faculty meeting. She interpreted this response as a sign of readiness to move forward toward developing a more positive, collaborative workplace.

At another school, the values at the heart of the culture honored teacher seniority and protected teachers. Desiring to change the heart of the culture to revolve around students, the principal carefully studied staff members' daily behaviors. One thing she noticed was that there was fierce competition for a limited number of parking spaces. If you didn't arrive early enough to get a spot, you would have to park at the bottom of the hill and walk back up! One weekend, she painted over "Principal" on her marked parking space and stenciled gold stars all over the space. The following Monday, she posted a notice in the teachers' room where staff members congregated:

Star Studded Parking?

We are beginning a new practice here. Next Monday everyone will receive a stack of five blank handprints in his or her mailbox. Anytime you notice a colleague making a difference for a student, you are invited to write that person's name on a handprint and acknowledge what he or she did to make a difference. If you receive this "Pat on the Back" award, bring it to the office and deposit it in the Star Studded Parking box. Every week, a Pat on the Back will be drawn, and that person will be able to park in the Star Studded Parking space for the week.

Surprisingly, the staff members, who rarely expressed exuberance about anything, went out of their way to celebrate colleagues. The box was overflowing the first week of the program and in weeks thereafter! The principal had artfully woven something staff members valued with a reverence for efforts that make a difference for students.

ESSENTIAL UNDERSTANDINGS IN SHAPING CULTURE

Establish a Clear Picture. In shaping school culture, it is important that the leader has a clear picture of what he or she wants to accomplish in the end. "It is much easier to picture what you don't want," reflected one principal. "But it's essential to have an image of what you do want in front of you, to guide your actions."

Involve the Staff. Whenever possible, involve staff in decision making related to cultural practices. Although the principal sometimes initiates action, problems can be avoided or minimized if staff members are involved. For example, if the principal had engaged a teacher leadership team to redecorate the teachers' room, the information regarding the wreath would have been shared early on and the faux pas avoided. Plus, involvement generates ownership and models an important norm: collaboration.

Align Goals and Practices. Be sure the culture doesn't erode goals. That is, a culture that rewards individual accomplishments—Teacher of the Month, Student of the Week, Employee of the Week—over collaborative team efforts will unravel even the tightest knit faculty. Make sure what is rewarded or recognized is consistent with the goals.

Be Aware of the Interconnectedness of Cultural Elements. Most elements of culture are so interconnected that trying to change one element will affect others as well. Using time is a profound way to change a culture. If you change the use of time, you will change the values. For instance, if people perceive that having more time for collaboration is meaningful and productive, they will come to value time allocated for that purpose. This in turn will change the stories staff members tell about their experiences. Ultimately, rituals and ceremonies will be influenced as well.

View One's Own Behavior as a Culture-Shaping Tool. Leaders consciously and unconsciously shape school and organizational culture through daily acts. Consider what messages are communicated by behavior:

- What do you do first when you arrive at work?

- How do you greet people?

- How do you interact with students?

- What's on the front door of the building?

- What's on display in the office? In the halls?

- What's first on the daily bulletin?

- How is the faculty meeting agenda prioritized?

- How are day-to-day decisions made?

- What do you notice when you walk the halls or walk around campus?

- What do you pay attention to when visiting classrooms?

- What do you expect from others?

- What do you celebrate?

What leaders value and care about is communicated by their actions. In the end, it's the little things that matter in shaping school culture.

Use a Large Toolbox. Culture shaping involves a variety of situations, and no one tool will be appropriate for every context. Sometimes confrontation will be the appropriate tool. At other times, shaping culture will require hiring, firing, or transferring staff. At still other times, the right tool will be focusing energy and resources on positive aspects of, or members within, the culture. Tools can also involve inventing and relating new stories, creating and implementing new traditions and ceremonies, and designing new schedules that maximize common planning time for staff members and quality learning time for students.

View Trust as Key. "After a 10-year study of Chicago school reforms, researchers Anthony Bryk and Barbara Schneider have concluded that schools with a high degree of 'relational trust' are more likely to make the kind of changes that help raise student achievement. Improvements in such areas as classroom instruction, curriculum, teacher preparation, and professional development have little chance of succeeding without improvements in the school's social climate" (Gordon, 2002). Trust is built over time, particularly when actions match words, respect and honest acknowledgments are a part of daily interactions, confidences are kept, competence is celebrated and revered, people care for one another as professionals and as human beings, and there is a shared commitment to put students first, exemplified both in word and deed.

Communicate, Communicate, Communicate. The clarity and precision of communication is fundamental in shaping organizational behavior and practices. Individuals do not always interpret behavior through the same lens. Hence, it is important to be explicit. Let one example suffice. Lou was assigned as a new principal to an elementary school. The former principal rarely emerged from his office—a bit of history Lou soon discovered. Being a morning person, by 7:00 a.m. Lou had already been to the gym to work out, stopped at Starbucks for a cup of java, read the local paper, and responded to his e-mail. As soon as he got to school, he began walking the campus, interacting with students, and dropping into classrooms to greet teachers. Staff, however, interpreted his actions quite differently. "He's conducting bed checks," the self-proclaimed "historian" of the school noted, "Based on my years of experience, he wants to find out who's on time and who's tardy." Luckily, a teacher colleague shared this interpretation with Lou. At the next faculty meeting, Lou began by saying, "It has come to my attention that many of you are interpreting my early morning visits as 'bed checks.'" He continued, "Let me be perfectly clear about what I'm doing and why. I'm a morning person. I deeply value connecting with each and every one of you and our students. That way, I get a sense of the pulse of the school—what's happened in the neighborhood the night before—and become forewarned about any emerging tensions. In the long run, I hope that these actions—frequent contacts—will serve as building blocks for what I consider treasured relationships. I apologize if I scared you. I have learned an important lesson about being clear!"

At PS/IS 123 in the Bronx, New York, Principal Virginia Connelly creates a daily message board for staff that contains

- Everything that is going on in the school that day,
- Commendations for staff and students,
- Important upcoming dates, and
- A "word" of the day.

It has become a daily ritual for staff to check this board when they enter the school. This minimizes intrusions on classroom instructional time that would result if these same messages were communicated by intercom.

Culture in the Rearview Mirror

This chapter began with a look at how hidden history influences daily life in the culture of the organization. Indeed, the past is closer than it appears on a calendar! Culture can be a barrier or facilitator of change. One principal noted, "Culture is literally the stage on which leadership gets played out. If the shared vision for the school is to be a 'home' for the heart and the mind, one has to ask, 'To bring this reality, what will it take? What will be in the halls, on the walls, in the trophy case? What will the stories be like that are told to newcomers? What will the traditions and celebrations be? And, what's more, as principal I have to be aware of how my behavior—what I attend to, put first or last on my priority list, what I participate in, what I don't—shapes the culture of the school.' "

 **Activity** ———————————————————————

Assessing Culture and Action Planning

The purpose of this form is to provide an opportunity for the principal (and leadership team) to identify a vision or goal and then "assess" whether the culture will facilitate or hinder movement toward accomplishing that vision or goal. Such an analysis is a first step toward action planning to make that vision or goal become reality (see Figure 2.5).

——————————————— **Figure 2.5** ———————————————

Assessing Culture and Action Planning Form

Vision or goal:		
Elements of Culture	**Current Reality**	**Desired State (consistent with the vision or goal)**
• Values and beliefs • Norms • Rules • Celebrations and rituals • Rewards • Stories • Physical environment • Symbols and artifacts • Traditions • Cultural players (priest, priestess, hero, heroine, historian, storyteller) • Informal communication network		
General "health" of culture:		
Areas in need of transformation:		
Action Plan: What next steps are necessary to facilitate cultural transformation?		

Reflective Field Notes ─────────────

Please use this space to jot down notes that are important for your personal leadership journey. You may do this in a structured way, by responding to questions, or in an unstructured way, perhaps by creating a graphic organizer.

- Why might it be important to understand the *hidden history* as a newcomer to an organization?

- What strategies do you believe are most helpful in reading or assessing school culture?

- What are the tools you typically use to shape culture? What new tools do you wish to add to your toolbox?

- Create a T-chart. On one side, list positive aspects of the culture in which you work. On the other side, list potentially toxic features. Select one item from the positive list, and develop a strategy to enhance that aspect of the culture. Select one item from the potentially toxic list, and plan a strategy to minimize its negative impact.

- How will knowledge of culture affect your personal leadership journey?

3

Lessons Learned
from Previous Explorers

New principals beginning their first day on the job bring their individual talents to the position *and* face the unique principalship challenges that separate one school from another. Also, newcomers experience many common challenges simply because that is the *nature of the newcomer experience* (Alvy & Robbins, 1998). New principals need to recognize that others are experiencing similar challenges. They must not lose confidence and wonder, "Why am I making so many mistakes?" When explorers foresee hurdles, they can prepare proactively for the journey and take advantage of the experience rather than treating them as obstacles.

Sociologists remind us that newcomers are "strangers." As strangers, our personal antennae and radar go up as we carefully investigate and scan the territory. For new principals, this is a wonderful opportunity. Too often in life our everyday routines are so mundane that we barely recognize new and creative opportunities. Rookie principals with antennae and radar up sense everything that is taking place. This is even true for new principals hired from within their district or school. The territory is the same, but the relationships will be very different. New principals hired in-district often are surprised to hear the conversation in the teachers' room end or change when they enter. Aspiring principals serving as administrative interns also experience this change of their colleagues' behavior.

Newcomers are at a disadvantage when they do not know how an organization operates. This makes them more vulnerable, dependent, and willing to change. Being vulnerable to change can, of course, be good and bad. It is good because the newcomer might be open to ideas that can greatly improve a school. However, if leaders do not have a vision or sense of where they are going or values to anchor them, then any idea might sound reasonable! The process of learning the organizational ropes—the roles, values, expected behaviors, and social knowledge of an organization—is referred to in classical organizational development literature as "organizational socialization" (Schein, 1974; Louis, 1980).

The organizational socialization process takes most new leaders through three important stages or phases (Louis, 1980). Because Harvey Alvy (author) personally experienced these phenomena as a principal, he is hesitant to refer to the socialization process as *stages*, because stages are linear. The organizational socialization process might be more accurately described as "two steps forward and one step back." To better understand their own anxieties, fears, and behaviors, aspiring and new principals must be aware of these stages or phases. The stages or phases include

1. *Anticipatory Socialization*—when newcomers develop expectations about the new role and organization they are going to enter.

2. *The Encounter Stage*—when newcomers begin the role and enter the organization.

3. *The Insider Stage*—when newcomers are comfortable with their role and accepted in the organization.

The Anticipatory Socialization Stage

Louis (1980) describes an interesting aspect of the anticipatory socialization stage as *leave-taking*, when one is "letting go" of the old organization loyalties and values and "accepts" the values and loyalties of the new organization. Thus, it is normal to rationalize that we are moving to the new job because the grass is greener on the other side. Interestingly, understanding the possible consequences of leave-taking can be very helpful to anyone in a leadership role. When an individual decides to depart an organization, leave-taking might entail telling colleagues how happy one is to leave the present organization and move on to a better situation. In one school, the principal always discusses leave-taking with teachers who have decided to take a position in another school. The principal simply asks the teachers to consider the leave-taking phenomenon and expresses to the teachers how important it is to leave an organization positively, working for students until the last moment of the last day. This ensures that departing faculty leave on a positive note and remaining faculty do not feel that they are passengers on a sinking ship.

The Encounter Stage

The rubber hits the road during the encounter stage of the organizational socialization process. Janet Heller (Archer, 2002), a middle school principal in New York City, describes this reality shock: "Unfortunately, you don't go into the job knowing what it entails. . . . Only when you're in there, do you say, 'Oh my God! I have to worry about the budget, about construction, about the school plan, about the kitchen and the custodian.'" One of the goals of this book is to reduce the reality shock by giving a realistic portrait of the principal's role. For the encounter stage a good piece of advice is to expect anything to happen. When it does happen, recognize that you cannot pass the buck—even though you were not responsible for the school bus breakdown 20 miles away.

The Insider Stage

Each new principal seeks to become an *insider* as soon as possible. Reaching the insider stage usually takes a few months and, in some cases, up to a year (Duke et al., 1984). Remember that teachers, classified staff, and parents want their principals to succeed. When stakeholders feel good about their leader, everyone benefits. One principal commented that he reached the insider stage when a veteran member of the staff, often regarded as hostile to management, introduced the new principal at an informal gathering. The veteran teacher stated, "This is my principal; he is even putting up with me!"

Other indicators of the insider stage include understanding the values, norms, and routines that make up a school's culture; acceptance by students and the community; taking control of one's schedule; knowing the names of a good number of students; effectively handling daily routines or the big school events (e.g., holiday programs, special testing schedules for state assessments); and learning how the informal school network operates (e.g., "I need to check with Ms. Smith, the veteran English teacher, to discuss the pros and cons of scheduling an extra assembly next week for the famous alumnus who will be in town.") Successfully networking with colleagues at regional, state, or national principalship conferences and getting to know the veteran principals who are the expert practitioners are also important induction activities characteristic of the insider stage.

A fair question to ask about the insider stage is, How long does it take for new principals to feel confident about their job performance? Recently, a retired principal asked a newcomer, "How did you do on the first day of school?" The new principal said that she didn't know if she was successful. The veteran then asked, "Did all the kids arrive home safely on the first day?" The newcomer smiled and said, "Yes!" That little bit of encouragement from the veteran with a subtle message about school safety is an important starting place when considering building confidence. Malcolm Gladwell's (2002) notion of the "tipping point" in his bestseller,

The Tipping Point, can be a helpful concept when reflecting on confidence building or success in the principalship. Gladwell states, "The name given to that one dramatic moment . . . when everything can change all at once is the Tipping Point." He relates the tipping point to consumer fads, reduced crime rates, and the spread of epidemics. Although most principals cannot tell you the dramatic moment when they reach the tipping point that indicates "I am succeeding," consider the question reflectively: At what point do you feel successful or confident in your job performance?

Personal and Professional Experiences That Influence Success

In the preceding sections we explored some of the common stages that new principals experience. Now we will explore the personal and professional *baggage* that leaders bring to the job that can influence their performance. The four areas that we will investigate include personal background, teaching experiences, university training, and preprincipalship administrative experience (Alvy & Robbins, 1998). The activity at the end of this chapter will give you an opportunity to analyze this topic further.

PERSONAL BACKGROUND

We all bring our own history to the principalship—a history that includes personality and cultural factors such as schooling; learning style; self-confidence; family background; ethnic origin; religious training; gender; urban, rural, or suburban experiences; unique talents; personal hobby interests; and scores of friendships and professional relationships from childhood through adulthood. We need to recognize that these factors will influence our performance. Think about the following factors from your past:

• Reflect on your own experience as an elementary school student.

- Consider a teacher who greatly influenced your career.

- Think about how successfully you interacted with peers and made friends as a child and now as an adult.

And ask yourself the following questions:

- Are you shy or gregarious, easy to humor, comfortable or uncomfortable with groups?

- Was there an incident during your childhood with a school principal that you can learn from today?

- As a child raised in an urban area, would you be comfortable serving as a principal in a rural school district?

The purpose of exploring these factors is not to find the voids or weaknesses in your background but to consider how you can grow from the richness and unique experiences and perspectives that each of us brings to the principalship.

TEACHING EXPERIENCES

How you conduct yourself as a principal is affected by the assumptions, beliefs, and experiences you bring to the new administration from your own teaching experiences. Asking yourself the following questions will help you clarify the perspective you will bring to curriculum, instruction, supervision, and evaluation issues:

- What are your preferred teaching strategies?

- Is your teaching philosophy based on an essentialist view? progressivist view? existential view? Are you eclectic in your thinking?

- How would you characterize your classroom management style?

- How did you get along with the parents of your students? classified staff? other teachers? students?

- What was your first year on the job like?

- What kind of help did you receive from your principal or other school administrator during your first year?

- How effective were you as a teacher?

- How effectively were you observed and supervised as a teacher?

This last supervisory question is particularly interesting for several reasons. Unfortunately, traditionally teaching has been viewed as a solitary profession, involving little interaction with other teachers or administrators. Teachers often close their classroom doors and prefer no interference from other teachers and the administration. Teachers consider their classrooms private property to be occupied only by themselves and their students. If a newcomer enters the principalship with this belief, then it is only logical to assume that the same new principal might feel very uncomfortable visiting classrooms to observe student work and supervise teachers. This situation may be compounded if the new instructional leader had unpleasant experiences with supervisors during his or her teaching career. It is fair to ask, Would a new principal recoil from supervisory responsibilities—spending minimal time in classrooms to observe students and teachers working—if his or her own principals provided ineffective supervision?

UNIVERSITY TRAINING

New principals gain different experiences from their university training. For some, taking graduate courses is an opportunity to learn and apply new ideas. For others, the process is simply necessary to "jump through the hoops" to get administrative credentials. Some educators and researchers question the positive effects of graduate programs: "We have yet to develop a method for determining whether or not the graduates of educational leadership programs will be successful" (Young, Peterson, & Short, 2002, p. 151). Joseph Murphy, a key architect of the ISLLC Standards and long-time observer of educational administrative programs, maintains that programs often miss their mark, "reinforc[ing] the centrality of the university, . . . quite frankly, diverts energy from other much more needed work" (Murphy, 2002, p. 181). Murphy strongly suggests that programs need to concentrate on leadership roles that transform principals from managers to learners, underscoring the moral-steward, educator, and community-builder responsibilities of leaders. Previously, other analysts of university programs (Bridges, 1976; Sarason, 1982) noted that a student in graduate class has the time to argue a case study or reflect and write a paper on a topic, whereas a principal often has to make instant decisions (e.g., "Should I implement an immediate school lockdown based on the comments of two students who are often unreliable, or should I investigate the situation further?"). Also, in university courses students can discuss an issue abstractly and review a checklist of steps involving a teacher dismissal without personal emotions, which are usually involved in a real-life major personnel issue.

Each administrative candidate who serves as an intern and is involved in a practicum gains something different from the experience. Some interns work very actively with competent principals, who serve as excellent mentors, giving the interns a variety of responsibilities and preparing them effectively for the principalship (Alvy, 1997). Other principal mentors give interns few responsibilities, focusing on only one area (e.g., discipline). In some cases mentors are fine role models, frequently talking with aspiring principals and giving advice, while encouraging the interns to come up with their own solutions. As a consequence of an autocratic style, or more likely because of time constraints, some mentors may simply tell interns what to do.

During a leadership seminar of administrative interns at Eastern Washington University, the interns were asked to comment on some of their initial experiences. One intern was surprised by "the variance in school climate among schools in the district." Another intern observed, "It is amazing how many things go wrong when the principal is out of the building." And another stated, "The number of different roles that you are not an expert in was a real shock to me."

PREPRINCIPALSHIP ADMINISTRATIVE EXPERIENCES

There is no particular path that can ensure principalship success. Some rookie principals first serve as counselors; others, as athletic directors, department chairs, special education directors, grade-level leaders, or curriculum or media specialists. Other administrators come straight from the ranks of teaching, whereas in some alternative or nontraditional credential programs individuals are hired directly from the military or business. The assistant principalship is the likely preprincipalship post for many newcomers. Hartzell, Williams, and Nelson (1995) point out that discipline is the main responsibility of 90 percent of first-year assistant principals. However, one could argue that the assistant principal's role as disciplinarian limits the capacity to grow. If we are to support the notion that the principal should first be an instructional leader, then we need to do a better job of expanding the assistant principal's role to reflect the importance of responsibilities in areas such as curriculum, instruction, and assessment.

The kind of support aspiring principals receive as they "climb up" the administrative ladder can affect their eventual level of success. Traditionally, climbing the ladder has been more difficult for women, who have not experienced the support of the old boys' network and have needed more administrative experience and advanced degrees than their male counterparts (Lyman et al., 1993). On the one hand, individuals who are "anointed" by the central office or a supportive principal feel good about the support and the opportunities for advancement. On the other hand, individuals who do not receive obvious support for advancement may see themselves as bucking the system. It is important to encourage those individuals with leadership potential who do not represent mainstream thinking to enter administration because, one could argue, the support that anointed candidates receive may be linked to the bureaucracy's desire to avoid rocking the boat—whereas stormy seas may very well require new captains on board.

Surprise as Routine

As we noted previously, during the encounter stage first-year principals must recognize that anything can happen on the job—and many, if not most, of these surprises are events that new leaders cannot be trained to effectively handle. These events are both serious and humorous. For example, one principal successfully calmed, assisted, and rescued a student in a science class who had a snake's fangs in her neck! A principal intern smiled when recalling an incident in which a 12th grade student affectionately gave him a senior photo—immediately after he had suspended the student for a disciplinary referral!

Surprise can be very personal when graduate academic training confronts the emotional reality of a job. For example, aspiring principals hear from their professors and read in their textbooks that they will have to spend a great deal of time on the job. However, when first-year principals actually encounter the time juggernaut, they are surprised and frustrated. Their initial emotional reaction may include resentment and regret (e.g., "Why did I take on this responsibility; previously, I only had to worry about my class!"). A principal who is also a single parent and spends Saturday morning in the office can easily resent the missed quality time with his daughter—to meet the needs of other children. An administrative intern recalled a frustrating Friday afternoon experience when "the 3:00 p.m. bus came back to school because of several student fights; and I needed to go to my class reunion."

Professional and Personal Challenges

It is important to identify problems and challenges that newcomers encounter. One cannot articulate too often the importance of sharing this information with new principals. They need to know that they are not alone in their experiences and feelings (Alvy & Robbins, 1998). And, one can only hope that by examining the challenges, problems, pitfalls, and traps encountered by previous explorers, the voyages of future explorers will have fewer setbacks. Those challenges and problems include

Constraints on Instructional Leadership and Visiting Classes. Almost every individual who becomes a principal wants to be an instructional leader. Aspiring and rookie principals visualize themselves working with teachers and conferencing with individuals or groups about professional development, curriculum, instruction, and assessment issues. For many principals, however, managerial and logistical duties often overshadow instructional responsibilities. For example, it is important that teachers begin the school year with needed teaching supplies and that the first cafeteria lunch schedule works successfully. These managerial tasks can dominate each day. Unfortunately, if the principal is not careful, the first casualty of the managerial role may be visits to classrooms to observe students working and to watch teachers in action (Alvy & Coladarci, 1985).

Managing Time. Related to the issue of constraints is learning how to manage time. Kent Peterson (1982) observes that the principalship is characterized by "brevity, fragmentation, and variety." Principals make 50 to 60 decisions an hour, which is compounded into hundreds of daily tasks. A helpful metaphor is the principal as a circus performer, juggling numerous objects or simultaneously spinning several plates. As noted earlier, university training, even with in-basket exercises and creative simulation activities, cannot duplicate the pressure of reality. Learning how to control one's schedule is not easy. New principals need to work with their secretaries, get a feel for the rhythm and culture of a school, and develop time-management techniques that reflect their goals of leading with a mandate that each student is guaranteed meaningful and challenging learning experiences. The activity in Chapter 7, "Leading and Learning by Wandering Around

(LLBWA)," (see p. 179) is an important strategy to convert the brevity, fragmentation, and variety of the job into an effective time-management strategy.

Experiencing the Loneliness of the Principalship. There is no other position in a school like the principalship. New principals note that as teachers they were the first to know about something, but now they are the last. A common remark from rookie principals is that they are now "on the other side of the fence." This can be especially difficult for a new principal hired from within a school or district. The new principal may have worked for years with a friend who is an ineffective teacher—and dealing with this situation can be very lonely and emotionally draining for all. Colleagues of many years may expect special treatment.

Regardless of how much we discuss democratic leadership, distributed responsibilities, or site-based management, the principal is still accountable for the schoolhouse. In truth, it is a little insincere for us to talk about shared leadership, yet expect principals to take *greater* responsibility for a school's performance during this era of accountability. When President Truman said, "The buck stops here," he could have added, "the oval office is a lonely place." Further, Shakeshaft (1995) notes that with more male principals on every level of school administration, males and females have not been socialized to work together. Women and people of color who are underrepresented in the principalship may feel the loneliness even more if they are encountering gender, race, and ethnicity issues.

Struggling to Develop a Personal Vision. Hall and Mani (1992) suggest that it is important for new principals to develop a "strategic sense," or a personal vision to direct their actions during the first year. A personal vision can offer first-timers a reflective ideal to evaluate one's daily actions. It is easy to write a to-do list and cross off various items by the end of the day. The challenge is to develop a personal vision statement so one can judge whether the to-do list includes items of importance, such as talking with students about their work in class. At the same time that a personal vision is being constructed, a newcomer needs to relate to the organizational vision.

Meeting Expectations on the First Day of School. A major challenge for a new principal is the expectation to succeed from day one. This may seem unfair and unrealistic, but a student new to a school and that student's parents expect the principal to help them. This family, also new to the community, needs information about the master student schedule, the location of a particular classroom, and names of school clubs that would be best for their child who needs to make friends. New teachers in the school also need guidance and support from the principal. A doctor would never be expected to know all the answers on his or her first day. A rookie principal, however, is expected to be as helpful as a 10-year veteran.

Taking a Broad View of Responsibilities. Principals bring an expertise to the position based on their teaching field or most recent position (e.g., vice principal, guidance counselor, special education director, English as a second language (ESL) director, Title I director). Can that longtime ESL director who is now the principal objectively "fight" to reduce ESL funding to support school budgetary needs for new math textbooks, based on the recent curriculum review process? Can a guidance counselor who always advocated for students from a counseling perspective make the hard decisions to support a firm disciplinary program to counter school violence? Seeing the big picture and supporting the overall mission of a school is a principal's responsibility. The challenge is to reconsider a viewpoint and attitude that worked when the boundary of responsibilities was limited.

Coping with the Steep Learning Curve. When principals are hired, they are often selected from an exemplary candidate pool. The euphoria of being selected as the top candidate for the job can turn to a crisis of confidence if new leaders expect too much of themselves. The learning curve is incredibly steep because so many unforeseen responsibilities surface for which one cannot be trained. Consider the following questions: How many educational administration programs inform candidates about making special schedules for testing days? How many programs have enabled interns to cope with data-driven, decision-making responsibilities, or convince a student to hand over a weapon to the administration or the police? The key to understanding the challenge of feeling unprepared is to remind yourself that all principals experience this feeling, beginning *and* veteran principals. Developing effective strategies to cope with the situations that bring on this feeling is the important next step.

Learning About the Informal Communication Network. Chapter 2 examined school culture comprehensively. The challenge for new principals is to take the time to absorb the culture and learn about the values, norms, and routines of the school before making any significant culture-shaping decisions. Understanding the culture involves, also, gaining an understanding of and effectively using the informal school and district network. That is, whom should you contact to get precise help from the central office? It may not be the person noted on the organizational chart. Often the school secretaries are the key informal school network personnel, which can be a real benefit to a new principal *if* the secretaries are able to provide good advice concerning how things really work in the school. A visionary principal must examine the informal network and implement changes if students and staff are not meeting important goals.

Keeping Up with the Latest Mandates and Innovations. Today's principals have more responsibilities and are expected to know more than in the past. The emphasis on standards and accountability based on state and federal regulations and the demands of data-driven decision making are examples of increased responsibilities related to academic success. Home-grown professional development programs such as action research, lesson study, and critical friends groups have gained importance in recent years, and the need to facilitate teacher efforts to help students produce quality work also raises the bar for principals regarding their role as instructional leaders. Responding to school violence, the importance of bullying prevention, and the threat of terrorism have increased the need for crisis management strategies. Family problems faced by many students have forced schools to offer full-service programs that sometimes involve dental and medical care and parenting workshops. Interestingly, veteran principals are having to retool to address recent challenges; thus newcomers need to realize that experienced principals are feeling the same pressures and confidence issues based on expectations and implementing changes. A former Stuyvesant High School principal in New York City recently remarked, "It just became a situation where you felt that you were responsible for everything, without having any ability to effect change" (Archer, 2002).

Becoming an Instant Sage. An official title does not bestow instant wisdom. However, teachers and classified staff often take comfort in knowing that the individual in a leadership position can provide sage advice. A new principal, especially a relatively young one, may be puzzled when a veteran teacher, often quite a few years older than the new principal, asks the principal for advice concerning a particular problem. And the problem may have nothing to do with school. Topics may range from retirement issues to raising one's kids, working with a colleague, handling a divorce, or investing; it doesn't really matter. When an out-of-school problem is raised, should one say, "I really don't have experience with that issue?" A more helpful approach might be to just listen and brainstorm a variety of alternatives together.

The important point to keep in mind is that although a new leader does not become Solomon overnight, the school principal is a respected figure. A degree of wisdom is conferred on new principals by most students, much of the parent community, classified staff, and teachers. Whether one's instant wisdom becomes true wisdom may take a lifetime to answer.

Meeting the Needs of the Whole School *and* Each Individual. As a new principal gazes on the faces of hundreds of elementary school students in the cafeteria or stands on the stage speaking to a high school assembly, how does one make sure that individual student faces are not lost among the masses? This can be very difficult for the new principal or vice principal who is used to seeing individual faces in a classroom. In Patricia Hersch's (1998) heartwarming and heartbreaking book about teenagers, *A Tribe Apart*, she reminds us of the importance of treating and seeing all teens as individuals and not just as a tribe or mass.

Wise principals must consider how their decisions will affect the needs of the whole school. Decisions of right and wrong become more complex when hundreds of people are involved, instead of maybe two or three in a particular classroom situation. Often new principals accept the job because they want to make more of a difference for individuals than they could in the classroom. Yet school policy can lead to complex and troublesome decisions when the needs of an individual student seem to contrast or conflict with the school policy. Rushworth Kidder's (Kidder & Born, 1998–1999) ethical dilemmas of "right vs. right" can make it very difficult for the principal who wants to help the individual student *and* the whole school. In a classroom a teacher can usually monitor individual student behavior and make an exception when necessary. But can the principal do that, when the students involved cannot be counseled daily by the principal? This can be quite frustrating for the new principal who wants to appear personable, compassionate, and caring—yet firmly upholding school policy.

Introducing Change, but Maintaining Stability. New principals symbolize change. For example, veteran teachers have to readjust to the new principal. Secretaries have to determine the work habits and routines of the newcomer. Parents need to find out if the newcomer is approachable or distant. Students wonder,

Who is that new person standing by the bus with the walkie talkie, identification tag, and bullhorn? Is the new principal going to smile, frown, make school tougher for students, or let them hang out by the lockers? The culture is influenced by the newcomer's presence. As Ann Hart (1993) points out, newcomers shape the organization as the organization is shaping them.

If the first year of the principalship is an indicator of future success, then it is important for the newcomer to pursue a student-centered vision right from the start. But if that vision does not include first trying to understand the school culture, then a degree of organizational instability can occur, making it all but impossible for the new principal to develop a trusting relationship with the faculty. During leadership workshops, Harvey Alvy (author) sometimes shares an anecdote about a principal candidate selected by a school district that had carried out a national search. The top candidate impressed every stakeholder group during the interviews, including the faculty, and was hired for the job. However, the number of changes that he tried to implement during the first few weeks on the job—and this was a veteran principal—doomed the leader to failure. The advice gleaned from this anecdote cannot simply be to tell the newcomer to maintain the status quo—organizations that stand still do not move forward. Striking a balance between maintaining stability and serving as a change agent is difficult. Leading a smooth transition characterized by stability *and* meaningful change is indeed challenging.

Building Relationships in the School. Meaningful and quality human relationships are a key to any successful organization. Until those relationships are established in a school, day-to-day energy and long-range meaningful goals are difficult to pursue with passion.

Faculty Relationships. Veteran staff may be particularly critical players in the relationship-building phase, because anointing the newcomer may be necessary for significant progress to occur. Newcomers face some very complex issues, dilemmas, and questions while building relations. Important questions include the following: Whom should I meet with first? How can I make sure that my initial meetings with individual faculty members do not signal favorites simply because of the scheduled sequence of meetings? How can I make a positive and lasting impression on the faculty during our first August meeting? How can I affirm the veteran staff and also validate the new faculty? How can I get folks to trust me?

Student Relationships. Building trusting relationships with students is a challenge for new principals. The newcomer wants to connect with individual students and with students as a group. Grade level is a critical variable. With elementary students the principal might serve as a compassionate paternal or maternal figure, bending or crouching down to maintain eye contact with a 1st grader. With secondary students the principal may need to be firm, resolute, and compassionate all at the same time. Regardless of the age of students, setting a personal example of behavior sends a powerful message. The newcomer needs to relay a complicated message, "I am a caring person, and I am here to make sure you are challenged academically and engaged in meaningful work. I am here, also, to make sure you behave appropriately, care for classmates and adults, and respect learning and the school facility." A new leader cannot fully communicate this message on the first day of school—but must start on the first day.

Unfortunately, in many schools fear of the principal or vice principal is a dominant sentiment among the students. An individual who serves as a vice principal for discipline is especially vulnerable to being perceived as one to be feared! Gaining respect from the students and, at the same time, maintaining meaningful disciplinary standards without appearing too authoritarian may be difficult for new principals. Behaving both compassionately and resolutely is challenging even for long-time school leaders.

Today, new principals must make it clear from the outset that they are firm and resolute with regard to violence, harassment, intimidation, bullying, and bigotry. Students, faculty, parents, and the community must know that violence, bullying, and bigotry will not be tolerated. The whole school community, both internal and external forces, must know that the principal is unwavering concerning these issues.

In addition to relating to individual students, a school leader needs to relate to students as a whole, as an aggregate group. Setting a tone when speaking to a full assembly or a whole class, or kicking off a school event such as a field day, demands a particular persona from the school leader. Everyone wants to be proud of the principal. Newcomers are challenged immediately to step up to the plate at major school events, serving as public speakers and representing the students, teachers, and parents at important functions. When the principal is a skilled public speaker, the school community takes pride in having him or her represent what the school stands for.

Classified Staff. Building a trusting relationship with classified staff is another significant leadership challenge. Classified staff too often receive little recognition for the contributions they make on a daily basis. Yet, the secretaries, custodians, bus drivers, paraprofessionals, cafeteria workers, and security personnel make a difference each day. An immediate challenge for a new principal is ensuring that classified workers know that they are respected and will be treated with the same respect granted to the professional staff. Classified staff can play a vital role in helping new principals create a bridge with community stakeholders. For example, many bus drivers are in the community and coffee shops at times when the other classified and professional staff are working in the schoolhouse. They can send a strong message— positive or negative—about the school leader.

Dignifying Others Who Applied for the Principalship. In some schools, one sensitive challenge may be working with teacher or administrative candidates who applied for the principalship position. To say the least, this can be a thorny and complex human relations situation. Often, the reigning vice principal applied for the position. Harsh feelings may exist. The newcomer must immediately dignify these individuals and take advantage of their strengths to help students and staff. In reality, the new principal may be totally unfamiliar with the school and needs to work with the vice principal simply because the vice principal knows how the school works. Daily meetings during the first couple of weeks of school and weekly meetings afterward, as well as assigning the vice principal to important roles during faculty meetings, can help to mitigate possible harsh feelings. Two other vital points: First, do not behave in a condescending manner to soothe the feelings of an individual who is angry or disappointed about not getting the principalship. One's decisions concerning the individual must benefit the school. Second, principals are ethically bound to help others attain the skills needed to become future principals. Assisting others by helping them to fine-tune their skills and surrounding oneself with experts is a leader's responsibility.

Building Relationships with Central Office Personnel. New principals, although feeling the immediate need to communicate successfully *in* the schoolhouse, must, at the same time, make sure there is always two-way communication with the central office. Superintendents do not like to hear about significant school events, positive or negative, after they have occurred. Principals must keep the superintendents or the appropriate assistant superintendents informed about school events. It is easy in the beginning to become so engrossed with the issues at the school site that you may forget or put on the back burner the need to work with the central office. Keeping a wider educational personnel focus is critical, because much of the success of the school depends on human and material resources acquired through the assistance of the central office (Grove, 2002). Chapter 11 addresses relationships with the central office in greater depth.

Building Relationships with Community Stakeholders. Today, a major responsibility for each school principal is strengthening the relationships with the external school community. As we note in the preface, schools can no longer succeed without community help. Like an explorer, the new principal must survey and seek help from the human and material resources in the area. First-year principals should meet parents; business leaders; police, fire, medical, and other emergency personnel; social service workers; media representatives; community service-agency workers; and others who represent community-based organizations (CBO) that affect the school, or that the school can affect in a positive way. Chapters 12 and 13 contain strategies to interact successfully with these groups. For now, the message is to explore the community, finding out who the key stakeholders are and letting folks who work positively with the school know that you appreciate their efforts. Principals must convey that they honor constructive two-way conversation to provide the best education possible for the student.

Balancing the Principalship with Personal Responsibilities. In a very honest and valuable article by Boris-Schacter and Langer (2002), smartly titled "Caught Between Nostalgia and Utopia: The Plight of the Modern Principal," the authors note that new principals are frequently selected for their positions while they are raising families and fulfilling other crucial personal obligations. Setting a personal example is a primary leadership responsibility. Part of that responsibility is signaling to others the importance of dignifying one's own family by attending family events—even during the school day. Although it may not be popular to state this, principals should encourage teachers and other administrators to make the appropriate arrangements, *even during the school day*, to attend activities in which one's own child appears. How can principals sincerely encourage parents to take time off from work to attend a school function if they are unwilling to do the same for their own children? A principal can serve as a substitute for a teacher so that the teacher can attend a play featuring the teacher's child. This action sends a very powerful message concerning the value of each child, meaningful relationships, and building community.

Success Stories ——————————————

The success stories of beginning principals noted in the paragraphs that follow are helpful examples of leaders starting their journeys effectively. As you are reading, take note that the principals' actions can be interpreted as symbolic behaviors of the important leadership themes that we note in the preface. These include keeping students at the heart of organizational actions, being a learning leader, building quality relationships, dedicating oneself to instructional leadership, and orchestrating school–community partnerships.

ARTICULATING A LEADERSHIP VISION

The first faculty meeting for a new leader is a one-time opportunity for success. One new principal used this meeting to articulate his personal vision, review the research on successful schools, and share his thoughts on learning about the school culture. In his initial remarks the principal noted that teachers were the key to school success, and that it was a principal's role to serve the teachers. Consequently, his vision was of the leader who is a servant of the students, teachers, and community. He stated that he did not view becoming a principal as moving up the ladder, because that implies that the principal is more important than the teacher. Instead, the new principal indicated that he wanted to make a different contribution to affect the whole organization in a positive way.

The new principal then provided some personal reflections on the literature about successful schools. This gave the principal an opportunity to state how important it is to have a common vision of success based on agreed-upon learning goals; high expectations for all students; an emphasis on meaningful, quality, and engaging student work; successful relationships with parents; monitoring of student success; respect for instructional time; leadership throughout the organization; collaboration among faculty about teaching and learning; and a safe and orderly school environment. The principal purposely left out the part of the literature that stressed the "principal as instructional leader" and emphasized distributed leadership because he was concerned that some faculty might have interpreted these critical initial comments as a call for a dominant school leader—and Napoleon Bonaparte was not the image that he hoped to convey.

The principal noted that he had a lot to learn about the culture of the school. He mentioned that he had heard the school was very caring and was known as a place in which teachers were always accessible. The principal stated that he had a couple of pet peeves that he wanted to share with the faculty. One, he was very uncomfortable with publicly embarrassing someone. Thus he would not do that to faculty or students—and he hoped they would follow his lead. Two, he indicated that he was uncomfortable with cynicism and sarcasm about kids. The principal observed that a couple of faculty members were uncomfortable with his remarks on these issues. But, the principal was satisfied that he had articulated his views.

In his closing remarks the principal indicated that to learn about the culture, he would be visible, trying to meet students. He was looking forward to observing their successes in the classroom. He stressed that the important school events take place in the classrooms, the theaters, the gymnasiums, and on the playing fields—not in the principal's office. The new principal asked the staff to be patient with him because he would be asking lots of questions about how the school works—about curriculum, instructional resources, and other school-related issues—to get up to speed. He apologized in advance about all the questions that he would ask. He reiterated, "Please be patient with all of my questions." Finally, the principal stated that he would try to articulate and celebrate whenever possible how much he supports all of the good things the school has done and will continue to do in the future.

BUILDING COMMUNITY AND SETTING A CARING TONE

A principal new to a school district began serving a few weeks before the first anniversary of September 11, 2001. He was in a small school district on a Native American reservation. He asked the superintendent if it was okay to do an assembly program to honor those who lost their lives on September 11th and articulate important American values during the assembly. After receiving the green light from the superintendent, the new principal contacted tribal elders, police, military, and emergency service personnel in the area and invited them to attend and to speak during the assembly. In addition, the principal worked with the music teachers and others to prepare several songs for the occasion. The assembly was a great success. The principal hoped that this commemoration assembly would become an annual day of remembrance, bringing the school and community together and reinforcing for the students the precious nature of freedom. On a personal note, the rookie principal was pleased that so many teachers, classified staff, and community elders thanked him for organizing the worthwhile assembly. His principalship was off to a satisfactory start. Most important, the assembly had symbolized values meaningful to the new leader, the school, and the community.

 **Activity** ————————————————

Self-Assessment and Charting Your Course

It is important to reflect and consider strengths and areas needing improvement when making the transition to the principalship. Based on the earlier discussion of the personal and professional baggage one brings to an organization, examine the "Know Thyself Action Plan Assessment Grid" (Figure 3.1). Develop an action plan based on the far-right column of your self-assessment grid (i.e., "What Practical Steps Should Be Taken?"):

———————————————— **Figure 3.1** ————————————————

Know Thyself Action Plan Assessment Grid

"Baggage" Categories	Initial Thoughts	Implications for the Organization	What Practical Steps Should Be Taken?
Cultural and Family Background Issues			
Geographical Comfort Zone			
Formative Educational Experiences and Personal Learning Style			
Relationship-Building Skills			
Personal Teaching Effectiveness			

(continued)

Figure 3.1

Know Thyself Action Plan Assessment Grid *(continued)*

"Baggage" Categories	Initial Thoughts	Implications for the Organization	What Practical Steps Should Be Taken?
Supervisory Style of Former Principals Who Assisted Me			
University Preparation for the Principalship, Including Practicum			
Observed Leadership Examples, Models, and Mentors			
Personal Administrative Ladder			
Leadership Style: Beliefs About Human Potential			
Communicating Through Various Methods			
Professional Development Experience			
Supervisory Notions Related to Student Achievement and Teacher Growth			

Reflective Field Notes ───────────────

Please use this space to jot down notes that are important for your personal leadership journey. You may do this in a structured way—by responding to questions—or in an unstructured way. Use whatever approach works for you!

- As a new principal, you are going through some of the organizational socialization experiences discussed earlier in the chapter. Describe some of the personal and professional events that indicate aspects of the anticipatory socialization stage, the encounter stage, and, if you are there, the insider stage. (You may want to write about these events in a journal or share reflective thoughts with a colleague or mentor.)

- Considering your experiences this year, what personal success stories would you like to tell a group of aspiring principals?

- What have been your greatest surprises this year? Could you have prepared for these surprises? If yes, how? If not, why not?

- If you were teaching graduate courses in a university for aspiring principals, what would you add to the curriculum?

- What insights or new questions do you have as a result of reflecting on the issues raised in this chapter?

4

Developing Professional Learning Communities for a Productive Journey

It has been said, "To a certain extent, a school leader's effectiveness in creating a culture of sustained change will be determined by the leaders he or she leaves behind" (Fullan, 2002). One of the powerful roads to accomplishing this challenge involves developing a professional learning community in which administrators and teachers collaboratively engage in a relentless pursuit of excellence, focusing on what fosters student learning.

Portrait of a Professional Learning Community at Work

As individuals arrive in the Prestwood School parking lot, they can be seen meeting and talking about the student assignments they evaluated the night before. As they enter the building, they continue the conversation. "I tried using the comparison matrix from *Classroom Instruction That Works*, and I was amazed at the quality of the student work! It was as if having to fill in the matrix and compare and contrast the elements of the two short stories really caused them to analyze and think more deeply about the content than they might have without the matrix," reflected Lydia.

"I discovered the same thing when I modeled the use of the matrix with three explorers the class had studied and then asked students to complete the matrix. It was rewarding to see some of the connections they made!" said Mark.

Mark and Lydia are both teachers at a school that has evolved into a professional learning community. They are members of a study group focused on what fosters student learning that decided to use *Classroom Instruction That Works* (Marzano et al., 2001) as a text. Study group members read about the nine powerful teaching strategies linked to fostering student achievement and coplanned lessons based on state curriculum standards, in which they applied selected teaching strategies from the book they had studied. After they had taught their lessons, colleagues got together and analyzed the student work derived from their instruction. They problem-solved situations in which students didn't attain mastery and created new learning experiences to help students reach a particular standard. The study group posted their learning—the results of applying the teaching strategies they had studied—on the school's Web site and put hard copies in a binder entitled "Share the Wealth—Lessons Learned" which had a permanent home in the teachers' room.

This study group was one of several operating at the school. Two years before, the principal and three teachers elected by the staff had spearheaded an effort to develop a comprehensive, responsive professional development plan designed to increase the staff's ability to serve students. The plan was based on student data derived from a variety of sources. It involved engaging staff members annually in examining student test scores, attendance data, referrals to the office, socioeconomic statistics, student transiency rates, data regarding students with special needs, and percentages and distribution of English language learners across grade levels. This examination of data yielded important information on student need areas. Staff members then reflected on and analyzed their own strengths and weaknesses in relation to the knowledge and skills they would need to address student needs. This analysis led to the identification of several topics they wished to learn more about in an effort to serve students. The topic areas identified addressed curriculum, instruction, assessment, social and emotional learning, English as a second language, and the needs of students who have learning challenges. The staff then brainstormed the professional learning structures through which they could acquire knowledge and skills—study groups, book clubs, lesson study, conversations about student work, peer coaching, and action research. They brainstormed ways to find time within the duty day for these professional development activities. Then they compiled a list of human and material resources they would need to make this venture successful. School improvement funds were identified to support the schoolwide effort. Finally, all staff members had an opportunity to select what they were going to learn (e.g., professional learning topics), how they were going to learn about it (i.e., what learning structure), when they were going to learn, and with whom they would learn. They also had to create plans that revealed these choices as well as their visions of how their studies would support student learning. The final part of each plan was the place for teachers to write what types of student data they would collect to ascertain if their professional learning experiences were enhancing their collective capacity to serve students. Looking back on this process, the principal reflected,

> What brought passion to the professional learning experiences was that faculty members got to choose what they wanted to learn as it related to enhancing their abilities to serve students. As luck would have it, this differentiated approach also turned out to be one that several teachers later said enriched their understanding of differentiating instruction for students! That is, they experienced as adults the same differentiation of learning experiences that we were asking them to

provide for students. A second source for fueling staff passion was that by identifying student data they could examine to determine if their studies were paying off, they could actually see the ways in which their learnings were helping students learn. When they did, their enthusiasm spread to colleagues. They celebrated their success! It was so much more powerful than if I had designed the professional development experiences I thought they should have. That was an important learning for me. You can give people skills, but it's much more difficult to create their will to apply them if they haven't been actively involved in the total professional development process.

Because staff were genuinely engaged in professional learning experiences and seeing tangible results of their efforts in terms of student learning, a collaborative community of colleagues emerged at this school, focused on and dedicated to the pursuit of learning. The experiences of this professional learning community are evident in the culture that has been shaped by staff members' toil. A shared valuing of student learning is now at the heart of the culture. It is now the norm to look to other staff members to tap their expertise when problems arise, another person's perspective is desired, or resources are needed. The teachers' room conversations are alive with stories about teaching and learning or knowledge swapping. Faculty meetings now begin with a segment of time dedicated to study-group or book-club reports so that those outside the formal learning structures also can reap the benefits of the groups' discoveries. Learning is celebrated in formal ceremonies. Veterans and newcomers alike have access to vibrant professional learning opportunities that challenge and enrich their lives.

Barriers to Professional Learning Communities

The preceding scenario is but one example of how a professional learning community might develop over time. (Expect a minimum of three years.) There are a multitude of approaches that schools have pursued, largely dependent on their unique contexts. What does seem to be a common thread across all of these approaches, however, is a relentless staff commitment to unraveling the mystery of what fosters learning and a shared belief that collaboration among colleagues is the only way to take on the complex challenges of life in the classroom. In schools where professional learning communities thrive, there is

- Dialogue characterized by mutual respect,
- Time for reflection,
- Study and analysis of student and schoolwide data,
- Problem solving,
- Knowledge construction,
- Nonjudgmental listening, and
- Time and effort dedicated to the development of shared meaning—all on behalf of making a difference in students' lives.

But professional collaboration is often not the norm in schools. In fact, exploring the roots of the privatization that typifies some classrooms and induces schoolwide norms of isolation, Carl Glickman, a noted author, once observed at an ASCD annual conference gathering, "It seems as if the historical one-room schoolhouse is repeated every few yards down the corridor!" Several conditions perpetuate the norm of working alone. First, teachers' schedules often preclude shared planning time. Second, the large physical structure of some schools sometimes makes opportunities for dialogue among colleagues scarce. Third, many teachers have never experienced the benefits to be reaped from collaboration. At the same time, they may fear that they may not be competent in the many areas of expertise required by state mandates. To play it safe, lest their self-perceived inadequacies be discovered, they retreat to solitary life in the classroom. Fourth, there is often a fear of competition. That is, norms of equality have historically characterized the teaching profession. "If I share something I do," some teachers fear, "it may be judged as trying to look better than my colleagues." Finally, there is a sense in many schools among staff members that there is so much to do that teachers don't have time for collaboration.

Breaking Out of Isolation

One key to transforming norms of isolation into norms that reinforce collaboration is presenting staff with a moral purpose for engaging in collaborative work. Sharing research with faculty members can help accomplish this. For example, Jan O'Neill and Ann Conzemius (2002) ask, "What is the difference between schools that are learning and making progress and those that aren't?" They report that "schools showing continuous improvement in results are those whose cultures are permeated by a shared focus, reflective practice, collaboration and partnerships, and an ever increasing leadership capacity characterized by individuals who focus on student learning, reflect on student assessments and learn as a collaborative team."

Fred Newmann and Gary Wehlage, professors of education and colleagues at the University of Wisconsin–Madison, conducted a five-year study published in the book *Authentic Achievement: Restructuring Schools for Intellectual Quality* (1996). They report

> In schools that placed the intellectual quality of student learning at the center of their restructuring efforts, the language of student learning became the focus of daily discourse. Staff did not restrict aspirations for more ambitious learning to traditionally high-achieving students; their commitment extended to all students, based on the belief that all students can meet the higher standards. This commitment translated into teaching that contributed to higher levels of achievement for all students.

In addition to research, a second key to promoting collaboration is to point out that many teachers now report that for a variety of reasons, their work is becoming increasingly difficult: a wide spectrum of student needs, high-stakes testing, increasing classroom demands related to unmet social and emotional needs, and a discontented public. Given these conditions, the need seems never to have been greater for colleagues to join together in addressing classroom challenges and ease the individual burden they pose. Further, when professional colleagues collaborate, the resources and expertise available to serve students are magnified dramatically.

Essential Understandings

For the principal and other school leaders engaged in planning, implementing, and sustaining professional learning communities, there are some essential understandings that will influence success.

Recognize that it will take *time* to develop a professional learning community—a minimum of three to five years. The presence of *trust* among colleagues has a dramatic impact on the collaborative venture. One vital tool the principal possesses is the capacity to build trust by making sure one's actions match one's words. This congruence is reassuring to the staff and builds trust over time. *Quality training* is essential so that staff members develop the skills requisite to work together around issues of teaching, learning, and assessment. In a recent study of the effects of staff development activities, "a survey of 1,000 teachers revealed that those features of staff development with the strongest relationship to reported change in teacher behavior are (1) focus on content knowledge, (2) opportunities for active learning (opportunity for teachers to apply new learnings in their classrooms and observe their effect on student behavior), and (3) overall coherence of staff development [staff development experiences that build on one another versus disjointed, unrelated sessions]" (Garet, Porter, Desmone, Birman, & Yoon, 2001 in Marzano, 2003). Making sure that these attributes are characteristic of the staff development experiences for those striving to become a professional learning community is vital to its ultimate success and the likelihood that staff endeavors will affect student learning. Finally, *tangible support* is critical for staff to believe that collaborative work is indeed important. Tangible support is conveyed when the principal attends training with teachers, when time for collaboration is placed first or given priority on the faculty meeting agenda (not at the end when people are kicking each other under the table, saying, "If we talk too much we'll never get out of here by 4:00!"), and when individual and collective efforts on behalf of enhancing student learning are celebrated.

Another key to success is to recognize that simply providing staff with new ways to behave professionally will not necessarily produce the desired outcome of collaboration. After a professional development session, each individual's thoughts will be influenced by a deeply held value system (Cubbage, 1995). For instance, if an individual deeply values and believes in the benefits of competition, a workshop on approaches to collaboration usually will not transform that person's behavior. It is not until an individual experiences the value of collaboration—obtaining new perspectives or strategies that can enhance one's "toolbox" as a result of collaborating with colleagues—that he or she begins to change professional behavior and become more collaborative. Hence, when planning professional development activities, the principal in collaboration with the staff development facilitator needs to be sure that activities are planned so that participants can experience the value of collaboration. Figure 4.1 illustrates the

Figure 4.1

The Influence of Experiences on Beliefs, Values, Thinking, Behavior, and Outcomes

effect of experiences on beliefs, values, thinking, and ultimately behavior and its results in the workplace.

Leaders need to ensure that the teachers who will be responsible for providing those experiences must first experience those outcomes desired for students. That is, if we want neurally stimulating, nurturing classrooms for students, we must ensure that the schoolhouse provides a neurally stimulating workplace for adults. The focus of collaborative work must be its ultimate effect on the student. To that end, colleagues must engage in work that ultimately leads to a heightened awareness of the conditions necessary for learning to occur.

The workplace context has a tremendous effect on how willingly professional colleagues will collaborate as a community of learners. Each school differs in how it evolves to become a culture characterized by collaboration. Leadership, the history of professional development experiences of the staff, and existing norms, values, and beliefs will influence how the development of a collaborative workplace begins. However, there are some specific activities that tend to take place in a developmental way. Collaboration tends to emerge as staff members move from relationships characterized by congeniality to cooperation and then to collegiality. How much time is spent in each of these stages is a function of the existing characteristics of an individual school. A teacher and principal, reflecting on how their staff grew to become a collaborative one, noted, "We had come to know each other as human beings . . . sharing about our families, interests, and sports. This was essential to build the trust so you can bare your soul with your colleagues and say, 'Here's the problem.' To be intellectually honest requires a foundation of trust." They describe a continuum (see Figure 4.2, p. 79). This continuum is significant in that it reminds one that if a basic respect for one another as human beings does not exist, people will experience a more difficult time collaborating" (Robbins & Alvy, 2003).

Spending time with staff—that is, interacting in a collaborative way around issues of teaching and learning—is a critical leadership function for the principal. Also, principals need to *be there* for

Figure 4.2

Continuum of Trust for Working Relationships

Congeniality	Cooperation	Collaboration

staff members when they are recovering from a serious operation or coping with a family tragedy or crisis. The principal's presence sends a strong message of personal concern and care. Over time, these incidents also contribute to the development of professional trust.

School culture has a tremendous effect on the development of a professional learning community. As the analysis of working relationships among colleagues (Hargreaves & Dawe, 1989) explained in Chapter 2 suggests, teachers often wonder, "How do I measure up to the teacher on the other side of the wall?" if they have worked only as isolated individuals. Therefore, when professional development sessions are planned, it is important to consider that the risk tolerance of these individuals may be low. When this is the case, the collaborative experiences should not require teachers to expose themselves professionally. Rather, they should be low-risk ventures, such as reading an article about closing the achievement gap and discussing the article's content with a colleague. If teachers have worked in a balkanized setting or one characterized by contrived collegiality, their risk tolerance is generally a bit greater because they have worked with a select group of colleagues. Hence, it would be appropriate to plan collaborative activities that offer medium risk. An example of a medium-risk activity is "Mail Call." Each individual in a faculty meeting is given a # 10 envelope on which to describe in writing (on the outside of the envelope) an instructional challenge with a student. The authors of the problems do not reveal their identities. The envelopes are collected and redistributed, so everyone will have someone else's envelope. Each person reads the problem described on the envelope, writes possible solution strategies on individual index cards, and then places the cards in the envelope. The envelopes are then passed to three or four other colleagues, who also review the problem on the envelope and, without reading the previously deposited idea cards (after all, it's rude to read someone else's mail), add their idea cards to the envelope. After envelopes have been passed among at least four colleagues, they are spread out on a table for Mail Call, wherein the problem owners retrieve their envelopes and read the idea cards within them. This develops the belief among colleagues that "if only I reach out, perhaps the answer to the problem I've been grappling with exists just two or three yards down the corridor!"

If professional colleagues work together frequently and view collaboration as a way of life, obviously their risk tolerance becomes greater. Hence, they may engage in high-risk activities, which would require them to demonstrate, analyze, and reflect on their professional knowledge and skills. Examples of high-risk activities include peer coaching, mentoring, lesson study, and conversations about student work, in which their professional practices and the consequences of those practices, in terms of student learning, are reflected on and analyzed for effect. Figure 4.3 elaborates on low-, medium-, and high-risk activities.

To the extent that there is a match between an individual's risk tolerance and the collaborative activity offered, attitudes toward professional collaboration will grow more favorable, the frequency of collaborative work will increase, the quality of collaboration will be enhanced, and staff and students will learn and grow.

Faculty Meetings as a Forum for Capacity Building

Finding time for collaboration is one of the biggest challenges associated with the development of a professional learning

Figure 4.3

Matching Risk Tolerance with Activities

Risk Tolerance	Description	Examples
Low Risk	Activities that do not require individuals to expose their professional knowledge and skill. Activities designed to raise an awareness of the value of multiple perspectives and resources that may exist in neighboring classrooms.	• Developing ground rules regarding how staff members will treat one another while collaborating • Communication skills training (conflict resolution, problem solving) • Reading professional journal articles and talking about implications
Medium Risk	Activities that require individuals to expose some of their knowledge and skill. These activities usually occur outside the classroom. They tend to build a desire for more knowledge about content areas, teaching practices, or assessment.	• Sharing successful classroom practices • Curriculum mapping • Problem solving regarding dilemmas with specific students and how to support their learning needs
High Risk	Activities that require individuals to expose their professional knowledge and skills. These activities might include a rigorous examination of curricular, instructional, or assessment practices and their consequences.	• Peer coaching • Mentoring • Conversations about student work • Lesson study • Demonstrating model lessons • Coteaching

community. Faculty meetings provide a natural context for such collaboration to occur. If you are a principal new to the profession or to the school, and it has not been the norm to use faculty meetings this way, expect resistance. Look for ways to ease into using the meetings as an invitation to learn. For example, one new principal, while visiting classrooms, noted that there was a need to develop a staff understanding of differentiated instruction, because most staff members were delivering one-size-fits-all instruction. "To openly address this," the principal reflected, "would probably generate some defensiveness." So, he decided to introduce the concept of differentiation gastronomically! He prepared different refreshment stations for the meeting. There were individual stations that featured chocolate, junk food, healthy snacks, high fat, vegetables, fruit, and high-protein snacks. The beverage stations were differentiated as well. As people entered the meeting room, they smiled and immediately began piling food on their plates. When the meeting began, the principal asked staff members to compare and contrast what they had selected to eat with what others seated at their tables had chosen. Then he asked what it felt like to have their individual eating preferences honored. He then said, "Today I'd like us to examine the concept of differentiated instruction. Just as I addressed your dining preferences with the refreshments, differentiated instruction offers a way for us to address the increasingly diverse learning needs of students with variations in the complexity of content, instructional approach, and assessment models." Following this brief description, the principal said, "I wouldn't be modeling what I'm preaching if I didn't offer you differentiated avenues to learn about this important topic. Hence, here are some choices I would like to offer." The principal proceeded with an explanation of these options: "Some individuals may wish to go to the media center and watch a video on the topic; others may want to analyze and dialogue about case studies of differentiation; others may wish to partake in a cooperative learning group wherein different group members read a variety of journal articles and then prepare, for each article, a written summary with implications for practice; still others may wish to begin a book club and select a book on differentiation to begin reading."

Within six months, the principal observed changes in the conversations among teachers in the teachers' workroom and in faculty meetings. He saw teachers sharing insights about differentiation, swapping teaching strategies, and talking about the results they were realizing with students as a consequence of differentiated approaches.

Expanding Professional Learning Communities Beyond the Schoolhouse

Ray McNulty, former superintendent of the Brattleboro School District in Vermont (and former Vermont Commissioner of Education), believes that "Education doesn't start in kindergarten. It starts a long time before that. Schools of the future need to think about this. We need to get out of the box and begin to engage very early with young children" (*ABC News Nightline*, 1997). In accordance with this belief, as a superintendent, McNulty wrote every child born in his school district's jurisdiction a letter of welcome. For the children born in 2003, it was a letter of welcome to the graduating class of 2020! Within a month of birth, that child would have received a visit from a representative of the school district. The visitor would have spoken to the parents about the importance of reading to the child, cuddling the child, playing games with the child to stimulate creativity, and singing to or playing music for and with the child.

Although all the children born in a given year are eligible for this visit, the district also has a special center that specifically targets the families of children most in need—from single parents and teenage moms to families with a history of drug abuse or domestic violence. District personnel believe that helping children means helping adults. Volunteers at the center teach parenting skills. They are also trained to recognize stress, which can contribute to neglect and abuse, and teach strategies to help parents cope.

Parents can receive job counseling or advice on purchasing a house or obtaining a high school diploma at the center.

As a result of this outreach effort, most children whose parents participated in this program are earning higher-than-average test scores in kindergarten. And statistics indicate that child abuse is down by 30 percent. Many of the individuals attending the job skills training have increased their family's income significantly. And some of the moms helped by the center now work for the center helping others.

In Harrisonburg City Schools (Virginia), Betsy Dunnenberger, principal of Spotswood Elementary School, reached out to community members to help support students. In the winter many children attending the school did not have warm coats or mittens. Betsy got the word out, community members donated winter clothing, and the school now has a well-stocked clothes closet. "When we run out of mittens," she noted with a smile, "we always have nice, warm wool socks that will do the job!" When Betsy became aware that families on assistance were not able to purchase shampoo, hairbrushes, toothpaste, or toothbrushes with Food Stamps, she let community members know about this need, and their generous response produced so many items that other schools were able to benefit as well.

A Final Note on Collaboration

Pondering the tall order of developing professional learning communities, the adage "It takes a village to raise a child" comes to mind. By harnessing the collective talents of staff, central office personnel, families, and community members, a principal can garner tremendous support in the quest to ensure that no child is left behind on the learning journey.

 **Activity** ——————————————————————————

Assessing Opportunities for Collaboration

Professional learning communities emerge as a result of striking a focus that resonates with individual members and their experiences with helping all students achieve and learn.

• Please take a moment and brainstorm key role groups who interact with students and potentially influence their learning experiences (see Figure 4.4).

—————————————— **Figure 4.4** ——————————————

Brainstorming Key Role Groups
That Influence Students

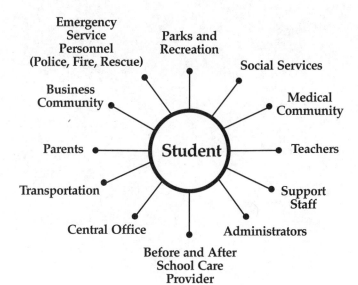

- Develop a plan to learn about what each role group is currently doing to support students, what additional roles they might wish to play, and how the school, in turn, might support their efforts. (Some schools have implemented a similar effort by designating committees to work with different role groups and report back; then they have implemented measures to take action—with incredible results!)

Reflective Field Notes ————————————

Please use this space to jot down notes that are important for your personal leadership journey. You may do this in a structured way—by responding to questions—or in an unstructured way. Use whatever approach works for you!

- Why might it be important to develop or enhance a professional learning community?

- Reflect on the organization in which you work. What are the current structures in place that encourage and support collaboration? What new ones might be needed?

- As a leader in the organization, how do you currently support staff members who are trying to develop professionally? How do you encourage professional collaboration focused on student learning?

- What connections do you see between building relationships among professional staff members and building relationships with students?

- How will your knowledge of professional learning communities affect your leadership journey?

5

Instructional, Curricular, and Assessment Leadership: The Helmsman in Action

Instructional leadership is a moral responsibility, where leaders are unwaveringly committed to student success and teacher growth. When individuals consider becoming school principals, they need to know that their job performance can help a marginal teacher become skilled or an average teacher become exceptional. One cannot overstate the effect this will have on students. Consider Marzano's (2003) research on school and teacher effectiveness. Marzano poses a scenario of a student entering a school at the 50th percentile and predicts the school and teacher effect on student achievement during a two-year period. His conclusions are compelling:

> ... this student attends a school that is one of the least effective and has a teacher that is classified as one of the least effective. After two years the student has dropped from the 50th percentile to the 3rd

percentile . . . [In another scenario] the student is in a school that is considered one of the least effective, but she is with a teacher classified as one of the most effective. The student now leaves the class at the 63rd percentile—13 percentile points higher than she entered. [In a different scenario] the student is not only in a school classified as one of the most effective but is with a teacher classified as one of the most effective. She enters the class at the 50th percentile but leaves at the 96th percentile. . . . Regardless of the research basis, it is clear that effective teachers have a profound influence on student achievement and ineffective teachers do not. In fact, ineffective teachers might actually impede the learning of their students. (Marzano, 2003, pp. 74–75)

Marzano's research supports what we intuitively know: Teachers make the difference. Consequently, school principals can affect student success by helping teachers be the best they can be. If we want students to grow and develop their skills, then we must want the same for teachers. *Teachers have a right to grow.* Beginning with their first day on the job, new principals must send a message of instructional support. As noted in Chapter 3, the principal's initial behaviors can set the stage for later behaviors. Visiting classes the day school opens and complimenting teachers for their effective instructional, curricular, and assessment strategies are critical beginning practices. A faculty meeting during the first week can provide an opportunity for teachers to share "first-week instructional successes," focusing on beginning-of-the-year teaching strategies. This sharing underscores the notion that collaboration and conversation about teaching and learning are valued.

Changes in Instructional, Curricular, and Assessment Practices

Major instructional, curricular, and assessment shifts are occurring to help students and adults succeed in schools. These shifts cannot succeed without effective instructional leadership from the principal. Of course, teacher leadership must permeate the school, but if principals are ineffective, they become major obstacles to school success. Principals can facilitate teacher leadership by supporting human and material resources used to assist teacher and student efforts. Thus, effective instructional leadership is a long-standing component of the effective schools research (Glickman, Gordon, & Ross-Gordon, 2001). Let's examine the instructional, curriculum, and assessment shifts (Robbins & Alvy, 2003) that effective principals need to support as instructional leaders:

- There is a shift toward observing quality, meaningful, and engaging student work; previously, supervisors concentrated primarily on the teacher delivery system.

- Supervisors and teachers are addressing the notion that quality, meaningful, and engaging work must be offered to *all* students—with success for *all* as the goal.

- Formative teacher supervision is *focusing* more on state standards, benchmarks, and frameworks. Summative evaluation practices need to follow a similar path.

- The clinical supervision process, traditionally focused on teacher behaviors, is now refocusing around quality, meaningful, and engaging student behaviors during class, and pre-observation and postobservation conferences on student work samples, state curriculum standards, data-driven decisions, and traditional and alternative assessments.

- Data-driven assessment decisions are influencing supervision and evaluation.

- State level assessments *and* alternative assessments, including portfolios, performances, and exhibitions, are increasingly valued by educators and the general public.

- Schools are addressing the "best practices" research on instructional strategies and curriculum standards.

- Differentiated supervision is customized for novice, experienced, and at-risk teachers needing intensive assistance.

- Continuous teacher growth, in contrast to mastery, is a more suitable approach for addressing the complexities of teaching, learning, and assessment.

• Teachers are initiating and directing collaborative professional development practices such as peer-coaching teams, mentoring, critical friends and lesson study groups, teacher curricular and instructional breakfasts, and action research projects.

• Supervisors are supporting teachers engaged in individual reflection, self-evaluation, and goal setting.

• Building-level teacher leadership is expanding regarding instructional, curricular, and assessment decisions.

New principals must support these shifts to succeed as 21st century instructional leaders. This chapter will explore how principals can facilitate staff and student success by examining these important instructional, curriculum, and assessment trends.

OBSERVING QUALITY, MEANINGFUL, AND ENGAGING STUDENT WORK

Although it is embarrassing to admit, many of us who trained to be principals were encouraged to observe the teacher, not the students. Supervision was about the teacher delivery system. Effective supervisors did not ignore students and their work, but the students and their work were not emphasized. Frequently an observation checklist was used with little emphasis on quality, meaningful, and engaging student assessment. During postobservation conferences, the conversation was about teaching decisions and lesson delivery, not samples of student work. Today, principals, other supervisors, and teachers involved in peer observation and lesson study groups are observing the teacher delivery system *and* students engaged in meaningful work.

In *Shaking Up the Schoolhouse*, Schlechty (2001) asks, "What then are the qualities, or attributes, that are likely to make schoolwork more engaging?" (p. 107). He provides 10 process standards for teachers and administrators to promote quality, meaningful, and engaging work. These process standards, part of his "Working on the Work" framework (WOW), provide an excellent source for those observing students to gauge the quality of student work:

1. *Content and Substance*—teachers and administrators share an understanding of what students need to know and be able to do;

2. *Organization of Knowledge*—content organized to maximize learning possibilities for all students;

3. *Product Focus*—the work and the tasks that students engage in, the "problems, issues, products, performances and exhibitions";

4. *Clear and Compelling Product Standards*—students' understanding how the results of their work will be evaluated;

5. *Protection from Adverse Consequences for Initial Failure*—a climate that encourages risk taking and supportive analysis when "failure" occurs;

6. *Affirmation of the Significance of Performance*—involving the significant public (students, parents, teachers, and community members) who participate in the affirmation of student work;

7. *Affiliation*—supporting student opportunities to work in groups of two or more with classmates, parents, or others in the community;

8. *Novelty and Variety*—providing a substantial range of learning opportunities that are exciting, challenging, and employing simple to complex technologies;

9. *Choice*—giving students opportunities to choose tasks to reach the intended goals of the school curriculum; and

10. *Authenticity*—supporting tasks and consequences that are meaningful to students.

New principals need to know that Schlechty's framework is not a checklist or algorithm. Schlechty states,

> The WOW framework is not a lesson plan format, nor does it assume that all students respond to the same qualities in the same way. It does not assess the "goodness" of a lesson. It is intended to be used by

teachers and school administrators when evaluating programs, classroom activities, and units of work intended to be assigned to students.

Too often we search for the one right way to make teaching and
learning easier to evaluate. For a new principal just learning the
ropes, it would be nice to have a simple formula to follow, but
teaching is one of the most complex of human endeavors. To
accomplish the process standards, Schlechty maintains that teachers need to be leaders and creative inventors of engaging work.

Schlechty's framework can be used as a valuable professional
development tool. In Central Valley School District, outside of
Spokane, Washington, more than 50 principals and central office
administrators used *Shaking Up the Schoolhouse* and the WOW
framework in a book-study group. In the group, school leaders
developed strategies to share with interested faculty after analyzing the 10 product standards.

OFFERING QUALITY, MEANINGFUL, AND ENGAGING WORK TO ALL STUDENTS

We opened this chapter noting that the moral purpose of
instructional leadership is to help teachers be the best they can be.
Because the standard has been raised for all educators, school
leaders cannot be satisfied with a system that accepts limited student success. Glickman and colleagues (2001) call this moral purpose a "cause beyond oneself." The objective of success for all is
more than a moral imperative; it is a component of the effective
schools research—all students can learn (Glickman et al., 2001).

New principals must hold a vision of success for all students as
a core belief, exemplified in their daily actions and conversations
with teachers, students, and parents. New principals are frequently unsure about a policy or action taken. Take comfort in
knowing that this goal—the success of all students—is one idea
that can be supported without question. Success for all does not
mean that every student will reach the same level of success. It
does mean that each student will be encouraged and provided
with the human and material resources to reach his or her

potential. The cornerstone of President George W. Bush's initiative "No Child Left Behind" (NCLB), signed into law on January 8, 2002, is success for all students. Regardless of whether a school leader agrees or disagrees with any aspect of the initiative, all can agree that, ideally, the intent of the initiative is to pursue the American Dream: that all individuals will reach their potential through support and hard work. Schools and school leaders can facilitate this ideal by working collaboratively with others and using bold, educationally sound, and innovative strategies to firmly pursue a vision of success for all students.

FORMATIVE AND SUMMATIVE TEACHER SUPERVISION FOCUSING ON STATE STANDARDS

While a large workshop group of elementary and secondary principals examined a draft version of the shifts described in this chapter, several members mentioned that although the shifts were accurate, summative evaluation forms were not reflective of the changes taking place in education concerning standards, benchmarks, and assessment procedures. One principal noted that although she fine-tuned her school's pre-observation form to address important educational trends, the end-of-the-year evaluation form did not reflect the changes because it was a compromise document reflecting the collective bargaining agreement and traditional state expectations. New principals need to know that this is not a recent phenomenon. The formative supervisory process *is* different from the summative evaluation process because the purpose of each process is different. It is not surprising that summative process changes in a state lag behind the formative process changes; the formative process is very personal and can be informal, whereas the summative process is tied to legal, institutional, and standardized needs. Formative supervision is concerned with

- Enhancing thinking about teaching and learning;
- Personal reflection, self-analysis, and self-improvement;

- Reflection on individual or group student work;

- Contextual changes based on adult development needs;

- Descriptive inquiry about what is taking place in the classroom; and

- Continuous personal improvement.

On the other hand, summative evaluation is concerned with

- Quality assurance that organizational expectations are met;

- Judgment of performance;

- Public recognition;

- Mastery of specific standardized objectives; and

- Legal guidelines.

Because the formative process is more personal and contextual, reflecting an individual teacher's needs and the specific classroom, a supervisor can customize the process when working with teachers. Formative supervision includes a range of professional development options. A common option involves supervisors observing teachers and students during class. The clinical supervision process, discussed in detail in the next section, is a valuable tool to observe teachers. Our clinical supervision process model, adapted from the seminal work of Cogan (1973), includes four steps: the pre-observation conference, the observation, reflections on the observation, and a postobservation conference. A pre-observation conference form should be developed to reflect teacher needs, observation of student work, and state expectations.

Before embarking on their official supervisory activities, new principals need to explore the cultural norms in their schools and ask questions about the teacher observation process. For example, can you develop your own pre-observation form or will you be tied to a form used in the district? If a new principal has the opportunity to develop a pre-observation form, the following elements are suggested for inclusion:

1. Lesson objectives—What do you want the students to know and be able to do as a result of the lesson? (Invite the teacher to bring student work samples to the pre-observation and post-observation conferences that reflect the objectives.)

2. How does this lesson align with the course curriculum? What state standards or benchmarks will be addressed during this lesson?

3. Describe the special needs students in the class and how you will address their needs.

4. What background knowledge or skills do the students have for this lesson?

5. Do you anticipate any particular difficulties that the class or specific students may encounter during the lesson?

6. Describe the key aspects or steps of this lesson. What specific activities will students engage in during the lesson to meet your objectives? Remember that each lesson holds its own surprises and the steps of the lesson may be altered. (You need to know that as the observer I am comfortable with the *surprise* possibilities.)

7. What teaching strategies, student engagement activities, curriculum issues, assessment procedures, specific student issues, and general educational issues do you want me to concentrate on during the observation? We will discuss these strategies, activities, and issues during our pre-observation conference and post-observation conference. (It is recommended that only two or three issues be selected for the observation.)

8. What else would you like to discuss concerning the lesson?

9. If you want to make arrangements for videotaping, let me know several days in advance.

10. Date, room, and time of lesson: _____ .

As an aspiring or new principal, you should review these suggestions and examine the pre-observation forms used in your school or district. Consider brainstorming pre-observation form possibilities for your school with other administrators, teachers, and central office personnel.

REFOCUSING THE CLINICAL SUPERVISION PROCESS

The shifts in instructional, curricular, and assessment practices provide an opportunity for supervisors to reinvigorate the clinical supervision process. The process, formerly used primarily to observe the teacher delivery system, is now used to engage teachers in a conversation about quality student work, standards, data-driven decisions, and assessment strategies. A review of our four-step process will shed light on these changes:

1. The Pre-observation Conference—The teacher and supervisor take the opportunity to discuss the lesson objective and the type of engaged work the teacher hopes to facilitate. Whether the conversation is honest and about taking risks with an innovative instructional idea will depend on if the teacher and supervisor trust each other. An experienced teacher should be more comfortable taking ownership and have more to say during this conference than a novice, but you never know. Some new teachers, having experienced success with student teaching and fresh out of the university, are very articulate about teaching and learning. If teachers are unsure about what they would like to have you observe, you can provide a menu of possibilities including

- Examining student work samples;
- Focusing on recent data-driven class information;
- Addressing a particular state standard or benchmark;
- Using traditional or alternative assessments;
- Checking lesson transitions;
- Observing questioning techniques;
- Documenting student participation;

- Beginning lesson strategies;

- Checking for understanding;

- Using closure;

- Watching the pacing of classes;

- Using technology;

- Assessing that student work is engaging;

- Using brain compatible learning;

- Incorporating multiple intelligences;

- Facilitating effective classroom management; and

- Addressing special needs students.

If the teacher would prefer a structured framework of ideas, the supervisor might introduce appropriate components of Schlechty's (2001) 10 process standards; Marzano's (2001) nine instructional strategies; or the planning and preparation, and environmental and instructional domains in Danielson's (1996) work. It is critical, however, that the teacher take ownership of the conference and decide what should be observed. The pre-observation form suggestions, reviewed earlier, can provide a framework for the conference.

We cannot overstate the importance of a collegial conversation about teaching. New principals can make significant contributions if they stimulate discussions about teaching and learning. During pre-observation conferences teachers should do most of the talking. Principals need to listen actively and help teachers clarify and reflect on their intentions. As Art Costa and Bob Garmston (1991) note in their Cognitive Coaching workshops, "A good pre-observation conference is worth six observations." The conversation between two colleagues about teaching and learning is more valuable than having a colleague observe a lesson. As noted on the suggestions for the pre-observation form, the teacher should select no more than two or three areas for feedback. This is particularly important for many new principals who may not yet be experts at recording observation data. If a teacher decides to videotape a lesson, the menu of feedback possibilities can be expanded, because videotape can be reviewed repeatedly.

2. *The Observation*—An observer (e.g., principal, supervisor, or teacher) records and gathers data for feedback on the areas agreed on during the pre-observation conference. Supervisors need to mitigate the fears that many teachers have about being observed. For example, when principals are visible around the school and visit classes frequently, even for a few minutes, there is much less concern when they enter the room. Schlechty (2001) reminds us, based on the shifts discussed,

> Rather than observing the classroom to see how the teacher is performing, the principal observes the classroom (and perhaps interviews students and reviews assignments as well) to determine the extent to which students are engaged, persist, and experience a sense of accomplishment and satisfaction as a result of what they are asked to do. (p. 144)

3. *Individual Reflection by Supervisor and Teacher*—Principals need to encourage teachers to reflect on their teaching. The clinical supervision process can facilitate reflection. In one scenario a principal might say, "It was a pleasure watching you teach today. Because we have scheduled the postobservation conference for tomorrow after school, why don't you examine and reflect on the work students completed during the lesson and bring some samples and your reflections to our conference?" In another scenario the principal might state, "I took notes during the lesson (e.g., possibly script-taping) based on our pre-observation conference discussion. I'll make a copy of my notes and place it in your mailbox. Please examine my notes and add your ideas for our scheduled meeting tomorrow. I'm really looking forward to your comments. I have a copy of the state benchmarks in my office. We can use that to concentrate our discussion on the benchmarks you asked me to observe."

4. *The Postobservation Conference*—The teacher should do most of the talking and data interpretation during the postobservation conference. Again, how much "conference ownership" a teacher takes may depend on his or her experience and level of trust between the supervisor and teacher. As a new principal, one should not expect teachers to open up during the first conference about what worked and what did not; more than likely, the teacher will focus on what worked. Postobservation conferences are challenging, refreshing, and intriguing when the trust level is high and a teacher can walk into a principal's office and state, "Mary, wasn't that great the way Billy, sitting in the back of the room, helped Diane? I could not believe it, he usually doesn't help her at all. I have really been feeling like cooperative learning has not been working, but now I will have to reassess my thinking. What did you see?"

If teachers ask to have their lessons assessed based on state benchmarks, samples of student work can be very helpful. The discussion will likely be productive if examples of best student work, average work, and work needing considerable improvement are examined. Toward the end of the conference, some variation of the question "Where do we go from here?" will likely emerge. Whether another clinical conference or some other professional development practice will occur needs to be discussed. Chapter 6 reviews a variety of professional development practices that will enrich our discussion of supervisory ideas. The following general guidelines for conferencing with teachers will help aspiring and new principals succeed:

- Ensure that teachers are familiar with the clinical process before you begin. As a new principal you need to inquire about the culture and find out if your predecessor used a similar professional development strategy. Depending on the culture and the school's size you may want to share your philosophy about supervision and the clinical process during a faculty meeting, with small groups of teachers (e.g., department or grade-level teams) or with individual teachers.

• Be visible and visit classrooms frequently to help students and teachers be more comfortable during formal observations.

• During the conferences, create a positive climate for thoughtful decision making and risk taking.

• When possible, hold the conference in the teacher's classroom or another place of the teacher's choice.

• Support clinical supervision focused on teacher ownership of conference objectives and important decisions.

• When appropriate, student work should be examined during the conference.

• Emphasize that the conference dialogue and reflections may be more critical than the actual observations.

• Refrain from dominating conferences—supervisory dominance inhibits teacher reflection and honest communication.

• Recognize there is no Holy Grail of effective teaching. If teachers believe that you prefer one style of teaching or are enamored with a particular instructional fad, you will lose them.

• Although emphasis on state standards and benchmarks is critical, remain open to observing lessons that are a stretch from the explicit curriculum. Remember, seek a conversation about teaching and learning. If a teacher has an idea for a lesson that will result in engaging students, that lesson could serve as a springboard for instructional growth. Later, one can align the instructional ideas with important standards and benchmarks.

• Demonstrate lessons, team teach on occasion, and encourage lessons involving groups of teachers observing one another.

- Promote staff development—the clinical process should not be a "box canyon" limited to the four-step process, but an opening to other professional growth possibilities.

DATA-DRIVEN ASSESSMENT DECISIONS

Part of the accountability movement is tying teacher performance to student results. Although the alternative assessment movement is popular among many educators, the hard data characterized by norm-referenced and criterion-referenced tests (NAESP, 2002) are usually the focus of attention when considering data-driven assessment. In general, a positive aspect of assessing is the process of disaggregating data and searching for group or individual student trends or patterns to help teachers pinpoint needs. In theory, if needs are pinpointed, teachers can modify their practices to meet the needs of individual students or groups of students. Contracted software companies (or homegrown central office software developers) that develop assessment analysis software for use by local and state education agencies have opened up a whole range of resources to track student progress. A multitude of demographic variables can be disaggregated to discern patterns, including gender, ethnicity or race, student mobility, economic standing, teacher experience, behavior referrals, student disabilities, dropout rates, English proficiency, and attendance patterns.

Thus, teachers and supervisors can begin a healthy conversation about patterns and trends. Discovering that a specific group of students is performing above or below a standard can influence teacher and supervisory decisions concerning strategies and resources. Whether inappropriate or unfair pressure could be placed on a specific teacher, school, or district because of the data-driven testing results is hard to predict. *Teaching to the test* is expressed often as a negative consequence of the accountability movement. Of course, if the test is engaging, aligned with meaningful curriculum standards, and not just a regurgitation of facts, then important educational outcomes may result.

On a practical note, No Child Left Behind requires the publication of testing data. The law is intended to exert pressure on school districts to perform. Supervisors and teachers recognize that public accountability is an important part of the law. To illustrate, Spokane School District 81, in Spokane, Washington, like all school districts in the nation, shared its 2001–2002 data with local constituents through a school report card:

> One of the act's [NCLB] new accountability measures is a requirement that all schools, school districts and states publish "report cards" that contain specific data elements highlighting the progress of public schools. These report cards provide disaggregated data on the state's assessment, the Washington Assessment of Student Learning [the Washington State test based on the state's curriculum standards], by the five major racial/ethnic subgroups: gender, disability, English proficiency, migrant/bilingual status, and economic standing. These reports also include data on school improvement status and school demographics: teacher qualifications; graduation and dropout rates for secondary students.

Sharing this data-driven information with parents on such a large scale is new for schools. New principals are not alone in trying to figure out how to share the data with the public, what to do about "good and bad" results and how to analyze the data to help students. Understanding how to navigate most effectively to assist students in the data-driven world is also a challenge for the most experienced principals.

One final note: Testing data can be misunderstood and misused. Our nation's history of using testing data has a negative side. Beginning in the early part of the 20th century, fascination with IQ testing and other standardized tests led to consequences that closed the door of opportunity for millions of Americans because of their ethnic or racial origins. "Earlier, during World War I, Terman [a pioneer of intelligence and achievement tests] and a group of psychologists had field-tested their exam on 1.7 million U.S. Army recruits. Scores on word and picture problems helped to determine which men would be assigned jobs in Washington, and which men would be sent to the trenches in France.

Psychologists concluded, based on IQ tests, that the average mental age of American adults was 13.7 years and that ethnicity affected intelligence. . . . By the 1920s over a million children were undergoing IQ tests each year" (Mondale & Patton, 2001). Schools have a history of tracking students, often based on tests, and placing them in differentiated academic or vocational programs that either optimize or limit possibilities. Julian Nava, raised in a Mexican American family in California during World War II, tells a story of how he was able to select college prep courses in high school. The classes became available only because his older brother, in a sparkling naval uniform, insisted in the school guidance counselor's office that the counselor let his brother take an academic program. Julian went on to receive a doctorate in history from Harvard and later was elected to the Los Angeles Board of Education and became U.S. Ambassador to Mexico. Nava states with sadness that as a result of classifying students, "It has been an enormous loss to our country. We will never know how many Doctor Salks or Pablo Casals or Picassos have been lost because children from minority groups were not inspired or challenged and given the chance to show what they've got" (Mondale & Patton, 2001).

STATE-LEVEL AND ALTERNATIVE ASSESSMENTS

An interesting aspect of the assessment movement is that two very different assessment paths are being supported concurrently. One path includes standardized high-stakes tests that are usually criterion-referenced and supported by the general public, the business community, and segments of the education community. The other path includes alternative assessment strategies, supported by much of the educational community. Most school leaders support both paths because each addresses particular needs. New principals may feel the pressure of the criterion-referenced tests because a school's performance can be perceived as a litmus test of the newcomer's performance. Judging a new principal on a school's test results during the principal's first administrative year may seem absurd, but the public may take that position. NCLB and the yearly report card on a school can place a new principal on the hot seat.

In theory, state standards and benchmarks are aligned with the criterion-referenced tests. A debate in the educational community concerning criterion-referenced tests relates to whether one test should serve as a gateway or barrier to the next grade level or graduation—hence the high-stakes classification. Some educators maintain that most state tests assess only minimum competencies and lower-level skills. Others believe that these state assessments are different and raise the bar for expectations and higher-level thinking.

For more than a decade we have seen the emergence of alternative assessments including portfolios, exhibitions of mastery, and performance assessments. These assessments are frequently created at the class or building level. The presence of an audience to observe or participate in the assessment activity is a dynamic aspect of the alternative assessment movement. For example, the traditional parent-teacher conference has been transformed in schools where students display their portfolios—their progress over time—to parents during the conference.

At the high school level in some states, a senior project has become a requirement for graduation. Senior projects typically contain alternative assessment components, although traditional paper-and-pencil tests and the high school transcript might be included in a portfolio. A successful senior project could include a research paper on a possible career path, a physical project with required hours in a school-to-work setting, a plan for the "13th year," a portfolio including exemplary high school work and career artifacts such as a résumé, a service component, and finally, a culminating presentation demonstrating competency to a group of significant adults from the school and business community.

BEST PRACTICES RESEARCH

"Thirty-five years of research provides remarkably clear guidance as to the steps schools can take to be highly effective in enhancing student achievement" (Marzano, 2003). This is good news for teachers, students, and administrators. For example, Marzano, Pickering, and Pollock's (2001) book, *Classroom Instruction That Works*, provides nine "best practice" instructional strategies that can significantly affect student achievement. Systematically implementing and practicing these strategies will have a significant positive effect on most students. New principals should share this information with the faculty in a supportive manner to demonstrate a commitment to important research with practical application. The nine instructional strategies are shown in Figure 5.1.

Figure 5.1

Strategies That Affect Student Achievement

Rank based on effect size	Nine Instructional Strategies
1	Comparing, contrasting (identifying similarities and differences), classifying, analogies and metaphors
2	Summarizing and note taking
3	Reinforcing effort and providing recognition (giving praise)
4	Homework and practice
5	Nonlinguistic representations
6	Cooperative learning
7	Setting objectives and providing feedback
8	Generating and testing hypotheses
9	Questions, cues, and advance organizers

Source: Adapted from Marzano, Pickering, and Pollock (2001).

Danielson's (1996) framework of four domains to enhance instructional practice—Planning and Preparation, the Classroom Environment, Instruction, and Professional Responsibilities—provides schools and teachers with 22 research-based components that can help create a common professional vocabulary and professional development activities based on what we know about the behavior of effective teachers. Stronge's (2002) research review of qualities of effective teachers, including "the teacher as an individual, teacher preparation, classroom management, and the way a teacher plans, teaches, and monitors student progress," adds to the knowledge base that school leaders can share with faculty about teacher success. New principals can immediately help new teachers by sharing the work of Marzano and colleagues (2001), Danielson (1996), and Stronge (2002). The faculty will take pride in a leader who can provide a strong knowledge base of effective teaching and learning strategies.

A corollary to the best-practice instructional strategies is the work of Zemelman, Daniels, and Hyde (1998) in the curriculum field. New principals will find their work useful because the researchers examined the major curriculum standards from the various disciplines and arrived at a consensus concerning emphasized and de-emphasized trends. Zemelman and colleagues note the importance of developing standards: "As a nation, we stopped for a moment and asked each school subject area field to define itself, to identify its key content, processes, and habits of mind. No matter how imperfect and controversial the results, this has been a rare episode of national reflection." A compelling conclusion drawn by Zemelman and colleagues (1998) is that "polarities do not characterize these [national curriculum] reports. . . . [T]he fundamental insights into teaching and learning are remarkably congruent. Indeed, on some key issues, the recommendations from these diverse organizations are unanimous." In this sampling of their conclusions, best practice curriculum includes *more*

> hands-on learning . . . diverse roles for teachers . . . higher order thinking . . . learning a field's key concepts and principles . . . deep

study of a smaller number of topics . . . primary sources . . . responsibility transferred to students for their work . . . choice for students . . . enacting and modeling of the principles of democracy in school . . . developing the classroom as an interdependent community . . . heterogeneously grouped classrooms . . . .

. . . but it includes *less*

one-way transmission of information from teacher to student . . . attempts by teachers to thinly "cover" large amounts of material in every subject area . . . rote memorization of facts and details . . . less tracking or leveling students into "ability groups" . . . use and reliance on standardized tests.

DIFFERENTIATED SUPERVISION CUSTOMIZED FOR NOVICE, EXPERIENCED, AND AT-RISK TEACHERS

Generally, our profession has failed to honor teacher differences in professional expertise, personal life experiences, career goals, life-cycle stage, and gender (Glickman et al., 2001). The fifth-year teacher and the 25-year veteran often encounter the same evaluation system and staff development opportunities. Danielson and McGreal (2000) observe, "Teaching, alone among the professions, makes the same demands on novices as on experienced practitioners" (p. 5). Fortunately, a shift is taking place, and customized professional development opportunities are being offered that also meet district or state accountability needs. This is good news, especially for expert teachers. Mentoring opportunities, for example, enable school districts to use the strengths of their best teachers to help new or veteran teachers. Danielson and McGreal state,

Thus, schools and districts should differentiate their evaluation systems for teachers, according to their professional needs. Many schools have designed systems with three "tracks": separate activities and time lines for *novice* (or probationary, or nontenured) teachers, *experienced* (or career, or tenured) teachers, and for those *needing intensive assistance* or a plan of action (experienced teachers for whom the next step is dismissal for inadequacy in teaching).

CONTINUOUS TEACHER GROWTH

Stated in different ways, a cautionary note is expressed in many of the instructional works published today: *This document is not a checklist for success.* This warning is necessary because too often a framework or instructional model has been fashioned by a school district or state, and supported by school administrators, as the only yardstick for success. A teacher who receives all checks on the form reaches "mastery" and has little incentive for further growth.

As professionals, we recognize that a community of learners can thrive when the goal is continuous growth. Whether we are referring to an individual, a group of teachers, or an organization's culture, continuous growth is a model and philosophy right for the times. Our pedagogical knowledge base related to instruction, curriculum, assessment, and classroom management continues to grow. New principals can take comfort in knowing that as learning leaders, it is their responsibility to the teachers and students in the organization to model an inquisitive and questioning style of leadership. Continuous improvement is a requisite goal of all learning leaders.

COLLABORATIVE PROFESSIONAL DEVELOPMENT PRACTICES LED BY TEACHERS

A shift that all of us in education are pleased with is the leadership role that teachers are taking in the organization. It is foolish to think that principals alone are the school leaders. The old administrative model of the principal at the top of the pyramid directing the teachers is as outmoded as the old schoolmaster using a paddle to rein in the boys fighting behind the one-room schoolhouse. Breaking down the barriers of teacher isolation that have characterized our profession since its inception is a healthy aspect of the emerging teacher-leadership culture. It would be a monumental accomplishment if we could move from a profession characterized by isolation to one characterized by collaboration. The research base supporting a shift toward a collaborative model firmly indicates that when the faculty functions as an effective learning community, student success is enhanced (Newmann & Wehlage, 1995). Important teacher-led professional development practices, such as peer coaching, lesson study, action research, and mentoring, will be discussed in detail in Chapter 6.

TEACHER REFLECTION, SELF-EVALUATION, AND GOAL SETTING

Teachers make thousands of decisions each day. Each day is filled with a series of decisions, events, and episodes, from which we can learn if we take the time to reflect. If we reflect, then the decisions, events, and episodes can become valuable experiences, some of which we will recall many years later as markers, or transition points, in our lives. Students will suffer if we do not reflect on these decisions and refine our skills. For some individuals, keeping a reflective journal can serve both the professional need to elaborate on an issue and the personal need to step back and slow down to gain perspective.

A teacher portfolio can be an effective vehicle for reflecting on your professional practice. Danielson (1996) recommends the following components for the professional portfolio: a three-week unit plan, an instructional plan for a single lesson, samples of assessment procedures reflecting knowledge of students and resources for students, videotape of the class, instructional artifacts of assignments given to students in the classroom and at home, samples of student work, a reflective sheet to assess the lesson, logs related to family contact, participation in school and district projects, professional contributions and professional development activities, and finally a log of possible action research activities. A portfolio might also include a list of inspirational quotes or personal comments and observations acquired from meaningful books, articles, and conversations; a list of Web site addresses linking you to helpful resources; pictures of meaningful school events, and notes from students or parents that help you celebrate the profession.

BUILDING-LEVEL TEACHER LEADERSHIP

Site-based management (SBM) has become an empowering tool for teachers, parents, and other community stakeholders, resting on the notion that those affected by decisions should be involved in the decision-making process. Along with administrators and sometimes students, SBM teams are often responsible for developing and implementing a school improvement plan (SIP), "designed to improve how a school functions and operates, with the intent of increasing and enhancing teaching and learning; often required by state departments of education and local school districts" (Morrison, 2003). Morrison suggests that a SIP should include the following components:

- School mission and goals
- Baseline data necessary to identify needs
- Expected student learning outcomes
- Strategies and time line for improvement
- Participatory management model
- Description of how resources will be used
- Training and technical assistance necessary to support the SIP
- Report on the status of current year's plan

The range of possibilities for SIPs is unlimited. A school might be considering a technology plan, a senior project, a new math program, a looping model, a differentiated professional development plan, a parent-education program, an innovative extracurricular program, a reorganization of a large high school into family units, or a change from a traditional to block schedule. Teachers, because of their expertise, exercise considerable influence on most teams. Administrators can facilitate the process by ensuring that issues are raised that reflect the schoolwide implications of SIP decisions, meeting venues are comfortable, material resources are provided, a record is kept of the planning sessions, budgetary and educational decisions follow legal principles, proper steps are followed if the plan is steered by state time lines and regulations, and substitute teachers are provided for important SIP meetings. Teachers are very busy, and often the most creative and dedicated individuals are reluctant to serve on SIP teams because meetings divert energy from their classroom responsibilities. Administrators must support these bright and valuable individuals, encouraging them to take leadership roles to influence the schoolhouse.

 ## Success Story

The new principal was appointed on August 6. The appointment came because of a veteran principal's illness, resulting in a late decision by the veteran to apply for retirement. The retirement papers did not arrive until early August, at which time the veteran could officially announce his retirement, and the rookie principal could move into her new office. As the new principal looked over the schedule for the two days of professional development workshops planned for the faculty before the opening of school, she was impressed: two nationally known educators were scheduled to speak and conduct day-long faculty workshops. She had heard both educators speak at conferences and knew they would be successful.

A couple of weeks before school, a veteran teacher walked into the new principal's office and wished her good luck. She was pleased until the veteran mentioned with a cynical smile,

> You'll just have to go through the torture with us of listening for two days to some speakers who will discuss nothing of interest. We just want to work in our classrooms and prepare for our students. Bill was a good friend and a fine principal, but I don't know why he insisted on finding these speakers who just waste our time each year. Maybe you can change things next year.

The rookie principal thanked the veteran for stopping in but did not mention that the speakers were first-rate. The principal decided to take a wait-and-see attitude, knowing that the literature on the principalship suggests observing the culture before making significant changes.

The two professional development days received mixed reviews. Four new teachers seemed to enjoy the workshops, as did a few of the experienced faculty. In general, most of the staff just sat and listened, looking at their watches and sneaking off for extended periods to work in their classrooms. Although the principal previously had been impressed by the speakers, she had not seen them in action during full-day workshops. She was not impressed with the workshops, and she thought the time could have been used more effectively.

Three weeks after school began, the principal asked the veteran teacher who had visited her before school about organizing a committee of teachers to work with her on professional development issues. The principal indicated that she had no "agenda" but wanted the teachers to have significant input in professional development decisions at the school site. The veteran said he was willing to get involved and raise the issue at the next faculty meeting. After the faculty meeting several teachers agreed to get involved with the staff development committee. They met for the first time a couple of weeks later and discussed several possible staff development ideas. The ideas included workshops on instructional strategies to align with the state benchmarks, wellness workshops, a book-study group, technology workshops, and strategy sessions for working with students who have limited English proficiency. One faculty member said she was excited about an article she read recently about Japanese teachers watching one another teach a lesson with similar strategies and then working together to refine the lesson. The principal told the teacher that she would have copies of the article made for all faculty members because the teacher was so impressed by the article. Toward the end of the meeting a veteran teacher reflected, "You know, we have teachers at the school who have an expertise in almost all of the areas mentioned for possible staff development topics. Maybe we could sponsor our own workshops during the staff development day in February." The teacher looked at the principal and said, "What do you think? How about we use some of the expertise around here?" The principal knew that the central office had already contracted a speaker for the February meeting but wondered if something could be worked out: "Maybe we can talk to the presenter about our needs or do two half-day sessions. Let me check with central office, and let's talk about it with the faculty." When the staff development committee meeting ended, the rookie principal knew that the staff was on the right track. She would have to work with them to capitalize on their ideas and the emerging commitment to homegrown staff development. Finally, she wrote down a couple of thoughts concerning changes she was going to implement with the help of the teachers in the planning of the two-day professional development workshop in late August.

 **Activity** ――――――――――――――――――――

Disaggregating Test Data to Assist Students

The table in Figure 5.2 includes a number of variables and essential questions that can help schools, principals, subject-area colleagues, special service teams, grade-level teams, and individual classroom teachers make thoughtful, data-driven decisions. The table can help drive decisions based on criterion-referenced tests aligned with state standards. Assessment results for all of the variables listed in Figure 5.2 may not be available. Feel free to modify the variables and create your own template depending on how the data are reported in your state, district, or school. The table can be used to develop a framework or action plan for analyzing disaggregated data. To demonstrate how to use the table we have walked through the process with the gender variable.

Figure 5.2

Disaggregating Data: Analyzing Test Results to Assist Students

Demographic Variables: A particular variable may have several components with aligned testing data.	Results of Assessment (e.g., percentage of 7th and 8th grade students meeting the math standard).			What critical issues emerge from these assessment results?	Where do we go from here? Consider appropriate groups and strategies to analyze the data.
		7th	8th		
	Female:	75%	65%	Why are the 7th grade results significantly different from the 8th grade results?	Let's have the 7th and 8th grade math teachers meet, analyze data, and develop strategies.
Gender	Male:	76%	60%		
Racial or Ethnic Subgroups					
Economic Standing					
Disability					
English Proficiency					
Migrant or Bilingual Status					
Attendance Patterns					
Behavioral Referrals					
Student Mobility					
Teacher Qualifications					
Teacher Mobility					
Extracurricular Participation					

Reflective Field Notes —————————————

Please use this space to jot down notes that are important for your personal leadership journey. You may do this in a structured way—by responding to questions—or in an unstructured way. Use the approach that works for you.

- Review the shifts in instruction, curriculum, and assessment at the beginning of this chapter. What would you add to the list of shifts? Which shifts do you believe are in place in your district or school? Which are most difficult to implement?

- What is your feeling concerning the parallel interests of various school stakeholders in both criterion-referenced assessments based on state standards and the alternative assessment movement?

- Consider some questions or issues that you would like to address during pre-observation and postobservation clinical supervision conferences.

- Consider the research on best practices. How would you use the research during a faculty meeting? With a grade-level or subject-area team? With an individual teacher?

- Develop a brief professional growth plan for a new teacher; a successful, experienced teacher; and a marginal, experienced teacher. Share your ideas with a colleague.

- What insights or new questions do you have as a result of reflecting on the issues raised in this chapter?

6

Improving Student Learning Through Supervision and Professional Development

As individual staff members increase their craft knowledge, their capacity to serve students is enhanced tremendously—if, of course, teachers and other professional staff have the will and support to apply their new knowledge and skills in the classroom. Chapters 2 and 4 addressed the ways in which the workplace context can hinder or support professional learning within the schoolhouse. As Chapter 5 illustrated, two other ways to move forward on the path to learning are through *supervision* and *professional development practices*.

Chapters 5 and 6 are seamless regarding the importance of supervision and professional development. New principals who really want to make a difference as instructional leaders strive to expand their instructional repertoire beyond classroom observations to include professional development initiatives. These practices also enable the principal to model lifelong learning for faculty and students to observe.

Supervision is embraced as a growth-oriented, formative process; teacher and supervisor engage in a rigorous examination of what content and practices can best create the conditions under which all students will learn at high levels. In the process of talking about, observing, and reflecting on teaching and its consequences, both parties gain new insights, develop new perspectives, solve problems, and learn. The new principal, often a former teacher, usually has credibility in this process because he or she has recently been in the classroom. An important stance to model in the supervisory role is to seek to understand the content to be taught, the learners in the classroom, what experiences preceded this observation, what teaching and assessment strategies will be used, and the way the teacher thinks about the planning process prior to instruction. Developing this understanding is vital in observing in an unbiased way and engaging in meaningful, reflective dialogue about the teaching episode. Because this process often reveals areas in which those seeking to understand teaching and its effects wish to grow professionally, supervision and professional development are addressed in an intertwined manner.

Supervision as a Tool to Foster Staff and Student Learning

Several years ago, Carl Glickman, playing with the word *supervision* suggested that the act of supervision should be guided by a *Super Vision* of effective instruction (Glickman et al., 2001). These words serve as a guiding light for the principal who has the important task of spending time in classrooms and ascertaining if effective instruction is taking place. As noted in Chapter 5, instruction is effective only if it contributes to student learning. In addition to what the teacher does, it is critical to consider what the student is being asked to do. Phillip Schlechty (2001) writes,

> Teachers do not cause learning; they do not make learning happen. Rather, they design activities for students that they believe students will find engaging and from which students will learn. When teachers design the work right and when they provide the right work (work that contains the right content), students do learn. The primary source of variance in student learning is the quality of the work the teachers and the schools provide to students.

As mentioned in Chapter 5, Schlechty lays out 10 qualities in a framework called WOW (Working on the Work) that are likely to make schoolwork more engaging for students. As teachers and principals engage in ongoing dialogue about teaching and learning in schools and in classrooms, this framework can guide their conversations. This framework can also be used as part of a staff study group or book club, such as the Central Valley example mentioned previously, and can lead to lesson study and lesson development.

Scheduled Supervisory Visits

To build on the previous discussion of supervision introduced in Chapter 5, before engaging in a scheduled supervisory visit, it is essential to begin with a *pre-observation conference*. This session is designed to "unpack the teacher's thinking" about the upcoming class lesson. This enables the principal, who will observe, to have a perspective of the thinking that precedes the actual teaching performance. This understanding also provides a strong foundation for questions constructed to foster teacher reflection in the postconference. The principal and teacher may wish to seek answers to essential questions that they believe are critical to experiences designed to foster student success. Often simply asking a question will help a teacher fine-tune a lesson about to be taught. Examples of questions principals, other supervisors, and teachers have asked include the following:

- What will students be expected to know and do as a result of the lesson?

• By what standards will students be assessed? Will students be engaged in the analysis of their performance? Is it appropriate to use rubrics? If so, how will they be constructed? Will students be involved?

• Regarding the content to be taught and how students will be required to demonstrate this understanding, how does this align with the content, benchmarks, and processes students are expected to master on the state assessment?

• What curriculum materials and resources (human and material) will you be using? Will technology be used? How?

• Is an interdisciplinary approach appropriate for this lesson? Please explain.

• What activities have you designed to motivate students to learn? Are they based on prior knowledge? How specifically? Are they linked to critical thinking, problem solving? Are they social and interactive?

• Will students have the opportunity to select activities in which to engage? How do the activities planned reflect students' interests?

• What will be some artifacts or products of the lesson (e.g., performance, experiments, projects, journal entries, or inventories)? Will students work on these alone or with peers? In person or linked by technology? If students will be working interdependently, what ground rules for their interactions have been established? By whom?

• How will the students' products be assessed? By what criteria? Who will conduct the assessment? Teacher? Teacher and student? Student? Student groups? Will anyone else view the products? In what context?

• If a student is unsuccessful, how will you decide on next steps? If a student fails, in what ways might you create within the student the desire to try again? What additional resources might you provide?

• What methods will you (or students) use to present information in this lesson (e.g., experiments, video clips, cooperative tasks, reading, technology)? Emphasize the use of a variety of learning styles and multiple intelligences when possible.

• How do the instructional strategies you plan to use reflect best practice?

• Tell me about the learners in the class. What was the lesson they experienced prior to this?

• How will learning experiences be differentiated to address the developmental needs of learners?

• What plans do you have to revisit this lesson's content in the future?

• What do you believe students will remember about this lesson?

• What would you like me to focus on in the observation? How, specifically?

• How would you like me to collect data?

• If students ask me to interact with them during the lesson, what are your preferences?

• When's the best time for us to dialogue about the lesson?

Note: The preceding questions were inspired by Phil Schlechty's WOW framework.

Although this and the conferencing strategies are not an exhaustive list of possibilities, they provide ideas about the type of background information that would be useful to understand a lesson that is about to unfold in terms of its content, process, and context. How many questions will be asked and the type of questions will generally be dictated by the level and trust and type of teacher with whom the observer is interacting. That is, the more reflective and self-analytical a teacher is, the less the principal will probably have to speak.

During the observation process, trust is created if the observer focuses only on what has been identified during the pre-observation conference. The only exceptions to this are if the content presented is incorrect, inappropriate teaching strategies are being used, or the students are being harmed—emotionally, psychologically, physically, socially, or intellectually. Though these issues occur rarely, they must be addressed directly.

The postobservation meeting should be conducted within 24 to 48 hours. After that, memories of what transpired seem to fade. As Chapter 5 indicated, both teacher and principal tend to reflect after the teaching episode and prior to the postconference. Often this period of reflection leads to new understandings or connections that will be shared in the postconference. The goals of the postconference are to

- Invite reflection about the lesson and its effect on student learning;

- Foster analysis of teaching practices and their consequences;

- Provide a forum for problem solving;

- Create opportunities to dialogue about next steps;

- Develop autonomy as it relates to the capacity to reflect, analyze, and infer in ways that will contribute to and inform future lessons;

- Expand instructional repertoire; and

- Continue the trust-building process.

Some questions that have been addressed by principals and teachers in postconference settings follow. Again, they are not exhaustive but rather are intended to serve as examples from which to develop one's own. Sample questions to inspire dialogue between supervisor and teacher include

- How do you feel or think the lesson went?

- Were there any surprises?

- Were there any particular segments of the lesson that are lingering in your memory? What's your hunch about why?

- What do you believe students learned as a result of the lesson? Were there additional learnings that happened incidentally?

- Looking at the quality of student work derived from the lesson, what are your impressions? If you were to teach the lesson again, would you modify any of the assignments?

- What did you learn as a result of teaching the lesson?

- If you had the opportunity to reteach the lesson, what would you do the same? Differently?

- What new insights do you have as a result of this experience?

- What will you do next with students?

- If you were to identify something from the lesson that really was successful that you could share with colleagues, what would it be?

- You asked me to collect data about (whatever was discussed in the preconference). What do you recall about that?

- Present the data and provide time for the teacher to examine them. Are there any surprises? How does it compare with your recollections?

- Is there anything else you'd like to dialogue about?

Whereas a scheduled supervisory visit is useful, it is a time-consuming process. New principals often bemoan a lack of time to conduct meaningful supervisory visits. The next section describes strategies to provide effective supervisory feedback within short periods of time.

Supervising with Limited Time

Given the sense of fragmentation that often typifies the principal's work reality—that is, the frequent interruptions and tremendous task variety—how can you find ways to inspire teachers to reflect, gain a sense of the taught curriculum, develop a sense of the climate of classrooms and the general emotional health of the school, build relationships with staff and students, build schoolwide norms of practice, and enhance your storytelling capacity? One strategy that uses the fragmentation as an opportunity is called "Leading and Learning by Wandering Around" (LLBWA). This strategy involves using short time segments—some planned, some unplanned—to get out of the office and into classrooms or campus areas to observe. Some principals make a doorknob hanger for the office that reads "Out Learning" while they are doing LLBWA. This sends a strong message to anyone who comes looking for the principal that this is a task that has top priority! There are many approaches to LLBWA. The paragraphs that follow address a few, and Chapter 7 describes additional approaches.

8–10–12–2–4

This approach simply means the principal visits classrooms or the campus at 8:00, 10:00, noon, 2:00, and 4:00 on selected days. These visits provide several types of information, as the principal reflects on questions such as these:

- How do teachers begin class? By engaging students immediately in a meaningful activity or just taking roll?

- How do classes conclude? With an activity that invites students to summarize their learning?

- What is the nature of the taught curriculum (versus that which is tested)?

- What do transitions look like?

- How does instruction in the morning compare to instruction in the afternoon?

- What happens in the cafeteria?

- What procedures are in place to protect academic learning time? What should be put into action?

- Are there logjams at passing periods? Why or why not?

- Who lingers after school? Why?

A new principal at a high school in Michigan who was using the 8–10–12–2–4 strategy became aware that the previous administration had assigned lockers by hallways—for example, seniors in the A-wing and juniors in the B-wing. Freshman and sophomore students who had classes in A- and B-wings were taunted and teased as they passed the senior and junior locker areas. As a result, several students began hiding out to avoid the torment—coming to class tardy after the seniors and juniors had made their way to class. This cut deeply into instructional time. (Just 5 minutes a day in a school year of 180 contact days adds up to 15 instructional hours!) To remedy the situation, the next semester the new principal reassigned lockers, so no one class owned a hall. This annoyed the seniors and juniors; yet, they came to accept it and focused on other things important to them. Tardies were reduced significantly, enhancing time to learn.

STUDENT INTERVIEWS

This strategy is designed to provide the principal with a student's perspective on the classroom. Student interviews can be targeted to specific students, such as following up on a referral for a special-education inclusion student. Or they can be random—the principal selects a student to interview at random in the classroom. The focus on the student calls faculty members' attention to what is important, and it provides an opportunity to build relationships with students.

A new principal in an inner-city school interviewed students in math class and discovered that students did not perceive the content as relevant. Yet, because they liked their first-year teacher, they were doing most of the work assigned to them. The principal engaged the teacher and a couple of students in grant writing to solicit funds to energize the existing math program. They received the math grant to support a special program to make math come alive. In a follow-up interview with the students, they explained how the model suspension bridge they were constructing was making geometry meaningful.

PARENT OUTREACH CALLS

This approach is designed to build positive home–school relationships and celebrate student success. The principal visits a classroom and identifies a student who has demonstrated effort or improvement. The student is called out of class, and the principal and student make a quick celebratory call via cell phone to the parent at home or work. (For those parents who do not have phones, a note is written and sent home.) This strategy serves to accentuate the positive and builds positive attitudes toward the school—especially among parents who have been conditioned only to receive bad news from the principal!

After three weeks of using parent outreach calls, a new principal observed that the returns of surveys sent home to parents increased dramatically. A parent approached the principal one Saturday morning at a grocery store and reflected, "It was such a nice surprise to get a positive call from you instead of one telling me my son was in trouble. I believe it's influenced my son to work toward positive ends as well."

COLLECT WORK SAMPLES

This approach provides the principal with an opportunity to collect a sampling of student work. The samples yield invaluable information about the quality of work assigned to students, the content that is addressed (and whether the content and performance requirements are aligned with state standards), whether the work reflects student interests, and the nature of expectations for student performance. A variation of this strategy is to collect and analyze unit plans or lesson plans, providing that cultural norms or contract agreements permit this kind of activity.

A new principal reflected that she was more attuned to channeling appropriate resources—articles, books, conference advertisements—to staff members as a result of collecting work samples, which increased her awareness of what staff and students were focused on. And she noted that the quality of student assignments increased substantially as a result of this process. Her presence focused teachers' attention on what was valued.

THE 7-MINUTE CLASSROOM SNAPSHOT

This strategy is a quick way to collect data regarding curriculum, assessment, and instruction across the school. It also provides focused opportunities for dialogue with selected staff members. Here's how it works.

- *1-Minute Preconference:* Establish the focus of the observation and how and when data will be collected.

- *5-Minute Observation:* Collect the data (based on the focus identified in the preconference).

- *1-Minute Postobservation:* Ask questions designed to promote teacher reflection, share data, compare and contrast teacher's perceptions and data, and share insights.

Principals who have used LLBWA often describe a practice of simply dropping into a classroom, observing a teacher action that fosters student learning, and writing a Post-it note that describes what the teacher did and the student behavior that followed: "When you began class with storytelling, all eyes were on you. Later I heard several students referring back to the story as they worked in small groups. Storytelling brought the history they were studying alive!" The Post-it note is left for the teacher. One principal talked about the effects of this process: "At break, all the teachers gather in the teachers' room and swap notes. I don't leave notes in those classes where good things are not happening for kids. It's been a wonderful way to build schoolwide norms of practice. At faculty meetings, I always mention how many classes I've visited and I talk about the excellent practices I've observed in individual classrooms. I don't mention specific teachers' names— but they know who they are. It's also a strong message to those who aren't doing good things for students [about] what our expectations are." Principals report several benefits when using LLBWA:

- Early warnings about problems.

- An avenue to celebrate success.

- Knowledge about the congruence between desired or agreed-on behavior and actual behavior.

- Increased storytelling capacity.

- Elevated staff awareness of key cultural values and beliefs.

- Greater principal believability and clout.

- An expanded sense of control.

- Sanity—the pleasure of being out and about.

- Increased contact with students.

Principals using LLBWA share one caution: it's important to communicate with staff about what you are doing and why you are doing it, lest your actions be construed as "bed checks."

Differentiating Supervisory Practices

The goal of supervisory visits is to promote reflection on practice and foster staff and student learning. But just as in the classroom, no one lesson will meet the needs of all students; no one supervisory approach will meet the developmental needs of every faculty member. Hence, the principal as instructional leader differentiates supervisory practices to address individual needs. Some teachers by nature are more reflective; others may need reflective opportunities modeled or taught explicitly. Some teachers are autonomous—able to analyze their own practices. Others initially rely on the administrator to guide their reflections. Some teachers are defensive. The administrator needs to build trust and invite dialogue, but be very firm with these folks. And a very few teachers have retired on the job but have forgotten to announce it! These individuals either need to be revitalized or counseled out of the profession.

Modeling differentiated supervisory practices is a great way to simulate for teachers the expectation that instructional practices for students need to be differentiated as well. One principal reflected on the connections he sees between supervisory practices and student learning: "I believe we have a moral responsibility as professionals to make a positive difference in every student's life. If you've ever counted the number of years you've taught and multiplied that figure by the number of students in each of your classes, it becomes crystal clear that most of us have touched thousands of students' lives!"

Promoting Best Practices

The supervisory process provides one powerful way to promote the use of research-based best practices in individual classrooms. Chapter 5 cited several well-documented areas of focus. In addition, as Pat Wolfe (2001), notes in *Brain Matters*, "The more we understand about the brain, the better we will be able to design instruction according to how it learns best." The following brain-compatible teaching practices offer teachers (and administrators) specific strategies to maximize student learning:

- Immediately engage the attention of learners when they come into the classroom. The activities need to be of high interest and anchored in benchmarks or standards. They can build readiness for a lesson about to be taught or review a previously taught concept. The brain remembers best what comes first and next best what comes last. Information lingers in the sensory memory only three-fourths of a second. Then information is either forgotten or sent to short-term memory. If the teacher doesn't engage the attention of the learners, something else will!

• Routinely post lesson outcomes, benchmarks, or standards in a specific place on the chalkboard so students can refer to these. An agenda for the day and homework assignments should also have a regular place on the board. Advance organizers trigger attention and are linked to promoting memory.

• Use state standards to design curriculum and instruction and assess student work. Research indicates that high-performing, high-poverty schools implemented this practice with notable results. Making the brain aware of performance targets increases attention.

• Involve students in active learning experiences that engage a variety of learning channels: auditory, visual, and kinesthetic. Seek ways to structure activities so that students may have an opportunity to use a variety of intelligences: visual-spatial, mathematical-logical, verbal-linguistic, musical, bodily kinesthetic, interpersonal, intrapersonal, naturalist (Gardner, 1995). We remember only 10 to 20 percent of what we hear. Active involvement focuses attention and increases the probability that students will remember what they have rehearsed.

• Engage students in learning tasks, such as experiments or experiential activities, that require them to actively construct meaning. The brain actually forms new neural connections when it is actively engaged in "meaning making" based on experiences.

• Chunk curriculum content appropriate to the developmental age of the learner. The capacity of short-term memory appears to develop with developmental age. This understanding has major implications for the design and delivery of curriculum.

- Change activities at least four or five times within the context of a lesson. For example, students may first be actively engaged in a warm-up activity, report out, experience direct instruction, create a graphic organizer to summarize learning, stand, pair and share their work (with other students), and respond to a prompt in their learning journals. The more *firsts* and *lasts* within a lesson, the more memorable its content.

- Provide opportunities for meaningful *rehearsal*, or practice, after initial content has been introduced. Periodically provide review activities to distribute rehearsal opportunities over time. The more opportunities a student has to meaningfully rehearse, the greater the chance that information will move from short-term to long-term memory. Providing rehearsal opportunities using a variety of learning channels will maximize the probability that long-term retention will occur.

- Structure opportunities for movement during learning experiences. Movement provides oxygen to the brain, increases attention, and in some cases, integrates communication between the right and left hemispheres.

- Seek opportunities to integrate the curriculum. For example, using the *Dear America* book series, students read autobiographical accounts written by fictional characters based on actual historical events. So history comes alive in a language-arts context. Subjects are not found in isolation in the real world. Long-term memory stores information in networks of association. The more associations or connections a student has with a particular fact or concept, the more easily that information can be recalled.

- Use humor related to content. For example, concepts may be taught using a cartoon lecture. Humor increases retention up to 15 percent!

- Engage students in a variety of tasks that require higher-order thinking skills. Analysis, synthesis, and evaluation tasks require students to access and use remembered information to foster new neural connections in the brain.

• Provide for a variety of flexible grouping contexts that engage students in working with different classmates. Much learning occurs through social interaction. Students can receive instruction appropriate to their learning needs and pace in small-group settings. As students master academic content, they simultaneously develop skills in working with, and appreciating, others. For many students, a small-group setting reduces anxiety. According to brain researchers Caine and Caine (1991) the brain functions optimally in a state of "relaxed alertness."

• Assign and grade relevant homework that extends rehearsal opportunities and reflects how content will ultimately be assessed. Students learn more when they complete homework that is graded, commented on, and discussed by their teachers. Whenever possible, engage students in developing rubrics to assess their work. This increases their awareness of key attributes of quality work and lends credibility and authenticity to the grading process.

• Match instruction and assessment practices consistent with how standards and benchmarks ultimately will be assessed and the setting in which assessment will occur. Research on "state dependence" indicates that content will be most easily recalled when it is assessed under the same conditions as when it was originally learned.

• Use authentic assessment measures. Engage students in applying new and recent learning in a real world context. The brain remembers best that which is embedded in a particular context. For example, to remember what one had for dinner last Saturday night, most people will have to first remember where they were.

• Provide opportunities for students to summarize their learning in written or verbal form and communicate these to others. Summarizing strengthens neural connections. When students *rehearse* through reciprocal teaching, retention is enhanced 65 to 90 percent!

• Monitor and invite students to monitor their own progress. Self-monitoring and feedback can be a source for intrinsic motivation and may increase attention and focus.

• Select assignments that are challenging and interesting. Provide a support structure to help students achieve success in a psychologically safe environment. The brain learns best in an atmosphere of "high challenge and low threat" (Caine & Caine, 1991).

• Create a learning environment where students perceive that they are (1) safe from physical, verbal, or psychological harm; (2) free to experiment and take risks when learning; (3) "connected" in their relationships with others—including the teacher and other students; and (4) valued members of the class. Sylwester (1995) notes that "emotion drives attention which drives learning and memory." If students feel safe and cared for, and if teachers and others are responsive to needs, their ability to focus and learn will be enhanced.

• Encourage parents to stimulate their children's intellectual development and to provide a caring, responsive climate in the home. For instance, teachers can ask parents to help their children rehearse a report presentation to be given in class or discuss the results of a recent class science experiment. Environment plays a key role in brain development and intelligence. Verbal interaction with children, for example, has a direct impact on language and vocabulary development. A caring, responsive climate contributes to the development of a child's sense of self-esteem (Robbins & Alvy, 2003).

Addressing these strategies in faculty meetings, modeling them in professional development activities, and revisiting them in the supervisory process will serve to keep these significant practices in the forefront of staff members' minds.

Ensuring Staff Members Have the Opportunity to Grow and Learn

Robert Marzano (2003) conducted a synthesis of the research that indicated the effectiveness of an individual teacher and the effectiveness of the school both dramatically affect student achievement. Chapters 5 and 6 have examined the role supervision plays in contributing to individual and schoolwide effectiveness. Professional development activities, designed to promote continuous growth experiences for the adults in the school and enhance the individual and collective capacity of teachers and administrators to serve students, also serve this important purpose. Professional development consists of any activity that directly affects the attitudes, knowledge base, skills, and practices that will support individuals in performing their roles—present or future—to serve students. The National Staff Development Council (2001) has developed important staff development standards that should guide the intentional implementation of professional development activities. They address the importance of content, context, and process considerations when designing professional development. In general the activities created for the adult learners in the school should reflect and model those attributes of good teaching that we want to promote in classrooms: active learning, use of best practice, brain compatible instruction, time for reflection, differentiation of tasks, attention to the opportunity to use multiple intelligences, and meaningful assessment that requires learners to apply newly acquired knowledge and skills.

Approaches to Professional Development

Although one strategy to provide professional learning is sending staff to conferences, institutes, and inservice offerings, a potential downside of these experiences is that they lack follow-up in most cases. Nonetheless, some principals have combated this deficit by creating opportunities for continued dialogue at the school-level postconference or inservice experience, by asking staff members to talk about how the new ideas have influenced their thinking, teaching, and the work they have designed for students. Some have generated teachers' interest in bringing in lesson plans and artifacts of student work that have been inspired by the new ideas. Together, they compare and contrast their efforts and formulate next steps for the design of student learning experiences.

Chapter 4 introduced faculty meetings as a forum for adult learning, professional development, and culture building. Still another form of professional development consists of *job-embedded* learning structures. These structures provide a wide array of professional development opportunities that occur within the duty day—at work—from which staff can select. As Michael Fullan (2002) notes, "Learning in context has the greatest potential payoff because it is more specific, situational, and social (it develops shared and collective knowledge and commitments). . . . Learning in context also establishes conditions conducive to continual development, including opportunities to learn from others on the job, the daily fostering of future leaders, the selective retention of good ideas and best practices and the explicit monitoring of performance." Many principals have asked teachers and support staff to identify professional growth goals related to building their knowledge and skills to serve students as part of a Professional Growth Plan (see Figure 6.1, p. 137). Then, the teachers and support staff are provided with a menu of options from which to select how they will engage in professional learning. Finally, the principal asks them what indicators—in terms of student performance— they will look for as evidence that their professional learning is making a difference. As noted in Chapter 5, some staff members have developed professional portfolios as a way of demonstrating their growth.

The sections that follow detail a few of the professional learning options.

——— **Figure 6.1** ———
Professional Growth Plan

Name: _____

School and Location: _____

_____

Grade Level and Subject Area Assignments: _____

_____

_____

_____

Professional growth goals:

Relationship to student learning and achievement:

Professional learning structures you intend to use to grow
professionally:

Resources you will need:

Indicators of student learning and achievement that you will note
as evidence of the impact of professional learning:

Time line:

_____

LESSON STUDY

Lesson study engages groups of teachers to meet regularly over long periods of time to work on the design, implementation, assessment, and improvement of specific lessons. Often teachers group themselves for lesson study based on common interests, issues, or dilemmas related to the subject or grade level they teach. After teachers create the lessons, they teach the lessons. One or more individuals observe each teacher's performance. The observers reflect on the lesson with the teacher and offer feedback regarding what worked well, and what needs revision or reworking. This process adds to the collective knowledge base among teachers and enriches professional practice.

PEER COACHING

Peer coaching is "a confidential process through which two or more professional colleagues work together to reflect on current practices; expand, refine, and build new skills; share ideas; teach one another; conduct classroom research; or solve problems in the workplace" (Robbins, 1991). The forms peer coaching can take are limitless. They may involve professional colleagues in reflective dialogue about teaching and its effects within or outside the classroom.

MENTORING

Mentoring provides the newcomer to the teaching profession with a professional guide or mentor who offers support, guidance, feedback, and problem-solving strategies, as well as access to a network of colleagues who share resources, insights, practices, and materials. Mentoring also gives seasoned professionals the chance to leave their mark on the profession by passing along knowledge, "trade secrets," and experiences to the newcomer. Mentoring support enhances the probability that newcomers to the teaching profession will be retained and will grow—adding to the wealth of talent available to serve students.

ACTION RESEARCH

Staff members who engage in action research collectively select an area of focus, develop a research question, identify a data-collection plan, and create a plan for analysis of data. They identify who will assist in data-collection analysis and how findings will be posted and used. Data are collected and analyzed. Findings are described, summarized, and reported to colleagues at the school and often in professional journals.

STUDY GROUPS

This structure provides staff with the opportunity to select a topic or theme and identify ways that they will study it. For example, some study groups have identified the theme of *differentiated instruction*. The mechanisms for studying include discussions of current practice, analysis of case studies, selected journal readings, visits to classrooms where differentiation was in place, and reading books. Members of the group keep journals about insights and experiences. As they learn and apply ideas and practices in the classroom, they frequently meet to share experiences. Some teachers and administrators decided to begin student study groups as a result of their experiences as adult learners.

PROFESSIONAL BOOK TALKS

These talks focus on a particular book or article that a group of staff members identify of interest related to their mutual goal of enhancing their knowledge base to serve students. Generally, book talks involve

- Reading the book by sections,
- Dialoguing about key points,
- Discussing implications for practice,
- Trying out ideas or strategies in the classroom,

• Bringing back stories about implementation efforts and their effects,

• Reflecting on how the book has informed book club members' practice, and

• Sharing experiences with faculty members not involved in the book club.

CONVERSATIONS ABOUT STUDENT WORK

Conversations about student work involve small groups of teachers in examining the work they design for students and the results of student work. In conversing about student work, teachers usually follow a protocol. There are many varieties available. For example, Schlechty's (2001) Working on the Work (WOW) framework, mentioned previously, guided one group of staff members in examining the role of 10 design qualities in making schoolwork more meaningful and engaging for students.

Final Thoughts on Professional Development

Implementing professional development options recognizes the importance of nurturing every staff member's need to grow. Engaging staff members in a collaborative approach to professional development contributes to the development of a learning-focused community of professional colleagues. Not only do individuals benefit from this process, but the organization's knowledge base becomes richer, as does its capacity to ensure that every child will succeed.

 **Activity** ————————————————————

Keeping Track of LLBWA

One of the goals of LLBWA is to be visible and available so that each staff member has the opportunity to have contact with and access to the principal. Keeping track of this is facilitated by a "pocket planner" approach (Figure 6.2), which can be done with index cards or electronically with a personal digital assistant (PDA). To create this tracking system, list staff members' names on the left side of the form. Create a column for every month—perhaps three months at a time. Every time you visit a classroom, indicate next to that staff member's name

- When you visited (date and time),

- What you focused on in your visit (e.g., math problem solving), and

- The approach you used (e.g., work sample, student interview).

This system allows principals to quickly identify the staff members they need to visit. Then, the next time an appointment is canceled and a few spare minutes are available, the principal can visit those individuals.

Figure 6.2

Tracking System for LLBWA

Staff Member	September	October	November

Special notes and things I want to remember:

Reflective Field Notes ──────────

Please use this space to reflect on the chapter's content by creating a graphic organizer to summarize your learning.

The following questions may serve to inspire further reflection.

• What are some connections you perceive among supervision, professional development, and student achievement?

• How does LLBWA fit with your philosophy of supervision?

• What other learning or growth areas do you wish to pursue as a result of reading this chapter?

7

Managing Human and Material Resources to Promote a Thriving Organization

Leadership and management go hand in hand. Indeed, as noted in the preface, management is an essential instructional leadership tool. Yet, aspiring or new principals are often led to believe that the logistical or management aspects of the job are of minor importance. The popular expression "Managers do things right and leaders do the right thing" (Bennis & Nanus, 1985) can be interpreted as meaning that managers do not make important decisions—the "right" choices are made by the leaders. Principals, however, must "move" seamlessly between their management and leadership roles daily. To illustrate, consider whether the following situational questions relate to management or instructional leadership responsibilities:

- Is monitoring students as they are arriving or departing on school buses a management or leadership responsibility?

- Is supervising the cafeteria a management or leadership responsibility?

- How would you characterize a principal's role when leading a team that creates and develops the master high school schedule for students?

- How would you describe the role of a principal who hounds a textbook company to make sure the enrichment literature books arrive by the start of the school year?

These questions illustrate that principals are engaged in both leadership and management roles almost every moment on the job. Indeed, even bending down and picking up some trash in a school's hallway can send a powerful leadership message.

Protecting Quality Classroom Time

Unquestionably, protecting quality classroom time is at the top of the principal's list of responsibilities. One school leader combined the leadership and management roles and worked to protect classroom teaching time by fine-tuning the procedures for a high school's public address announcements, which were broadcast into each classroom. The school was trying to balance the "everyone needs to know" aspect of announcements with each teacher's desire to eliminate class-time interruptions. The traditional procedure reserved announcements for the morning homeroom period and during the last couple of minutes of a class period once or twice a day. This procedure sent a subtle message: The last few minutes of class were unimportant. After discussing possibilities during a faculty meeting, the teachers and administration decided to make class time sacred with everyone checking their e-mail around noontime for announcements that might affect their students. Equally important, a commitment was made by faculty and administration to *plan ahead* by sending announcements to the office by 7:30 a.m. for homeroom announcements. Everyone understood that, at times, emergency announcements would still be necessary. The administration had to remain firm and say "no" to a few last-minute announcement requests during the first few weeks (e.g., "Gee, I forgot to remind the chorus of the rehearsal after school. Can we just slip in a short announcement?"). The new procedures worked. Although fine-tuning public address announcement procedures may appear to be a minor management issue, the importance of keeping classroom instructional time sacred provided the administration with the authority to make decisions with overwhelming staff support. Aspiring and new principals need to know that resolving this issue was not a minor event.

Managing Resources Successfully as the Year Begins

Preparing for the hour when students arrive to begin their first day of school is a major endeavor that combines all of the human and material resources available to a school. If they can successfully coordinate the opening of school, new principals have a golden opportunity to make a good impression with all school stakeholders, especially teachers and classified staff. The following sections are lists of various beginning-of-the-year responsibilities—with an emphasis on rookie principal needs. Many of these ideas emerged from conversations with principals and from our book *The Principal's Companion* (Robbins & Alvy, 2003). Although we have organized these responsibilities into various categories (e.g., instructional leadership, students), many of the responsibilities may be aligned with more than one category.

INSTRUCTIONAL LEADERSHIP

- Review district policy manuals related to school mission, vision, philosophy, and disciplinary procedures. Note ambiguous sections, and seek clarity from experienced principals, the superintendent, or their assistants.

• Examine the supervision, evaluation, and professional development opportunities available to the staff.

• Review curriculum documents related to state expectations, benchmarks, frameworks, and assessment procedures. If possible, spend time with district testing personnel to discern your school's data-driven results, strengths, and areas needing special attention.

• Familiarize yourself with the student and faculty master schedules and how time is used, considering the full range of learning opportunities in the academic, visual and performing arts, athletic, extracurricular, and service areas. Obviously, differences will vary depending on the nature of the elementary or secondary program.

• Plan the beginning-of-the-year faculty meetings as professional development opportunities. Use the meetings to make a meaningful first impression that underscores your determination to be an *instructional leader in a school of leaders.*

• Check to see if the faculty workroom, department, or grade-level teams receive professional journals. If not, use professional development funds to subscribe to important schoolwide journals (e.g., *Educational Leadership, Journal of Staff Development, Kappan*) and specific subject journals (e.g., math, social studies, foreign language, reading).

• Fine-tune your own educational philosophy or personal mission statement.

• Block your schedule a couple of weeks before school begins to ensure that you are particularly visible during the first few days of the school year. This will help you develop the visibility habit all year.

• Consider how daily communication has been conducted in the school. Examine the formal and informal sources of communication, and determine how you will effectively keep others informed and receive accurate information.

- Consider how you will continue to "sharpen the saw" (Covey, 1989) professionally and personally (e.g., reading, remaining healthy, attending to your family).

MANAGEMENT

- Take several quiet walks through the school on your own. This is especially valuable if you are working in a large school. (You may be the newcomer—but on the first day of school everyone else who is new will be expecting you to know the facility!)

- If possible, spend a reasonable amount of time with the person you are replacing—asking about logistical issues and concentrating on the strengths of the school.

- Meet with the school secretary and review beginning-of-the-year resources: files; activity schedules; calendars; memos; and newsletters to staff, students, parents, and other stakeholders.

- Review important forms and software with the secretary to minimize the bureaucratic maze. Even before the school year begins, ask, "Do we need this form?"

- Review the school budget with the appropriate central office business manager.

- Review new faculty hirings and, with appropriate human resource personnel, last-minute vacancies that must be filled.

- Pay particular attention to the teaching responsibilities, classroom locations, and resources for new teachers. Are they being provided with sufficient support?

- Walk through the school facility with the head custodian (e.g., hallways, classrooms, bathrooms, locker rooms, offices, athletic fields, playgrounds, libraries, auditoriums, gymnasiums, labs) to get an update on the summer maintenance work, the condition of student and faculty chairs and desks, office equipment, and fixtures. Review the safety, health, and cleanliness aspects of the facility, including indoor air-quality issues.

- Let the custodians know that they are critical to the success of the school.

- Meet with district supervisors of security, transportation, and food services—let them know how much you appreciate the work they do to contribute to student success.

- Thoroughly review the collective bargaining agreement, and if appropriate, meet with the building union representative before the school year.

- Review the crisis management plan and emergency equipment concerning safety, health, and security issues (including intruder procedures); update faculty phone tree numbers, and fire, ambulance, police, child protective services, and poison control phone numbers.

- Working with the appropriate personnel, ensure that teachers have basic instructional and housekeeping supplies in their classrooms *before* the teachers arrive.

- Ensure that technology personnel have examined hardware and software and implemented upgrades for school information systems and educational software.

- Become familiar with the substitute teacher guidelines and logistical procedures for the district.

STUDENTS

- Review enrollment figures, trends, and class lists.

- Review orientation for new students with appropriate faculty. Try to promote veteran student involvement in the orientation if that is not already part of the program.

- In creative ways, try to have student work displayed throughout the school when the year begins. Display exhibits, projects, portfolios, artwork, science experiments, athletic accomplishments, exemplary photographs, and craftwork. Ask teachers for work from previous years that they may have filed away.

- Meet with high school or middle school student counsel groups either before school starts or during the first few days to communicate your support for their activities.

- Consider your remarks for the first week of student assemblies (e.g., orientation events or activities) or for your visits to individual classes.

PERSONNEL

- Send a letter to or call the central office personnel to let them know that you will be seeking their advice and asking questions.

- Prepare a "welcome back" letter to professional and classified staff to let them know how much you appreciate what they do for students; include a preview of your goals.

- Make sure there are beginning-of-the-year orientation, mentoring, and professional development opportunities for new teachers and staff.

- If appropriate, meet with the vice principal, athletic director, and other members of the school leadership team before the year begins. (It is also important to learn if any of these individuals applied for your position. If this proves to be the case, make an extra effort to seek honest advice from them about the school.)

- Meet with directors or coordinators of special service teams.

- Seek out veteran staff and ask, "What makes this school unique? What are the strengths of the school? What must be preserved?"

PARENTS

- Before school begins, meet with parent leaders so that they can help assist new parents (and the new principal!).

- Ask parents to help create signs and also help with orientation during the first days of school.

- Seek information about parent involvement in the school to promote volunteerism, tutoring, career day assistance, and other resources.

BROADER COMMUNITY STAKEHOLDERS

- After checking with veteran principals or district personnel, call a few community stakeholders and important school partners to let them know that you are looking forward to working with them on behalf of the students.

- In particular, contact organizations that provide services to the schools (e.g., child protective services, police and fire departments), and tell them in advance that you appreciate their assistance.

- Take several walks in the community during the summer. If appropriate, introduce yourself to community stakeholders.

Time Management

Each time we, the authors, speak to groups of principals about time management, we note that the job is characterized by "brevity, fragmentation and variety" (Peterson, 1982). As we state these descriptive words, heads begin to nod affirmatively, as if someone is saying, "Yes, that is my typical day. I am glad someone understands what I experience." Aspiring and rookie principals need to know that a so-called normal day is fragmented, has interruptions, and includes surprises and unpredictable moments. Although this is unnerving for some, many principals thrive on the atypical nature of the job. Each day brings excitement, unplanned events, and meetings—opportunities to creatively make a difference in the lives of students and adults in the schoolhouse. Still, principals need to take ownership of the *where, when, how,* and *why* aspects of the job—otherwise, the unpredictable excitement and the unplanned events and meetings will fill their days. If principals do not consciously and proactively monitor their schedules, then other individuals will dictate how principals spend their time.

Where Should Principals Spend Their Time?

Aspiring and new principals need to know that their offices are not the center of the school. Everyone in the school (and many stakeholders outside of the school) know and notice where principals spend their time. Principals send a very strong symbolic message of what is important simply by where they choose to spend their time. When we use the phrase "Leading and Learning by Wandering Around" (LLBWA), we are promoting the importance of navigating around a school in a purposeful manner. *Principals need to witness student and teacher success and verbally affirm the important work of the school.* They must work hard to make the classroom the centerpiece of their day. However, we know that visiting classes each day is not easy because so many other responsibilities and daily occurrences conflict with this classroom responsibility (Alvy, 1983). In addition, principals need to purposely decide where they should be on particular days to stay in touch with the organization (e.g., the cafeteria, playground, halls, buses, auditorium, gymnasium, labs, entrances, guidance office, nurse's office). Some may consider this approach micromanaging, but observing how an organization operates on each level is the responsibility of the principal.

When Should Principals Visit Different Areas of the School?

Sounds like a simple question, with a simple answer: all the time. But, a principal cannot be everywhere all the time. Again, purposeful visibility means carefully considering when to visit different areas of the schoolhouse. If principals are going to control the time when they will visit a particular area then they must block the time out in advance on their schedule. Principals should plan to spend time in certain areas days or weeks in advance so that these visits really do occur. Also, principals should vary their times for visiting particular places, so that they can feel the nuances of the school culture. For example, where are students congregating before school? After school? During the lunch period? Which students arrive early each morning? Which students seem reluctant to go home at the end of the day? Who hangs around the computer labs? the gymnasiums? library? the theater? When are teachers in the faculty work area? Which teachers prefer to work in their classrooms?

HOW SHOULD PRINCIPALS SPEND THEIR TIME?

Principals need to set a personal example of building trust and quality relationships in the school. They should spend their time talking to people—students and staff—reinforcing the positive values and norms of the school. *The essence of leadership is positive human relations and effective communication.* Principals need to spend their time building quality relationships. This means, of course, that much of the paperwork that is required of principals cannot be completed during the "8:00 a.m. to 3:00 p.m." school day. Principals must also spend their time observing what is working and what is not. Principals should watch how students and teachers are getting along, looking for the student who needs to hear a positive comment, seeking the at-risk student who needs some support, and, of vital importance, observing the classroom to see effective teaching and learning. Observing is also critical to recognizing inappropriate behaviors such as intimidation, bullying, or harassment.

WHY SHOULD PRINCIPALS SPEND TIME BUILDING QUALITY RELATIONSHIPS AND OBSERVING?

It is easy to answer, "Because that's their job!" Actually, school leaders need to spend their time building quality relationships and observing because human beings are social—we perform effectively with support from others. The leader of an organization can have a profound effect on organizational members by supporting or discouraging their efforts (Goleman, Boyatzis, & McKee, 2002). As authors, we are not shy about suggesting that part of a leader's responsibility is to serve as a team cheerleader, helping to motivate and celebrate student and collegial work.

Time Management Strategies

There are numerous techniques and strategies that principals can use to fine-tune their time management skills. Consider the following suggestions.

PRIORITIZING BEYOND THE "TO DO" LIST

Covey (1989) expertly reminds us that it is easy to create a "to do" list and convince oneself that a day of accomplishments has occurred because all the items on the list are crossed off. Covey suggests that we ask ourselves if the listed items represent important accomplishments based on our prioritized goals. He is particularly concerned about important goals that relate to professional growth ("sharpening the saw") that are neglected because of less urgent and unimportant tasks that absorb us. For example, in one high school the principal and assistant principal check all of the combination locks and match locker numbers with the locks before the school year begins. This activity can take a couple of days. Shouldn't this task be assigned to someone else, so the administrative team can plan a worthwhile faculty meeting? Therefore, we suggest that you reflect on your personal vision or mission statement and compare your goals with how you actually spend your time. A time audit will help.

THE TIME AUDIT

Assessing how you are using your time is a helpful tool, and there are several popular time audit techniques. One method is to simply carry a small pocket tape recorder and take one minute every 30 minutes or hour to briefly describe what you did during the previous 30 minutes or hour. Continue this audit for one week. (Some time management experts recommend recording your behaviors every 15 minutes.) Another method is to briefly write what you are doing (possibly on a small pad or your personal digital assistant), again approximately every 30 minutes or hourly. It is recommended, also, to simply examine your daily calendar for a two-week period to see how you are spending your time. However, the problem with examining your calendar is that it does not include all the interruptions or unexpected events that occur during the course of a day. A compromise might be to review your calendar at the end of each day, adding additional unplanned events to your audit notes. Regardless of which time-auditing method you use to record the data, it is important to assess what the data mean. Again, the crucial step is to consider Covey's (1989) notion of comparing your valued goals with how you actually spent time. Some key questions to consider when assessing your audit notes include these:

• How much of your time was devoted to instructional leadership?

• Did you spend time in ways that contributed to student achievement?

• How much time was spent building relationships?

• Did you spend time in classrooms?

• Did you visit various parts of the school?

• Did you spend time talking to students? Faculty? Classified staff? Parents?

• What have you omitted that is important? (e.g., Have you spoken with the counselors lately? What about a visit to the school library? Have you spoken with the custodian recently? What about the central office personnel? Have you spoken with security personnel or school crossing guards?)

TIME AUDITING YOUR MENTOR

Aspiring principals who are serving as administrative interns might consider asking their mentors if they would like to be involved in an experiment to assess how their mentors are using time. This could be a helpful activity for both the mentor and mentee. Of course, a trusting relationship and confidentiality would probably both be necessary for this activity to be success-fully implemented. This activity would entail having the mentee shadow the mentor for one or two days, taking notes, tape record-ing, or possibly videotaping during appropriate times. Following this one- or two-day period, the two colleagues would get together and assess how time was used.

BLOCKING YOUR SCHEDULE BASED ON SCHOOL GOALS

As noted earlier, principals need to block their schedules in advance to meet important obligations. It is critical that principals explain their time management philosophy to the secretaries, other administrative staff, and faculty (probably during a faculty meeting). The secretary needs to know that the principal values visiting classrooms and purposefully circulating in the school. To support this approach, principals need to let the secretary know that when the principal is visiting classes, if someone asks for the principal, the proper answer to give is, "Mrs. Smith is visiting stu-dents at work." The secretary needs to value the importance of stu-dent achievement and teacher success, just as the principal should value the contribution that the secretary or receptionist makes to the school as a link to the community.

TOUCHING BASE WITH STUDENTS AND STAFF

One of the authors was very impressed by a principal, David Miller, who always remembered and followed up faculty requests. Although every request was not implemented to the full satisfac-tion of each teacher, David consistently touched base with teach-ers, letting them know that he had not forgotten about their requests. Amazingly, David did this without writing all the requests down—at least not in the presence of the teachers. The point is, as principals walk through schools, they are constantly asked to fulfill requests from faculty, classified staff, and students. Most of us cannot always remember the details of a conversation with a colleague or remember a request. When he was a principal, Harvey Alvy (author) always carried a small pad in his pocket to write comments, suggestions, or requests from teachers, classified staff, students, and parents. Teachers would sometimes smile and gently remind Harvey to write their request on his pad at the end of a conversation. The notepad even became a cultural artifact in the school as faculty humorously impersonated Harvey with the pad during the end-of-the-year faculty skits. One year a veteran staff member gave Harvey a gift of three notepads to make sure the school year started off smoothly! Whether a principal uses a personal planner, a PDA, or simply a notepad doesn't matter. What matters is that requests need to be written down (unless you are David Miller!).

THE CUSTOMIZED AFFIRMING NOTE

A variation on the notepad, and a time saver for some principals, is the customized affirming note. A principal can use these notes when dropping into classrooms for short visits or when observing noteworthy teacher behavior outside the classroom. The notes also can be customized to write the affirming note to students. It's simple to have school stationery printed using a format similar to the note in Figure 7.1 on p. 158.

Cutting Through the Red Tape

Probably one of the most frustrating aspects of taking on a new job is learning the ropes. Little things that others don't even concern themselves with are major obstacles for newcomers. Simple tasks such as finding a parking spot, remembering the right code for the copy machine, or figuring out which keys to use can be frustrating until you are comfortable and familiar with the setting. Experienced principals can make things happen for teachers, students, classified staff, and parents simply because they have learned to work the system. New principals do not know how to work the system. For them, the system, the red tape, is more like the old Berlin Wall! Interestingly, this is part of the bifocal nature of the principalship (Deal & Peterson, 1994). On the one hand, school

Figure 7.1

Customized Affirmation Stationery

Abraham Lincoln Middle School
From the Principal, Pat Wolfe

Dear _____

I really enjoyed visiting your classroom today and noticed:

_____ How patient you were with each student.

_____ The time you spent with _____, carefully reviewing the work.

_____ The wonderful displays of student work.

_____ How engaged all students were in the lesson.

_____ Students interacting effectively during the group work.

_____ How helpful students were with their peers.

_____ How you encouraged a variety of solutions to the problem discussed.

_____ What a wonderful atmosphere you have created in the class.

_____ How effectively you were using each minute.

_____ How much you seemed to be enjoying the class.

_____ The variety of activities you used to pursue the instructional goals.

_____ How effectively you used questioning during the lesson.

_____ The variety of instructional resources during your lesson.

Comments _____

_____

Date _____

Time _____

Room _____

leaders need to use the formal system and learn the proper line and staff aspects of the bureaucracy. On the other hand, experienced leaders manipulate the system so that things get done. What makes this particularly sensitive is that often principals are asking others to "follow the proper channels."

In Chapter 3 regarding organizational socialization, we described the insider stage as the period when newcomers are accepted into the organization by veteran teachers. Part of the newcomer's prestige will depend on when veterans believe that the principal can make things happen. Thus, learning how to cut through the red tape is a critical goal for aspiring or new principals. Cutting through the red tape is necessary to address questions such as these: "How do I get specific instructional supplies if I need them tomorrow morning?" "How much do I *really* have in my budget?" or "Is it possible to 'creatively' use funds earmarked for one program to help students who desperately need assistance in another program?" There is no organizational policy manual written for new principals concerning these questions. The following list contains a few unofficial suggestions for cutting through the red tape (but it is important that you do not share these ideas with others—only kidding!).

- Get to know the folks who work in the supply rooms and technology offices and, in larger districts, individuals who are ordering resources for the district.

- If you have an opportunity to spend time with the principal you are replacing, simply ask the principal which members of the faculty are most helpful concerning specific areas. Also, ask for contacts in the central office for help in specific areas.

- Meet with the most veteran school counselor. Frequently, this veteran is a valuable link between faculty and students, and faculty and administration. Tell the counselor that you will be depending on him or her to provide you with insights to help students and faculty.

- Find out if there are particular parents or community stakeholders who can be of assistance.

- Meet with the athletic director or other individuals involved with activities, athletics, and services to determine which extracurricular activities are crucial to the school's traditions and culture.

- Review the central office organizational chart with a veteran principal (or a mentor principal if available) and ask for descriptions of each person's responsibilities. You will likely get a lot more information than appears on the chart.

- During your first few central office administrative meetings, notice which principals and central office personnel seem to be the experts on particular topics. If they are willing to talk about a topic in front of their peers, there is a good chance that they *do* know the issue.

- Visit other schools in the district and simply ask the principals how they accomplish particular projects.

- Have a good talk with your secretary. Ask the secretary to describe what takes place in the office area during a typical school day. Also, ask about the busy times during the year. You should get a feel from the conversation about what the secretary perceives as important.

- Be patient and observant. Create and develop your own informal network. Keep it legal and ethical.

The Caring and Ethical Manager

Part of managing human resources is ensuring that decisions are ethical and follow legal principles. Additionally, carrying out budgetary duties, working effectively with unions, and maintaining a facility that accentuates student and adult possibilities are all responsibilities that caring and ethical principals must effectively administer. The next section addresses all these issues.

Legal Issues

Almost all aspiring and new principals have taken at least one graduate course in school law. Depending on the state requirements and a particular professor's curriculum, courses range from an emphasis on constitutional landmark cases to stressing state or district statutes affecting schools. Also, university classes spend time on issues of media interest because of a rash of incidents (e.g., violence in schools) or because schools have seemingly abandoned common sense (e.g., suspending a 5-year-old for harassment for kissing a classmate). When newcomers begin a principalship, it is difficult to know which legal issues to emphasize to prepare for the year. To exacerbate the situation, some of the state school law policy documents and manuals are several inches thick! How is a new principal to cope with all that?

The following review of important legal topics and guidelines can help new principals deal with the legal issues they will face. The list is not totally inclusive and specific issues will surface that no one can predict. The review does, however, cover many of the major landmark issues that have confronted schools during the past 50 years (Morrison, 2003; Zirkel, 2001–2002; Iller, 1996; Aquila & Petzke, 1994).

DESEGREGATION

The desegregation laws, beginning with *Brown v. Board of Education* (1954), blazed the trail for so much of what schools do. Equal access for all groups and other civil rights issues were given a major legal and moral boost when *Brown v. Board of Education* struck down the notion of "separate but equal" as an accepted U.S. law or value. The *Brown* decision was a pioneering act, directly and indirectly leading to a variety of laws and legislation that has included the right of equal school entry for all races, ethnic groups, and religions; the importance of gender equity; fairness for students with disabilities; and issues relating to limited English proficiency. The legacy of *Brown* is that U.S. schools must pursue excellence and equality for all students.

Gender Equity

"Under Title IX the Department of Education can investigate complaints of sexual discrimination and can curtail funding to programs and agencies that discriminate" (Morrison, 2003). Since Title IX legislation was enacted in 1972, gender discrimination in activities, athletics, counseling, marital status, and admissions has been prohibited (Aquila & Petzke, 1994). Providing women with equal opportunities to participate on the athletic field has made the greatest impact on the public. However, the principal must think beyond sports and consider the effect of Title IX on the academic program and ask: Are females and males provided equal access to math, science, and literature classes? Are the school guidance counselors (who can have an immense effect on a student's future) scheduling students for classes that meet present student needs and future pathways—regardless of gender? Are teachers treating students in a fair manner without any preconceived notions of gender limitations? New principals can directly affect the culture of their schools by taking a strong and proactive stand on gender equity through their personal behavior, verbal remarks, and questioning perspective.

Serving Students with Disabilities

Beginning with the landmark legislation PL 94–142 (1975) and Section 504 of the Rehabilitation Act of 1973, schools were put on notice that students with disabilities have the right to an education that maximizes their potential. As disabilities legislation has evolved, more doors have opened. "Perhaps the most significant change in the new Individual with Disabilities Education Act [IDEA, 1997] is the clarification of special education as a service and not a place" (NAESP, 2001). Principals must make sure that students are provided the proper services, including defined evaluation procedures, parental involvement and consent, a specific Individualized Education Plan (IEP), and due process to qualify for federal funds for the 13 disability categories defined by IDEA 1997. These categories comprise autism, deaf-blindness, deafness, hearing impairment, mental retardation, multiple disabilities, orthopedic impairment, other health impairment, serious emotional disturbance, specific learning disabilities, speech or language impairment, traumatic brain injury, and visual impairment. Additionally, IDEA expects schools to focus more on the specific school curriculum so that students can receive a "free and appropriate public education" and an Individualized Education Plan (IEP) that, as much as possible, is aligned with the curriculum standards intended for the whole student body.

Although the Section 504 legislation does not mandate federal funds or a specific IEP, nor list specific disabilities covered for servicing, the broad nature of this civil rights law is exactly what gives the law its strength. The law protects persons with physical or mental impairments that substantially limit one or more major life activities such as "walking, seeing, hearing, speaking, breathing, learning, working, caring for oneself, and performing manual tasks" (www.kidsource.com.ada.idea, accessed April 28, 2002). Each day, new principals should remind themselves that the commitment of schools to students with disabilities is an opportunity to celebrate diversity and serve all students. It is shameful that one or two generations ago students with disabilities were isolated and often unable to attend schools. Again, by their actions—in this case supporting school efforts to equalize the playing field for students with disabilities—principals can send a strong message of what is valued in the schoolhouse.

SERVING STUDENTS WITH LIMITED ENGLISH PROFICIENCY

In *Lau v. Nichols* (1974) the Supreme Court "required school districts to take affirmative steps to rectify the language deficiency of students with limited English proficiency (LEP). Carefully avoiding dictating a particular methodology, the Court left the remedy to the local level, where teaching English as a second language is often favored over a bilingual curriculum" (Zirkel, 2001–2002). How to teach LEP students is a complicated and sometimes highly charged issue. For example, in 1998 California voters passed Proposition 227, "which outlawed bilingual education in California schools" (Morrison, 2003, p. 137). As a result of this proposition, schools have been applying for waivers to assist the students. Using waivers in other states (to address LEP or other educational needs) is also practiced to assist local students when needs appear to be outside of the mandates set by state or federal regulations. Because flexibility is necessary to meet the needs of students, the school principal, working with the district, can be a strong voice in local application of statutes. To illustrate, principals and school personnel need to decide how many students it takes to create a program, the curriculum path of the program, and whether funding is available to provide students with the needed services, because the courts were not specific concerning the implementation of LEP laws.

SAFETY, NEGLIGENCE, AND CHILD ABUSE ISSUES

"When a person intentionally or negligently causes an injury, they are held liable for that injury. Teachers are negligent when they fail to use proper standards and care to protect students or fail to foresee and correct potential harm in a situation" (Morrison, 2003). Behaving proactively is critical in safety and negligence issues. Principals need to let teachers know that facilities must be safe. Thus, if teachers notice faulty lights in a hallway or a sharp edge on playground equipment, they need to report the problem immediately. Further, adults must be present and vigilant when students are involved. Whether students are practicing in a formal setting for a gymnastic competition or just running on the playground, teachers or aides must be present and supervising. One principal, in a candid moment, shared with his staff that during the school year he expected minor injuries during playground recess. He noted that it was not the minor injuries that worried him, it was whether an adult was present to ensure immediate care for the injuries.

Sadly, neglect and child abuse are major problems in contemporary life. "Teachers are required by federal law to report all suspected cases of child abuse" (Morrison, 2003). Types of abuse can include physical abuse, physical neglect, sexual abuse, emotional abuse, and emotional neglect. And, the U.S. Supreme Court has supported a ruling by a federal appeals court (*Lankford v. Doe*, Case No. 93-1918) that principals may not receive "qualified immunity" from suits and can be liable for their decisions as principals. The Lankford case involved a principal ignoring student evidence that a teacher was sexually abusing the student. The damaging effects of failing to report child abuse cannot be overstated. It is a principal's ethical responsibility to protect every child in a school.

FREE SPEECH AND CENSORSHIP

The *Tinker v. Des Moines* Supreme Court decision (1969) provides a general framework for free speech and censorship cases. The court ruled that teachers and students do not, in the famous phrase, "shed their constitutional rights . . . at the schoolhouse gate." "Immunity" from censorship associated with the Tinker decision was checked somewhat by the *Hazelwood School District v. Kuhlmeier* (1988) ruling supporting a principal's action limiting a school newspaper's content when sensitive issues were about to be raised concerning divorced parents and teenage pregnancy. While serving as a high school principal, Harvey Alvy (author) was able to comfortably use the guidelines of the Hazelwood decision to work with the student editor and faculty newspaper advisor to reshape an article on teenage drinking that resulted in a satisfactory solution and a responsible article in the school newspaper. Zirkel (2001–2002) summarizes the free speech issue eloquently: "In subsequent cases dealing with First Amendment protections of expression, from student dress to students' threats, lower courts have looked to the pole stars of Tinker and Hazelwood for guidance, with the distinct majority of the decisions favoring school authorities."

STUDENT DISCIPLINE: DUE PROCESS AND SEARCH AND SEIZURE LAWS

The school, as the primary institution for educating students in our society, has a responsibility to use its disciplinary procedures as an educational tool. Within limits, most disciplinary situations can be *teachable moments*. In most situations, *due process* can serve this purpose. School leaders are well aware of the importance of due process based on the Fourteenth Amendment to the Constitution and the Supreme Court case *Goss v. Lopez* (1975). As school officials that model proper procedures, principals, assistant principals, and teachers need to give students a chance to talk about an infraction, whether minor or serious, and try to use a student's unacceptable behavior as an educational opportunity. For example, a student who steals an expensive item from a classmate's locker is probably better off receiving the appropriate consequence in a school, with due process, and most likely counseling, than having the behavior go undetected, possibly leading to criminal behavior outside of school. The potential for very serious consequences in the criminal court system may be averted if a school responds firmly and compassionately. As wisely stated by the judges in the *Goss v. Lopez* case, "It would be a strange disciplinary system in an educational institution if no communication was sought by the disciplinarian with the student in an effort to inform him of his defalcation and to let him tell his side of the story" (Morrison, 2003).

Student searches are a more complicated matter. Although the Fourth Amendment protects public school students from unwarranted searches and seizures, the *New Jersey v. T.L.O.* decision (1985) also ruled that school officials can initiate searches depending on the objective to protect the students and the school:

> School principals are not law enforcement officials and are not held to the same standard as are police officers. When conducting a search to investigate a disciplinary incident the doctrine of reasonable suspicion applies to school leaders, whereas the doctrine of probable cause, a higher standard for a search, is applicable for law officers. (Alvy & Robbins, 1998)

Zirkel (2001–2002) summarizes the implications of *T.L.O.*: "Lower courts have applied the *T.L.O.* test to a variety of student searches, with mixed results for invasive strip searches and outcomes overwhelmingly in favor of school authorities for noninvasive searches."

Depending on the degree of inappropriate student behavior, a school's choice of disciplinary consequences or options includes, but is not limited to, in-class warnings, reprimands and restrictions often involving communication with parents or guardians, detention, an informal or official behavioral plan, school activity restrictions, limiting venues, voluntary school or community service, in-school suspensions, short-term suspension, long-term suspension, placement in alternative educational settings, and expulsion. Due process expectations increase when the inappropriate behavior and consequence are more serious. New principals must be particularly familiar with the school, district, and state policies and regulations regarding suspension, alternative educational opportunities, and expulsion. A rookie principal should not be shy about consulting experienced principals, central office staff, and district lawyers when difficult situations occur.

INTIMIDATION, HARASSMENT, AND BULLYING

Schools are taking a firmer stand concerning intimidation, harassment, and bullying behaviors as a specific disciplinary concern. To some extent this is because of a link some experts have drawn, connecting students who are the victims of bullying with severe reprisals, sometimes resulting in school shootings. However, principals do not need the justification of possible reprisals to stand firm on the issue of bullying, intimidation, and harassment. They should stand firm on the issue simply because schools should not and cannot tolerate behaviors that lead to fear and physical or emotional abuse of students. States and school districts have developed "zero tolerance" laws and policies concerning bullying, intimidation, and harassment. In Washington state, a new state law provides immunity to teachers, classified staff, students, and volunteers who report bullying incidents. This law mandates professional development workshops for teachers to deal with bullying and to provide positive strategies to their students to help reduce bullying behaviors.

Zero tolerance is a general position that many school districts have taken concerning issues relating to discrimination, alcohol and drugs, violence, weapons, and harassment. Although a strong stand on all of these issues must be taken in and around schools to protect students and adults, new principals need to understand and implement the laws properly with respect to due process and consequences, so that the schools are not accused of handling zero tolerance incidents inappropriately. Proactively informing everyone of the laws, supporting appropriate behaviors, consistently enforcing the laws, and using due process procedures to handle consequences become a school's best insurance policy to protect students and faculty.

LEGAL ISSUES AFTER SEPTEMBER 11TH

We are still processing how the tragic events of September 11, 2001, affect schools. For example, before September 11th and the shootings at Columbine, many schools prohibited students from carrying cell phones. Today, parents, students, and school officials believe that cell phones can provide a degree of comfort and security to students and their families. Cell phones can be very helpful in an emergency. Concerns relating to patriotism, the use of prayer in schools, preventing terrorism, and the treatment of minorities in our society have also emerged as issues with legal implications emanating from the September 11th events.

FINAL THOUGHTS ON THE LEGAL FRONT

A single practitioner cannot know all of the laws that apply to a school district. Lawyers spend their time researching cases, reviewing previous decisions, conferring with partners, negotiating settlements, and trying to figure out how a particular judge or jury will respond to their case strategy. New or experienced principals do not have the time to research legal precedent all day. Yet, there are general guidelines that one should keep in mind:

- *Behaving ethically.* If in your "gut" you feel that you are going down the wrong path, or circumventing the law, then avoid that path.

- *Using common sense.* It simply makes sense to find out all of the facts, exercise patience, and speak to those involved before taking disciplinary action with a student or responding to a parent's complaint about a particular teacher. Basically, step back for a moment and ask yourself, "Does this make sense?"

- *Setting a personal example that demonstrates support of the law and legal process.* Such a personal statement can have a powerful effect on the school community. To illustrate, although the principal may not be required to attend an IEP meeting, a principal's presence at the meeting indicates support for the process.

- *Keeping the key school policy manuals and state and district legal manuals in a convenient place in your office.* Also, insert tabs and use a highlighter to mark the policies and laws that are frequently needed for reference. This will save you a lot of time. As an aside, reflect on whether you and others are handling a situation in the most effective manner if it is necessary to frequently refer to the same policies and laws.

- *Asking questions of legal experts when you are unsure.* Use the craft knowledge of that experienced principal in the district, or a central office colleague, or the district lawyer. *Successful leaders ask questions* (Bennis & Nanus, 1985), so don't be shy when it comes to expanding your ability to handle the legal challenges.

Working with Unions

Today we recognize that collaboration and cooperation among the different stakeholders in schools is the only way we are going to succeed. Animosity between management and unions or employers and employees in schools is simply a no-win scenario. School administrators and unions must work together to achieve success for all students. The late Albert Shanker—who was so instrumental in helping teachers achieve better working conditions, decent salaries, and due process rights—stressed toward the end of his life that teacher unions should avoid confrontational tactics when possible. Unions need to be in the forefront of teachers' professional development efforts. Today, editorial pieces by the major leaders of the National Educational Association and the American Federation of Teachers often concentrate on professional development issues as opposed to adversarial bargaining issues.

However, unions and administrators have recently expressed some concerns about standards and testing issues. As Koppich and Kerchner (2003) note, "as education reform focused increasingly on test-score accountability, many unions hunkered down and management became even more protective of its turf." It is hard to say how this will play out in the future. An adversarial relationship is costly to all sides; everyone's goal must be the improvement of student performance.

Regardless of the political climate in a district, new principals need to begin their tenure seeking a healthy relationship with the union. To start, new principals must read the collective bargaining agreement. Many grievances occur because the principal is unfamiliar with the language and parameters of the contract. Also, principals should get to know, and have regular meetings with, the building union representative to keep the lines of communication open and positive concerning working conditions and professional development issues.

When a grievance is filed because of a principal's action and district policy, the principal should not take it personally. Remember, a grievance is an action taken, a complaint, based on *actual* or *supposed* circumstances. The circumstances must be investigated to see if the grievance has any merit. New principals, in particular, must remember to follow each step in the grievance procedure and pay particular attention to time lines. Principals are the official building representatives of the school district. It is their responsibility, regardless of their personal views, to carry out the district's position on an issue. When handling a grievance, a principal will be provided with assistance from the central office. Finally, if principals disagree with decisions coming from the central office or the school board concerning a grievance issue, they should express their views professionally, behind closed doors, and at the appropriate time.

Conflict resolution strategies can be very helpful when grievances occur. The following advice for handling conflict is based on our personal experiences, those of other principals and superintendents, and the work of Snowden and Gorton (2002, pp. 89–106):

- Conflict is natural and should be accepted as a feature of any vibrant organization.

- Conflict may be necessary to shake up an organization.

- Always ask, "How can we resolve the conflict to serve the needs of students?"

- Conflict resolution begins with identifying the real issues— from the viewpoint of both sides.

- Viewing conflict as a personal attack makes objective resolution difficult.

- Leaders must display self-control when conflict emerges.

- "Emotions are as important to consider in dealing with conflict as are facts." (Snowden & Gorton)

- Sometimes the best we can do is reduce conflict, not solve conflict.

- There is no specific algorithm, or one right way, to resolve conflicts.

- Trust building takes time.

- Many hours or days of frustration may be necessary before resolution emerges, so don't give up.

- Empathy cannot occur without active listening.

- Respecting and caring for the individuals involved in conflict is critical.

- Empowering others can reduce role conflict.

- Our society prefers winning over compromise, yet compromise and arbitration may be the only reasonable solution.

- Think outside the box for possible solutions.

- When conflicts end, feelings and issues must still be addressed.

Unions and school administrators must work together to provide a first-class education for all students. That has to be the ultimate purpose of all decisions. When the school district management team and the union are in an adversarial relationship, time, resources, and emotional energy must be spent to satisfy both sides. As long as time is spent on adversarial issues, students lose. When the management team and union turn to professional development and student success issues, students and teachers win. And principals can spend their time and efforts *serving* teachers and students.

The School Budget

Often, aspiring or new principals are more worried about the budgetary aspects of the job than any other area of responsibility. As teachers, most of us can recall seeing the principal examining coded numbers (e.g., 826X) and discussing budgetary issues dependent on FTEs or ADA (i.e., Full-Time Equivalent students or Average Daily Attendance) to calculate state funding available based on the number of students in a school. One might have thought there was a mysterious and secret system or formula that somehow provided funding to pay for a school's needs. Rookie principals learn quickly that the codes are pretty boring and refer to numbers associated with specific categories. The type of program (e.g., basic education, state or federal), specific school, and type of expense (i.e., instruction, food service, transportation, maintenance, or other service) are usually part of the coding system. In one school system the operating budget codes that the principals are responsible for monitoring include the following:

General Expenses	(8X4X)
Non-copyrighted Consumable Supplies	(8X5X)
Copyrighted Instructional Supplies	(8X6X)
Contract Services	(8X7X)
Travel Expenses	(8X8X)
Capital Outlay	(8X9X)

Specific subject areas are linked to these broad codes. Thus, language arts, math, science, vocational education, the arts, foreign language, technology, social studies, and physical education all have their own coded numbers. Each state and some school districts customize their system to keep detailed track of all revenue and expenses.

Although the coding system appears to be clear-cut, deciding on the expense category of a particular item is not always an easy decision. For example, what makes an item permanent or consumable? Is a consumable limited to one year of use? Two? Is software consumable? Can expenses for an extracurricular activity involving the debate club, which meets frequently during honors English, come out of English funds? Sometimes past practice and common sense are the best ways to resolve these issues. Again, seeking advice from an experienced principal and the central office financial officer is critical for a new principal. The following guidelines will help aspiring or new principals with the budgetary responsibilities.

• Remember that a budget is a *financial plan* intended to provide funds to effectively educate students in a school district. The objective of the financial plan is not to brag about how much money the school district saved; the objective is to wisely and skillfully use the funds to maximize student outcomes.

• Converse with the district financial officer and inquire about the particular budgetary philosophy and method used in the district. For example, is a Planning-Programming-Budgeting System used? Zero-based budgeting? Site-based strategies? (Kaiser, 1995)

• Review your school's budgets from the previous two or three years to discern patterns, especially relating to monthly expenses at the beginning and toward the end of the school year.

• Examine the district's budget development time line and highlight key dates on your personal calendar.

• If possible, before the school year begins, familiarize yourself with the district budgetary software program and the budgetary and expense forms. Often, a school secretary can be very helpful with these tasks.

• When seeking the cost of instructional items, always ask for written estimates. Also, check with the central office to find out if the district has particular suppliers and set price lists for the items.

• Try to determine, as early as possible, how much leeway you will have concerning budgetary decisions. If site-based management is practiced in the district, the principal needs to know how involved the site team is in budgetary decisions.

• Funds raised from student council activities should not be used for basic education. Also, a detailed paper trail of student council funds must be kept.

• Be transparent and explain financial decisions to the staff. Keeping budgetary cards close to the chest can provoke distrust among faculty and classified staff.

• Strongly support efforts to obtain staff development funding for teachers.

• Be creative and recognize alternative funding opportunities. Although private funding accounts for only about 3 percent of school revenue, grants from private philanthropic organizations and businesses can affect individual schools. (On a national average, revenue is 46 percent from the state, 44 percent from local sources, and 7 percent from the federal government.)

Maintaining a Facility That Accentuates Pride

What are students, teachers, and parents to think if they walk by a school and notice broken windows, graffiti on the school building walls, untidy lawns, poor lighting, a loose and hanging basketball rim on the playground, and a front entrance with a broken door handle? What impression will our same students, teachers, and parents reach if they walk by the school and notice beautiful windows, tidy lawns, sufficient lighting, efficient basketball rims, and a beautiful entranceway? Certainly, a favorable first impression is preferred. If our students, teachers, and parents walk into the school and observe beautiful display cabinets with student work, helpful direction signs, a brightly lit and welcoming reception and office area, and clean hallways, the first impression will likely be favorable. Clean classrooms, clean restrooms, suitable furniture, an inviting teacher work area, sparkling gymnasiums, clean labs, an inviting auditorium, and a comfortable student cafeteria are also important symbols of a first-class school facility. As a school's chief administrator, a principal has to take responsibility for the bleak facility description at the beginning of this paragraph—however, if the facility looks first-rate, then a good principal will make sure the credit goes to others!

Keeping a school facility in outstanding appearance and condition takes a tremendous effort by all. Pride in the school's appearance must be practiced daily in behaviors that extend from the custodians to administrators, students, teachers, and classified staff. Each person in the school must play a role. The principal, for example, should take regular walks in the school with the custodian, noting areas of concern and talking to teachers and classified staff about keeping the facility safe and clean. Probably the facility issue that is discussed least often is the condition of student restrooms. As Gewertz (2003) writes, "Administrative training seldom discusses bathroom management. . . . [A]dministrators feel far too busy with pressing issues to spend time on restrooms. . . . Paul Young, president of the National Association of Elementary School Principals, observes that, 'It [keeping restrooms clean] is one of the responsibilities of a principal. We are instructional leaders, but we also have to keep a balance with management.'"

A Clear and Present Danger: Air Quality in Schools

A graduate student in educational leadership shared with Harvey Alvy (author) that he developed health problems after moving to a new school and teaching in a particular classroom. The teacher found out that his new health problems were similar to the health problems suffered by the last teacher who used the same classroom. Indoor air quality (IAQ) and mold contamination may very well have been a contributor to each teacher's health problems. In recent years schools have recognized a particular and serious problem related to the air quality of the school facility. In 1995, the Government Accounting Office reported that 115,000 schools experienced difficulties from poor IAQ (Halverson, 2002). IAQ problems can develop from toxic chemicals, pesticides, biological contaminants, and odors from gas, propane, sewage, mold, glue, smoke, dust, and ammonia. Poor ventilation and leaking ceilings can also lead to serious IAQ problems. Halverson reported,

> Biological contaminants in the form of mold account for half of indoor air quality complaints according to Marilyn Black, chief scientist at Atlanta-based Air Quality Sciences. An estimated 7,500 public schools are infected by mold. Mold is on the rise and making children and teachers sick as a result of water infiltration. Mold can grow anytime there is water leaking. . . . Asthma, sinus infections, headaches, coughing, and throat and eye irritation are often reported in mold-infested schools.

An Environmental Protection Agency (EPA) economic analysis of repairs performed at an elementary school showed that if $370 per year over 22 years (a total of $8,140) had been spent on preventive maintenance, $1.5 million in repairs could have been avoided. The following tips gleaned primarily from EPA recommendations can help schools deal with indoor air problems (Sack, 2002; Dunne, 2001):

• Work with the maintenance and custodial staff to ensure that regular housekeeping and maintenance checks are done.

• Check for unexplained odors that may be caused by art supplies, laboratory activities, vehicle exhaust, kitchen or food items, chemicals, mold or mildew, pets, and carpeting.

• Regularly replace filters on heating and air-conditioning units.

• Adequately ventilate each classroom.

• Control temperature and humidity.

• Make sure exhaust fans are functioning properly.

• Clean up spills promptly.

• Control moisture.

• Ensure that drain traps are cleared regularly.

• Keep the administrative offices clean and pest-controlled as an example for other offices and classrooms.

 Success Story ————————————————

LLBWA is a purposeful leadership strategy that works. This success story uses the LLBWA strategy.

Once a month after the students are dismissed on a Friday afternoon, an elementary school principal and the school's head custodian walk through the facility. The principal and custodian drop into each classroom where teachers seem relaxed (it's Friday afternoon!) and ask about lighting, the condition of the furniture, and other matters that involve maintenance work. The teachers appreciate the visit, and a few usually have one or two suggestions. Because teachers know that the principal and custodian will drop by monthly, some keep a list of maintenance concerns. The teachers know that for serious problems, maintenance requests should be sent as soon as possible. For example, moisture observed in a ceiling tile should be reported immediately. If a problem needs considerable discussion (e.g., removing, redesigning, or renovating a bookcase area) the teacher and custodian plan a future meeting. Often a teacher's suggestion relates to preventive maintenance, with a possible repair or replacement during the December holiday or summer maintenance period. A Saturday repair is also a possibility. If it looks like a major summer job, the principal asks the teacher to fill out the summer work forms, which are distributed in the spring. The teachers may use this time to briefly share information with the principal that might relate to the class, a student, or some future activity. It is also an opportunity to wish a colleague a good weekend!

Activity

Leading and Learning By Wandering Around (LLBWA)

Review the suggested school visibility strategies in Figure 7.2. Then follow the directions in Theory to Practice on page 181.

——————— Figure 7.2 ———————
Visibility Strategies

A.   Select different times to wander around: 8 a.m., 10 a.m., noon, 2 p.m., 4 p.m.

B.   Engage in conversations to celebrate student and teacher success.

C.   Conduct focused observation drop-ins—7-minute classroom snapshots:

– student focus

– instructional focus

– curricular focus

D.   Conduct unfocused drop-ins:

– random

– planned

E.   Teach a class or group.

F.   Engage in a short pre-observation or postobservation chat.

G.   Monitor the hallway and yard at transition times.

H.   Schedule periodic one-to-one discussions.

I.   Conduct task group discussions.

(continued)

Figure 7.2

Visibility Strategies *(continued)*

J. Make parent outreach calls; while walking the hall, use the cell phone to share

– good news

– storytelling

K. Target student interviews—Look for that new student on campus.

L. Random student interviews—How are your classes going?

M. Sample lesson plans and comments (providing cultural norms permit this practice).

N. Make staff room visits.

O. Collect student work samples.

P. Collect specific schoolwide data (time on or off task, verbal flow, motivation).

Q. Follow up on referrals.

R. Wander by "black holes in space" that you monitor infrequently.

S. Go on a neighborhood walk and watch.

T. Observe display cases and consider what they say about the school.

U. Inspect cleanliness of bathrooms.

V. Examine safety of playground equipment and hallway lighting.

W. Examine safety features of bus loading and unloading areas while greeting students.

X. Check sprinkler system to ensure that landscaping is adequately watered; check timing to ensure watering does not occur when students are on the playground.

Y. Following severe rain, check roofing in areas that were previously problematic.

Z. What else?

THEORY TO PRACTICE

Consider the visibility strategies described in Figure 7.2 and school areas that you have not frequently visited during the past three or four months. (Do any of these visibility strategies or areas have important meaning relating to your school or district culture?) Jot down a reminder to use several of these strategies, and list areas that you will visit in your school during the next few days and weeks.

1.

2.

3.

4.

5.

6.

7.

Reflective Field Notes —————————

Please use this space to jot down notes that are important for your personal leadership journey. You may do this in a structured way—by responding to questions—or in an unstructured way. Use the approach that works for you.

• What else would you add to the phrase "brevity, fragmentation, and variety" to describe how a principal's day can be characterized?

• Take another look at the beginning-of-the-year responsibilities list in the first part of the chapter (beginning on p. 147). What responsibilities would you add to the list?

• Based on Covey's notion of formulating to-do lists based on important goals, create a list that describes actions you would take on a daily basis to support your vision of how a school should be managed.

• What current legal issues are particularly important to your school district?

• Find out about the budget management philosophy and strategy followed in your school district.

• What insights or new questions do you have as a result of reflecting on the issues raised in this chapter?

8

Emotions as a Gateway to Learning

At a middle school in the Bronx, New York, a second-year science teacher was abruptly deployed for military service. Her students were dismayed and angry. A young teacher at the school was asked to substitute for the class during one of his planning periods. The principal met him in the hall before he reached the classroom and said, "The class is really upset, and with good cause. Why don't you begin with offering them the option of writing to their teacher? I'll make sure the letters get to her. It would be therapeutic for the class and their teacher." The young teacher nodded and walked slowly into the classroom. Just before the end of that class period, the principal stopped by to chat with the class. She spoke compassionately to the students in a soft, calm voice. "I know you guys are really hurting. You were all very close to your teacher, and she adored you. She was very sad about having to leave. She spent hours getting lesson plans together so that you would continue to learn science, even in her absence. I hope you will choose to do so. And I will do all I can to get your letters to her. It will cheer her up, I'm sure. And we'll get her e-mail address so we can continue our conversations with her, okay?" The students, often unruly and outspoken, were silent. Many had tears in their eyes. They nodded in agreement with the principal's words and slowly filed out of the classroom. After they had left, the principal sat down with the teacher who had covered the class that period. "How did it go?" she asked. His eyes welled up as he said, pointing to the letters students had written, "Even the kids who usually are tough and belligerent had amazing things to say. Look at this one." He pulled a letter out of the pile and began to read, "You're the best science teacher I ever had. I didn't even think I liked science before you. I'll pray for you. I love you. Come back to us." He put the letter down. "You see," reflected the principal, "inside of every one of those rough, tough kids is a real human being with feelings. Those kids want to feel valued, cared for, loved and they are tired of being abandoned! We have to remember this—even when they are cussing at us—and seek to understand their feelings. At the same time, we can seize these moments as opportunities to teach valuable life skills as well as use the time to model handling our own emotions and empathy."

The preceding scenario, based on an actual episode, reminds us that emotions play a powerful role in the learning process. Driven positively, emotions can open the gates to learning. Driven negatively, the gateway to learning slams shut.

Understanding the role of emotions is a powerful tool for the principal—and especially for the newcomer who may be facing a faculty who has experienced a loss—for example, loss of a familiar former principal. Daniel Goleman and his colleagues, Boyatzis and McKee, remind us of these truths:

> Great leaders move us. They ignite our passion and inspire the best in us. When we try to explain why they are so effective, we speak of strategy, vision or powerful ideas. But the reality is much more primal: Great leadership works through the emotions. No matter what leaders set out to do—whether it's creating strategy or mobilizing teams to action—their success depends upon *how* they do it. Even if they get

everything else right, if leaders fail in this primal task of driving emotions in the right direction, nothing they do will work as well as it could or should. (Goleman et al., 2002)

Effective leaders act as a group's emotional guide. The principal in the opening scenario functioned as an emotional guide for students and staff, driving their emotions in an empathetic, productive way that would bring out the best in them, even at this time of great loss. Had she not intervened, the anger and upset that lingered within the students may have escalated and violence could have followed. "Leaders' moods and actions have an enormous impact on those they lead . . . to inspire, arouse passion and enthusiasm and keep people motivated and committed . . . and conversely, the power of toxic leadership to poison the emotional climate of the workplace" (Goleman et al., 2002).

The capacity to handle your own emotions and relationships with others is known as "emotional intelligence" (Goleman, 1995). Emotional intelligence can affect success at work and in life. Lack of it can cause demise of a career and unhappiness in life. The good news, according to Daniel Goleman, is that emotional intelligence is teachable!

Emotional Intelligence

Emotional intelligence involves competency in five domains. These include "self awareness, self-regulation, motivation, empathy, and social skill" (Goleman, 1998). *Self-awareness* involves the ability to put feelings into words, the ability to recognize and understand one's moods and emotions, and the skills to change one's moods to more positive ones. Self-aware individuals possess an accurate assessment of their strengths and weaknesses and often evidence self-deprecating humor. Competency in this domain also reflects an understanding of personality style and the effect of one's style on others. *Self-regulation* involves the skill of being able to manage emotions. This includes the ability "to control or redirect disruptive impulses and moods and the propensity to suspend judgment—to think before acting. The hallmarks of this domain include trustworthiness and integrity, comfort with ambiguity and openness to change" (Goleman, 1998). *Motivation* is the third domain of emotional intelligence. It involves the ability to delay gratification and the propensity to set goals and pursue them with zeal and perseverance. Researchers have found that the ability to motivate oneself even in the face of great difficulty is closely related to the spirit of optimism. Leaders who demonstrate this competency have high expectations for themselves, possess a strong drive for accomplishment even when confronted with failure, and "keep score" of their achievements. *Empathy* is perhaps the most familiar of the five domains. We are all familiar with the saying "Walk a mile in your neighbor's shoes." This competency enables one to understand the emotions of others and provides the skills to interact with others responsively, according to their emotions. This capacity reflects a valuing of diversity and cross-cultural sensitivity. Expertise in this area usually enables people to build community, retain talent, and deliver quality customer care. This influences school climate, which in turn influences productivity. It has been said, "Overall, the climate—how people feel about working at a company—can account for 20 to 30 percent of business performance" (Goleman, Boyatzis, & McKee, 2002). The fifth domain of emotional intelligence is known as *social skill*. This involves what some call interpersonal polish—the unique ability to read another person's verbal or nonverbal cues and respond appropriately. Individuals who show competence in this area easily create rapport with others and are skilled in networking. Expertise in this area lends itself to team building and the ability to work with leading change.

The ability to understand and model the five domains of emotional intelligence is a critical leadership skill. It also provides a valuable lens through which to view classrooms. In the ideal sense, one would want teachers to understand, model, and explicitly teach emotionally intelligent behavior to students. And, as a consequence, students should reflect these behaviors as well. Students are more likely to adopt the behaviors they view most frequently in their immediate learning environment. Maurice Elias (2002), professor at Rutgers University, often suggests to administrators that they take a "feeling walk" in the school. He asks them to reflect, "Are there some places that just feel better than others because good things are going on there for students?"

Emotional Intelligence and Community Building

Indeed, there is a "powerful connection between an emotionally healthy and exciting school environment and the propensity for learning to soar" (Wolfe, 2001). Principals can influence and promote these environments through daily interactions, supervisory visits, faculty meetings, and by building a sense of community within the schoolhouse. Research suggests that in schools where a strong sense of community exists, students are more likely to be academically motivated (Solomon et al., 2000). Staff is more likely to commit to professional learning and take collective responsibility for students in these contexts as well. Eric Schaps, president of the Developmental Studies Center in Oakland, California, suggests, "When a school meets students' basic psychological needs, students become increasingly committed to the school's norms, values and goals. And by enlisting students in maintaining that sense of community, the school provides opportunities for students to learn skills and develop habits that will benefit them throughout their lives" (Schaps, 2003). The principal plays a key role in ensuring that this happens. Because "schools are communities of human beings, bound together in an organic, continuously developing web of relationships" (Rooney, 2003), and because "without community nothing else matters" (Boyer, 1995), the principal's skill at building relationships among individuals and weaving together individual values and beliefs into a shared vision of care, compassion, and quality teaching and learning is crucial to student achievement and school success. An essential part of this effort involves not only building and nurturing bonds among adults, but also among adults and students, and among students. In fact, student learning is influenced profoundly by social and emotional factors in the environment. An alienated student often has diminished learning capacity because of a preoccupation with concern about lack of belonging. An inclusive school community that promotes close bonds among all stakeholders is a valuable antidote to bullying and violence and contributes to positive student learning and achievement. Roger Weissberg, executive director of the Collaborative for Academic, Social and Emotional Learning (CASEL), and his colleagues based at the University of Illinois at Chicago, underscore the important links between coordinated social and emotional learning programs for students, caring school communities of responsible and engaged learners, and benefits for students, teachers, administrators, parents, and community members (Weissberg et al., 2003).

In addition to forging the development of sustained, caring, responsive, professional learning communities, the principal also models care with a relentless concern about what transpires on a daily basis in classrooms. Understanding the role of emotions in learning provides valuable insights for the principal when it comes to assessing those processes and interactions designed to foster student learning.

The Role of Emotions in the Classroom

"Emotion drives attention, and attention drives learning" (Sylwester, 1995). "The brain is constantly scanning its environment, sifting and sorting through the incoming information to determine what to keep and what to ignore" (Wolfe, 2001). The brain is programmed to attend first to information that has strong emotional meaning. Its first concern is for safety. Proactive classroom management practices and social and emotional learning programs impact safety. If students perceive that the environment is safe—physically, psychologically, socially, and emotionally— they will be able to focus on learning. After a concern for safety, the next pursuit of the brain's attention is for that which has meaning. Joseph LeDoux (1996) reminds us "that explicit conscious memory of emotional situations would be stronger than the explicit memory of non-emotional situations." Because emotion does influence retention, an important implication for classroom practice is that the content addressed be delivered in a way that is emotionally meaningful and, hence, memorable. Simulations, role plays, problem solving in real life situations, guest speakers, field trips, and connecting academic content to students' lives are all strategies for accomplishing this important end.

And finally, another way that emotions influence students' learning in the schoolhouse, in the community, and in their homes stems from how it is embraced by others. When principals visit classrooms, they might examine these key points:

- The nature of relationships among students and teacher, and among students;

- How feedback is delivered;

- How value for students' work is demonstrated; and

- What opportunities are provided for parents and community members to affirm the significance of the students' work.

Many principals have adopted the practice of shadowing a student to gain important insights regarding how emotions are providing a gateway or a barrier to learning in the school.

Ensuring a safe, emotionally stimulating, significant environment for all members of the school community is indeed a tall task for the principal. But it is also a focus that will yield powerful, lasting results that will benefit all stakeholders in the schoolhouse.

 **Activity** ——————————————————————

A Visual Tour of the Building

Try taking a walk through the school in which you work. Imagine you are a visitor. Begin with walking from the parking lot to the front door, then into the building.

- What do you notice?

- What does the sign posted on the front door say? Is it welcoming, or does it read, "No Trespassing"?

- What is posted on the walls? In the halls?

- How does the building "feel"? Are there some places that feel better than others? Why?

- How are you greeted? How are others greeted?

- What impressions are you left with after your tour?

Reflective Field Notes ————————

Please use this space to jot down notes that are important for your personal leadership journey as a reader. You may do this in a structured way—by responding to questions—or in an unstructured way. Use the approach that works best for you.

• What suggestions might you make to other substitutes charged with the responsibility of covering the science teacher's class?

• See if you can recall the five domains of emotional intelligence. Assess your strengths and weaknesses in each of these areas.

• What additional insights do you have regarding emotions as a gateway for learning?

• What would you want a new teacher to understand about the role of emotions in learning?

9

Understanding and Working with Change: New Roads and Detours

Change is a constant. Change is inherent in life, in the schoolhouse, in business, in politics, and in nature. The new principal represents change within the organization. Change represents, in many cases, loss: loss of the familiar—familiar people, familiar ways of doing things, familiar traditions. The new principal quickly discovers it is critical to understand

- The change process,
- Basic principles regarding facilitating individual and organization change,
- Why change fails, and
- Strategies for working productively with resistance.

A critical and yet often frustrating reality is that change takes time. However, the school leader can create change friendly conditions to pave the way. Let's turn to an example.

During one of her first days in the role of new principal, Betsy examined student data. She noticed that the number of English as Second Language (ESL) learners in the school had increased dramatically. She immediately examined the material resources available to these students and inquired of staff members about how these students were currently being served. It became apparent to Betsy that the staff would benefit from opportunities to visit other schools that had similar ESL learners and examine those practices and resources that were making a difference. She also believed that providing staff development to teachers working with this new population of students would be beneficial. Yet when she offered these opportunities, she met with quiet, but nonetheless firm, resistance: "What we're doing is fine. But thanks for thinking of us." Betsy reminded herself that change was frightening to many and that some may have interpreted the invitation to learn new approaches as an indication that what they were currently doing was unsatisfactory or, in some cases, meant that they were inept. Yet she resolved that she must do something to create a desire to learn among the adults in the schoolhouse so that the English language learner students could be served well. She visited classrooms. When she dropped in, she often left Post-it notes for the teacher, in which she described what the teacher was doing and the student learning that resulted. During faculty meetings, she often showed a videotape and followed the video with dialogue about practices that seemed to make a difference for English language learners. At other faculty meetings, she distributed articles about programs for English language learners for staff members to read and discuss. At other meetings she invited guest speakers to share lessons learned from their experiences with teaching English language learners.

In March, seven months after her initial invitation to staff had been declined, a key group of staff members came to Betsy's office one afternoon and asked if they could "take her up on her earlier offer." She replied with a smile and a nod. "Sure. What would you like to do first?" she inquired, giving the power to make the decision about how to begin to the ad hoc faculty member committee.

The next morning was St. Patrick's Day. As she walked down the hall, Betsy was met by a first grader who spoke very little English, yet who shouted out, "Top of the morning to you, Ms. D!" Betsy smiled and responded, "Top of the morning to you!" She thought to herself, "My vision for serving these students is going to be realized! Yes!"

Change and Beliefs

As Phil Schlechty (2001) reminds us,

> Change begins with beliefs; beliefs about what the present circumstance of the system is, beliefs about what it should be, and beliefs about discrepancies between the way things are and the way they should be. . . . It is important for leaders to understand that in leading change, beliefs and the symbols by which beliefs are expressed are among the most basic tools of the leader's trade and that they must learn to express beliefs in clear and compelling ways as well as to hear and understand others' expression of beliefs.

Carefully chosen experiences provide one way the principal can express beliefs—such as the faculty meetings Betsy crafted—and begin to shape the beliefs of others. Over time, experiences can begin to alter belief systems so that gradually, individuals come to see how they can marry existing beliefs with new ones to heighten their effectiveness in meeting the needs of all learners. Recognizing that staff members did not share the initial sense of urgency she possessed, Betsy had two choices—forcing the change, which would clearly have met with resistance, or going more slowly and creating

- A sense of the need for change,

- A clear vision or "picture" of the anticipated results of the change,

- Inspiring experiences which provided images of what the change would be like in place, and

> • Strategic resources to make the vision of change become a reality.

In choosing the second path, she created valuable support among powerful members of the school culture. She provided the space, between stimulus and response, time for staff members to reconcile old ways with new, without introducing the element of fear. This was a key move, because "the fact is that people prefer habitual ways of doing things to new ways, and the deepest habits of people are embodied in the structure and culture of the organizations where they live out their lives" (Schlechty, 2001, p. 163). When change touches on these habits, people often perceive that their professionalism or sense of self-worth is in jeopardy. Recognizing this reality and reading the culture before attempting to change it garnered much support for a new way of functioning within the context of the culture. And, the decision about where to begin advancing toward a vision of serving all students was left to key cultural players.

Change and School Culture

Principals generate powerful support for change by creating opportunities for organizational members to take ownership in the change effort and attending to key cultural attributes. There are several roads to accomplishing this. Not considering the culture will, in almost all cases, lead to a short-lived change effort.

The California School Leadership Academy staff often shared the *R-FIT* principles when addressing the topic of facilitating change:

> R – Create opportunities for people to see the *relevance* of the change effort.
> F – Help individuals to perceive that the change is *feasible* or doable.
> I – *Involve* organizational members in fashioning what the change will look like, sound like, and feel like.

T – Build *trust* between the change initiator and those who will be affected by the change.

A Look at Change from the Individual's Perspective

It is critical that we go about facilitating change in a way that shows sensitivity to the individuals who will be affected by the change. As those individuals change, they will transform the school culture—one person at a time. Another valuable understanding for principals regarding the change process has to do with the notion that individuals' concerns about an innovation tend to differ but evolve in a fairly predictable way. And, that by recognizing a concern and addressing its specific focus, principals can support staff in moving through a variety of concern stages. To what extent that the concern can be assessed, and responded to accordingly, will facilitate one's understanding and experience of the change effort.

Gene Hall and his colleagues created a framework for understanding common characteristics that indicate one's concern related to an innovation or change experience (Figure 9.1). As can be seen from the framework, one individual may be concerned about how the change might affect him or her personally ("Self"), while another might be concerned about the "Impact" that the innovation might have on students. How the principal responds to these two individuals should clearly take into account the specific stage of concern expressed. One principal posted these concerns on a wall in his office and then created a column that indicated possible responses to each type of concern (Figure 9.2, p. 198).

Change and the Organization

Organizations change as the individuals within them change. It is important to view change simultaneously from both an individual and institutional or organizational perspective. Change takes

———— Figure 9.1 ————

Stages of Concern

Typical Expressions of Concern About Innovation		
	Stage of Concern	*Expression of Concern*
IMPACT	6. Refocusing	I have some ideas about something that would work even better.
	5. Collaboration	I am concerned about relating what I am doing with what other instructors are doing.
	4. Consequence	How is my use affecting kids?
TASK	3. Management	I seem to be spending all my time in getting material ready.
SELF	2. Personal	How will using it affect me?
	1. Informational	I would like to know more about it.
	0. Awareness	I am not concerned about it [the innovation].

Source: Adapted from Hord, Rutherford, Huling-Austin, and Hall (1987).

place one individual at a time but, if effective, positively affects the entire organization. This underscores the importance of systemic thinking. That is, changes in one part of the system have an impact on others. For example, one middle school elected to change to a 90-minute block schedule. Schedule changes had an effect on staffing, students, curriculum delivery and pacing, elective course offerings, assessment practices, budget, and parents. Whenever one high school principal examines a change effort being considered, she invites staff to create a visual map to think holistically about the ramifications of the change on different parts of the organizational system.

––––––––– **Figure 9.2** –––––––––

A Principal's Response to the Stages of Concern

Stage of Concern	Response Options and Opportunities
6. Refocusing	Revisit the change. Take stock. Make midcourse corrections to enhance it. Relate it to other, similar endeavors.
5. Collaboration	Create opportunities for individuals to work together, problem solve, share ideas.
4. Consequence	Demonstrate how using the change is impacting staff, students (share data).
3. Management	Show how the change might be implemented. Provide how-tos.
2. Personal	Share that others may have similar concerns. Illustrate how the change might support the individual and enhance practice.
1. Informational	Explain what "it" may look like in practice: guest speakers, articles, field trips, or site visits.
0. Awareness	Provide data; share examples, information.

Source: Adapted from Hord, Rutherford, Huling-Austin, and Hall (1987).

Often, mandates thrust an organization into a change process with little time provided to build awareness, understanding, and commitment—vital ingredients for the change process. This reality flies in the face of what research suggests facilitates successful change! The RAND study "set out to characterize the process by which an innovation is translated into an operating reality within school districts" (Berman & McLaughlin, 1978). In studies of successful change, three characteristic phases were identified: "mobilization, implementation, and institutionalization." As a principal, thinking about these three phases and speaking about them with staff when change is being anticipated or planned can contribute greatly to successful implementation of a change over time.

A Veteran Principal Offers Advice

A veteran principal was recently asked to give a few words of wisdom to a newcomer regarding change. He responded,

> I'll share this with you from the school of hard knocks! First, expect for major change to occur, it will take three to five, maybe six or seven years. Second, a little over halfway through a change effort, there's usually a state of entropy or running out of steam that occurs. So plan proactively—some type of celebration or 'hoopla' to get people jazzed up again—to recognize how much they've accomplished and to give them the energy to go forth—or you'll lose them. Be aware that sometimes starting change looks easy. Don't become overly confident! It could be that the opposition is just holding back. And, compared to sustaining change, starting it is easy! Another thing—be sure the change is consistent with the school's vision. If it isn't, revisit the vision to see if it needs to be changed. Revisit the change—maybe it's not right. Remember, sometimes rejecting a change is a bolder move than adapting one that's really a quick fix or inconsistent with the vision. And remember to be cognizant of the feelings of organizational members. Really, it all boils down to relationships. Think about it. If a staff member has poured 20 years of his career into a reading program, and we adopt a new reading approach, what's the message to this person? If you want him to remain on board, you better dignify the contribution he has made and look for ways to integrate the old and the new.
>
> This next point may seem rather simple, but if you want to know if change has really taken hold, look into classrooms on a regular basis. What you see there is your reality. And always remember to be true to your own leadership vision. Do the right thing, and do it right—or you'll lose a lot of sleep!

Rosabeth Moss Kanter (1997) offers an additional bit of advice, reflecting about how, if a change doesn't produce immediate results, it's tempting to move on to the next new thing. She writes,

> The difference between success and failure is often just a matter of time: staying with the project long enough to overcome the unexpected developments, political problems, or fatigue that can come between a great sounding plan and actual results. A basic truth of management—if not of life—is that nearly everything looks like a failure in the middle. At the same time, the next project always looks more attractive (because it is all promise, fresh, and untried).

Trust Is Key

Deborah Meier (1995), reflecting on the success of the middle school she created in Harlem, New York, spoke of building trust among teachers, school leaders, students, and parents as a key component in the change process.

After a year of studying Chicago school reforms, researchers Bryk and Schneider (2003) concluded that schools with a "high degree of relational trust" are more likely to make the kind of changes that help raise student achievement. Bryk and Schneider suggest four "vital signs" for identifying and assessing trust in schools:

1. *Respect.* Do staff members, parents, students, and community members acknowledge one another's dignity and ideas? Do organizational members treat one another in a courteous way during interactions?

2. *Personal Regard.* Do staff members and others in the larger school community care about one another personally and professionally? Are individuals willing to extend themselves beyond the formal requirements of the job or union contract?

3. *Competence in Core Role Responsibilities.* Do staff members, parents, and community members believe in one another's ability and willingness to fulfill role responsibilities effectively?

4. *Personal Integrity.* Can staff, parents, and school community members trust others to keep their word? Is there trust that the interests of children (their education and welfare) will be put first, even when tough decisions have to be made?

For the new principal, who may not have a history with a faculty, developing trust is an essential concern and priority. Looking for evidence of these "vital signs" among staff, and between principal and staff, can be a helpful guide to action:

Principals' actions play a key role in developing and sustaining relational trust. Principals establish both respect and personal regard when they acknowledge the vulnerabilities of others, actively listen to their concerns, and eschew arbitrary actions. Effective principals couple these behaviors with a compelling school vision and behavior that clearly seeks to advance the vision. This consistency between words and actions affirms their personal integrity. Then, if the principal competently manages basic day-to-day school affairs, an overall ethos conducive to the formation of trust will emerge. (Bryk & Schneider, 2003)

Working with Resistance to Change

Looking back on his first year as principal, Jeff reflected,

The ironic part of experiencing resistance was that it turned out to be a positive thing. Andy, for example, resisted almost any change we considered. But after I got past my initial anger, I realized that Andy usually was providing a perspective that we had not considered. By responding to and accommodating his concerns, the change effort was actually enhanced, and Andy became one of its ardent supporters! How we treated Andy became a cultural norm that gave people permission to express their values, beliefs, and opinions, even if they represented a conflict with a change we were considering. So I guess I'd say about my first year experiences with resistance and conflict, we "tilled the soil" so the environment permitted risk-taking and ultimately helped us experiment and make better decisions.

Another essential understanding regarding resistance is that it may stem from several possible reasons. Michael Fullan, in an ASCD workshop, "Implementing Instructional Innovations" (January 30–February 1, 1990), posed 10 reasons for resistance to change:

1. When the purpose is not made clear.
2. When the participants are not involved in the planning.
3. When the appeal is based on personal reasons.
4. When the habit patterns of the work group are ignored.
5. When there is poor communication regarding a change.
6. When there is fear of failure.
7. When excessive work pressure is involved.
8. When the cost is too high, or the reward for making the change is seen as inadequate.

9. When the present situation seems satisfactory.
10. When there is lack of respect and trust in the change initiator.
   (Fullan, 1990)

This list is helpful from two perspectives. First, when resistance to change is encountered, one might consider which of the reasons explains the resistance and respond accordingly. For instance, if the purpose is not clear, provide a clear vision of the purpose that takes into account the resister's current reality. Second, the list might be embraced as a way to reduce resistance by planning proactively, keeping these 10 reasons in mind. For example, because excessive work pressure can spawn resistance, help participants see how the change will align with their values and reduce rather than increase their work burdens.

Creating a climate of openness and one that encourages dialogue and mutual respect is a vital contextual consideration for successful change. Adopting a leadership stance that welcomes, embraces, and works productively with resistance is an important individual factor that will increase the prospects for successful change to occur.

Final Thoughts: Change and the Principal

Effective principals are essential for large-scale, sustained, successful change efforts in schools. "The principal of the future—the cultural change principal—must be attuned to the big picture, a sophisticated, conceptual thinker who transforms the organization through people and teams" (Fullan, 2001). "Cultural change principals display palpable energy, enthusiasm and hope" (Fullan, 2002). The principal of the future must

- Strive to make a difference in the lives of students and staff.

- Develop quality relationships and trust with all stakeholders—teachers, support staff, students, parents, community members—in the educational process.

• Support, collaborate with, learn from, and celebrate the success of other schools in the district. Remember, resources are in short supply!

• Understand the change process, anoint many change leaders, welcome resistance, and help create meaning for change.

• Cultivate change efforts and elements of the organizational culture so that needed changes are sustained over time.

• Align change with the vision.

• Model emotionally intelligent behavior.

• Forge valued relationships among colleagues to maximize resources.

• Promote the development of *Professional Learning Communities* focused on strategies to foster student learning.

• Create norms for lifelong learning.

• Be aware that change takes time. Often programs are "assessed for impact" before they are even implemented. Look into classrooms and engage in observation and dialogue to examine change.

• Be selective about change.

• Practice reflection.

• Place learning at the center of the schoolhouse.

And, in the words of Allen Haymon, director of leadership training for the Department of Defense Education Equity Division, "remember that real leadership is what remains after the leader has left"(personal communication, 2003).

 **Activity** ————————————————————

Understanding and Working with Change

Select a change effort that the organization in which you work is considering. Assess

- Readiness factors,

- Potential reasons for resistance,

- The "vital signs of trust,"

- The values embedded in the change and their relationship to the vision of the organization, and

- Opportunities afforded by the change.

Reflective Field Notes —————————————

Please use this space to jot down notes and reflect on your learning from this chapter to enhance its meaning for you. You may do this in a structured way—by responding to the questions that follow—or an unstructured way. Use the approach that works for you!

• Think about a change effort you are planning or involved in. Which of the ideas presented in the chapter are most relevant to promoting its success?

• Ponder a time when you expressed resistance to change. Examine Fullan's list of 10 possible reasons. Pinpoint the reason for the resistance you expressed.

• What do you believe are some pitfalls a principal can experience when implementing change?

• What new ideas or insights did you glean from reading and reflecting on this chapter?

10

Policies, Full-Service Counseling, and Crisis Intervention That Support Students

Public schools in the United States have always been institutions with a moral purpose. Jefferson's vision of a school included the dual notions of teaching children to read the newspaper so they could make democratic decisions and seeking out the talented among the masses for training as democratic leaders. Horace Mann dreamed that the free common school would educate the masses, end poverty, and save the juvenile delinquent from a life of crime and immorality (Spring, 2001). This moral purpose, however, did not extend to all. Irish Americans, finding the common schools of the mid-1800s anti-Catholic, formed their own parochial schools. As the 20th century began, millions of immigrants from Europe were educated to be "Americanized," as part of a melting pot, in schools that taught academics and moral lessons about behaving properly. The 19th- and much of the 20th-century history of schooling for Native Americans, African Americans, Hispanics, and Asian Americans is a tattered legacy of exclusion from schools, segregated schools, substandard schools, and forced boarding schools. Yet, the desire for knowledge was so powerful that even with seemingly impossible obstacles, stories of success emerged.

Despite school segregation and harassment from the white population, the African American population of the United States made one of the greatest educational advancements in the history of education after emancipation. Denied an education by law in slave states and facing inequality of educational opportunities in free states, only 7 percent of the African American population was literate in 1863. This 7 percent was composed mainly of free African Americans in Northern states. A small part of this 7 percent was composed of enslaved Africans who broke laws to become literate. Within a 90-year period after emancipation, the literacy rate jumped to 90 percent (Spring, 2001).

Today, we celebrate and take pride in the various ethnic and racial groups that are part of our schools. But principals must not forget this historical legacy when working with students, because it reminds us that the door of opportunity has not always been open. Considering this legacy, principals must hold to a *moral vision* that includes an unwavering commitment to helping all students reach their potential. The principal should *envision* each student successfully graduating from school with the academic skills and emotional strength to take advantage of the opportunities that the future holds. Success in school must include creating a climate of emotional safety so that students can succeed. Given (2002) reminds us that

> Unless teachers establish a classroom climate conducive to emotional safety and personal relevancy to students, children will not learn effectively and may reject education altogether. Teachers who nourish the emotional system serve as *mentors* for students by demonstrating sincere enthusiasm for their subject; by helping students discover a passion for learning; by guiding them toward reasonable personal goals; and by supporting them in their effort to become whatever they are capable of becoming.

School principals must support teachers by helping them establish an emotionally safe climate. The Florida Department of Education recommends that

> to establish this climate principals must support teachers' efforts to organize the classroom for quality learning and to exercise leadership in the development of a positive and healthy school climate. In addition to walking the halls and school grounds regularly, principals who have succeeded in creating peaceful schools out of previously violence-ridden campuses make themselves available to teachers, students, and parents and show a genuine interest in their students' lives and potential. They also emphasize prevention and nonviolent conflict resolution. (Office of School Improvement of the Florida Department of Education, 2002)

As a *moral leader* and part of a team, the principal must support a school culture of emotional safety that fosters student rights and responsibilities in a democratic setting. A dictionary definition of moral behavior can help new principals understand the purpose of balancing student rights and responsibilities. Moral behavior is "of or relating to principles of right and wrong in behavior: ethical judgments . . . expressing or teaching a concept of right behavior [and] conforming to a standard of right behavior." Synonyms for moral behavior include: ethical, virtuous, righteous, and noble (Merriam-Webster's 10th Collegiate Dictionary, 2000). Consider the words and phrases that emerge from this definition: "principles of right and wrong," "ethical judgment," "teaching a concept of right behavior," and "conforming to a standard." The synonyms tell us that moral individuals are ethical, virtuous, righteous, and noble. One can extend these personal moral expectations to a school community. Students should be taught principles of right and wrong, good judgment, and conforming to a worthy standard. Behaving ethically certainly raises the bar for a school, given that self-discipline—behaving as one should when no one else is watching—is a fundamental characteristic of the ethical person.

Balancing Student Rights and Responsibilities

Schools are expected to provide a safe and nurturing environment for all students. To do this, schools must balance student rights with responsibilities. As stated in one school district, "The basic right of all students is to receive the opportunity for an education. The conduct of one student cannot impair the rights of other students" (Cheney, WA, School District, 2002–2003). Responsible behavior must be expected and enforced so that students are comfortable in the classroom, in the hallways, in the bathroom, on the playing field, outside on school grounds, on field trips, and on school buses. Responsible behavior by the student community helps to provide a physical and emotional safety net for students to exercise their rights in a nonthreatening democratic community.

STUDENT RIGHTS

The historical legacy, discussed earlier, mandates that all students are entitled to equal educational opportunity regardless of national origin, race, religion, economic status, language, or gender. This fundamental student right, emerging from our nation's history, has expanded to include equal educational opportunity regardless of pregnancy; marital status; previous arrest; previous incarceration; or physical, mental, or sensory disability. Legal precedent and local customs, sometimes based on specific historical events, dictate how expansive or limiting the equal educational opportunity section of a school policy might be. For example, in American international schools, the student rights section may reflect issues relating to the host country culture. If modest dress is a fact of life in the host nation, then an American school in the host country will most likely require modest dress for students and faculty.

Chapter 7 reviewed several laws that relate to student rights and limitations based on legal precedent. These laws relating to due process with respect to disciplinary measures, suspension, and expulsion, search and seizure, and free speech must be addressed with clarity in school policy manuals and explained to new students in a proactive manner. Other student rights that policy manuals should address relate to student publications, freedom of assembly, and student and parental rights to student records. To create a supportive and democratic school climate, principals should address the following student rights, recognizing that age-appropriate language and expectations must be considered (rights and responsibilities are adapted from the Cheney School District, Cheney, Washington; The American Embassy School, New Delhi, India; and the Singapore American School). Typically, students have the right to the following:

- Appropriately express their opinions on school premises as long as it does not substantially disrupt the educational process or operations of the school.

- Be protected from all forms of discrimination from students and adults.

- Be free from harassment, bullying, and intimidation by students and adults.

- Pursue an education in a climate of mutual trust, respect, and interpersonal concern where openness and integrity prevail.

- Be assured of a meaningful education, which will prepare them to be confident and independent learners in the lifelong search for understanding.

- Access a quality education imparted by a highly qualified professional staff.

- Pursue as many educational and extracurricular activities as they are capable of and qualified for.

- Expect safety of both person and property, including the right to safe and clean school facilities.

- Engage in freedom of thought, conscience, and religion.

- Choose freely whether to belong to an association.

- Exercise freedom of inquiry regarding school policies.

- Be represented by a student government that has been elected by students.

- Have their views solicited and considered by teachers, administrators, and the school board.

STUDENT RESPONSIBILITIES

Involving students, board members, parents, teachers, and administrators in the development of the students' responsibilities section of the student policy manual helps build ownership and buy-in of school policies. The opening section of the student policy manual for the American Embassy School in New Delhi involves various stakeholders, including students: "Students safeguard their rights by taking full responsibility for their actions. Students are responsible for their own behavior. They must care for the individual rights of others and help to provide a safe and positive school environment within which to learn." Typically, students have the responsibility to do the following:

- Respect the educational process and learning environment by refraining from behaviors that diminish the rights of others to an education;

- Exercise self-control and take responsibility for one's actions;

- Act with integrity and honesty;

- Respect the ideas of others;

- Learn the rules and policies of the school;

- Attend classes and put forth their best effort;

- Contribute to a climate that is conducive to learning;

- Respect the rights of other students, the faculty and staff, administration, and others involved in the school community;

- Respect and care for the property of the school and property of others; and

- Contribute to a safe environment in and out of the classroom.

At the Amelia Earhart Elementary School in Lafayette, Indiana (Allen, 2003) 5th grade teacher Nadine Roush creatively involved students in developing class rules by holding a "miniconstitutional convention" and developing rights and responsibilities that become the school rules for the year. Students signed the document, which was then posted in their classroom. Roush also uses curriculum integration in science, reading, and writing to stress seven core democratic values during the year: "individual rights, the common good, justice, equality, diversity, truth and patriotism."

Students, teachers, and administrators at the American Embassy School in New Delhi developed the following code for elementary school students:

> Students care and come to school prepared to learn and to do their best. In order to do this we
>
> - Are polite and helpful
> - Take care of our school
> - Respect others—teachers, aides, students, secretaries, custodians
> - Care about ourselves and take responsibility for our behavior
> - Practice good health habits
> - Enjoy games in the proper areas
> - Are responsible for our belongings

Actively involving students in the democratic process is a powerful way for students to learn rights and responsibilities. At the Federal Hosking School in Steward, Ohio (Allen, 2003), students are involved in the teacher-hiring process, development of the master school schedule, curriculum decisions, and the creation of new school clubs. Federal Hosking principal, George Wood, stresses that high school is maybe the last place for all Americans to have a common experience in democracy. Wood views student involvement in each aspect of the school's programs as a primary principalship responsibility.

Leadership and Management Strategies That Promote Student Self-Discipline

A novice teacher having a difficult time with students may reflect, "If I have to send a student to the office, will the principal or assistant principal think I am an inadequate teacher?" If the school has a new principal, a veteran teacher may wonder, "Will the new principal be firm regarding disciplinary issues? Will the principal help us maintain the nurturing school that we have worked so hard to create? Or, will the principal take us back to the days when the student disciplinary policies were repressive?" New principals need to be proactive with the new and veteran teachers, building relationships and letting them know *before the school year begins* that everyone has to work together to create a caring school culture. Principals need to work on the *heartware* before *hardware*. When teachers need assistance with disciplinary measures, the message needs to be loud and clear: Together we will alleviate this problem.

Before developing a broad school policy statement with a specific code of conduct and accompanying disciplinary procedures, consider several points that should be used as guiding principles to formulate policy:

• Provide an inviting classroom environment that maximizes learning opportunities in a supportive and responsible climate. This environment includes engaging students in meaningful learning experiences, emphasizing cooperative and democratic principles, providing a nurturing environment in which students know they are cared for, offering choices and opportunities with academic and social activities, encouraging risk taking in the classroom and providing assistance when failure occurs, and allowing students to take responsibility for their behavior and for the behavior of their classmates.

• Remember the importance of heart when working with students. As the great Polish educator, Janucz Korczak, stated, "Children have a right to make mistakes." This does not mean that inappropriate behavior is acceptable; it is not. But, it does mean that we have a responsibility to work with students, talk with them, find out why the unacceptable behavior occurred, and provide the students with support and strategies to minimize the possibility of the behavior reoccurring.

• Recognize that the school is an ecosystem. Each aspect of the system can affect the balance or equilibrium of the school. Events and relationships must be perceived as connected. If the students and adults perceive the culture as democratic, supportive, respectful, and cooperative, then the vast majority of the community will perceive disparaging behavior as inappropriate. If a student is bullied on a school bus, then the bus driver, administrator, and classroom teacher need to show concern and stop the problem. In an ecosystem, activities in the cafeteria, corridor, playground, gymnasium, classroom, and bathroom are all related. Students are unable to learn when they know that someone will steal their lunch, or tease or bully them.

• Support self-discipline as the ultimate goal. Thus, intrinsic disciplinary strategies need to be part of the school and classroom repertoire. Otherwise, we are manipulating students to behave properly only because of a desirable or undesirable intervention. As Kohn (1996) notes in *Beyond Discipline*, "prefabricated interventions are rarely useful for getting to the bottom of problems since they usually turn out to be ways of punishing or otherwise controlling students."

• Shape the school culture so students view every adult as caring. The students must perceive the administration, teachers, and classified staff as allies. Students need to believe that the school is a safety net for them. One of the most disturbing statistics from the research on bullying is that students believe that teachers and administrators will not be helpful. According to Harris and Petrie (2002), "Findings show that [middle school students] perceived their teachers (59.5 percent) and administrators (73 percent) as 'not interested' or they 'didn't know' if they were interested in reducing bullying on their campus. This implies a critical need to build relationships between students and faculty to bridge this apparent communication gap."

The executive summary of the federal document, *Early Warning, Timely Response* (Dwyer, Osher, & Warger, 1998), provides excellent guidelines for formulating a schoolwide policy to support responsible behavior. These guidelines include the following:

• Establishing high behavioral expectations for students;

• Providing support for and reinforcing socially appropriate behavior;

• Highlighting sanctions against aggressive behavior;

• Enforcing schoolwide rules that are clear, broad-based, and fair;

• Ensuring that rules are communicated clearly to all parties and followed consistently by everyone;

• Developing a schoolwide disciplinary policy that includes a code of conduct, specific rules and consequences, a description of school antiharassment and antiviolence policies, and due process rights;

• Inviting staff, students, and families to participate in the development of fair rules;

- Providing schoolwide and classroom support to implement these rules;

- Creating a safe process for reporting threats, intimidation, weapons possession, drug selling, gang activity, graffiti, and vandalism;

- Promoting an antiviolence climate that includes students in schoolwide assemblies, student government, disciplinary teams, and peer mediation and conflict resolution activities;

- Making sure that when developing and implementing policies the consequences are commensurate with the offense;

- Combining negative consequences with positive strategies for teaching socially appropriate behaviors;

- Providing zero tolerance statements for illegal possession of weapons, alcohol, or drugs; and

- Providing service and support for suspended students.

BULLYING BEHAVIOR

"Most researchers say the key to cutting down on bullying may be to address the overall climate in a school. And that means convincing teachers and administrators, as well as every student, that it's not okay for students to bully others" (Viadero, 2003). The possible link between bullying behavior and school shootings is troubling. Viadero noted that bullying was a factor in two-thirds of 37 school shootings. However, as stated in Chapter 7, bullying should not be tolerated regardless of any link to school shootings. Everyone suffers from bullying. The bullies congregate with other bullies and become estranged from the school. The victims of bullying are apprehensive about attending school, and when they do attend, they are too scared or depressed to perform well in class. And, when bullying is a part of the school culture, it can affect the overall feeling that students and adults have about a school. Harris and Petrie (2002) synthesizing the research on bullying, make the following recommendations to reduce bullying in middle schools:

- Create a positive school climate that overtly and visibly addresses the problems of bullying.

- Develop an integrated school curriculum in which teachers and the principal regularly meet to address the issues.

- Train teachers to recognize bullies and develop behaviors to respond appropriately.

- Support cooperative learning and project-based curriculum and instruction.

- Develop schoolwide bullying policies.

- Provide high academic expectations for all students.

- Involve active participation of counselors as significant players.

- Increase parental awareness.

- Implement therapy for bullies and victims.

- Implement whole school strategies to help students develop empathy for victims.

- Provide peer mediation and conflict resolution strategies.

Finally, Harris and Petrie make a strong appeal to school principals: "Principal awareness of the problem leads to involvement; involvement leads to a reduction in bullying, and a reduction in bullying leads to an improved middle school experience for every child." (2002)

Full-Service School Guidance Counseling

New school principals should recognize a school's counseling program as an integral part of the student services program. A proactive student service plan includes the guidance program, community assistance and partnerships (discussed in Chapter 12), extracurricular or after-school program activities, and the school discipline plan. We have included extracurricular or after-school program activities as part of student services because for many elementary, middle, and high school students it is that connection with peers, teachers, and meaningful activities after school that make their school experience worthwhile. Guidance counselors and teachers can help steer students into certain programs and ensure that students get that extra attention from a coach, teacher, youth worker, paraprofessional, or mentor that may not be available during the school day. And, as full-service schooling continues to expand, elementary school children also benefit increasingly from the after-school experience.

The responsibilities of school guidance counselors vary a great deal depending on the grade levels, the number of students enrolled, budgetary constraints, cultural expectations, and the job descriptions in each school or district. Unlike classroom teachers, the defined job of a counselor can change depending on school needs. Their general role is to serve as a student advocate and help all students reach their potential and adjust to school and societal expectations. For students who are at risk because of emotional, social, and academic issues, a counselor's role is to provide advocacy and assistance until the student is able to cope successfully. Counselors also serve as advocates for students with disabilities.

New principals should expect counselors to be advocates for students and not view the advocacy as conflicting with a principal's responsibility. For example, when a serious disciplinary incident occurs in a high school, and it may be necessary to enforce a long-term suspension or expulsion, a counselor may intervene in a professional manner, appealing on the student's behalf. Principals should view this intervention as part of the counselor's job, which includes raising issues that may not come from any other source. Actually, if counselors are not student advocates, then the principal really has something to worry about!

The responsibilities listed in Figure 10.1 are generic for most counselors regardless of grade level. As aspiring and new

— Figure 10.1 —

General Responsibilities for Counselors

Generic Counseling Responsibilities K–12
- Student orientation.
- Individual and group counseling.
- Advocacy for students.
- Parent counseling.
- Working with teachers (sometimes informal counseling of teachers).
- Acting as a contact for Child Protection Services and other agencies.
- Placing and scheduling students for classes.
- Maintaining students' records.
- Interpreting and explaining testing programs to teachers, administrators, parents, and students. *Note*: Parameters of testing responsibilities will depend on certification qualifications.
- Being a member of the crisis management team.
- Engaging in conflict resolution mediation and training.
- Keeping the administration team apprised of important issues.
- Member of most special service teams.
- Keeping confidentialities.

High School Counseling Responsibilities
- College search and application process counseling.
- Writing recommendations.
- Career counseling.
- Usually assisting or supervising the creation of the master schedule.
- Coordinating peer counseling and service programs.
- Actively involved with scheduling and changing student classes throughout the year.

Middle School Counseling Responsibilities
- Advisory program coordinator or advisor.
- Sometimes involved with teaching values education and decision making.
- Managing peer counseling programs.
- May be involved with scheduling and some class changes throughout the year.

Elementary School Counseling Responsibilities
- Often involved in class activities relating to health, values, and decision making.
- Consulted in scheduling students with individual grade level teachers.

principals examine these responsibilities, consider the broad range of counseling duties. Because counselors are involved in most aspects of the school program, they are invaluable professional partners for school principals. Indeed, counselors may be the best people to consult other than the assistant principal about whole school issues.

Importance of Extracurricular and After-School Programs

Students can benefit considerably from extracurricular and after-school programs. According to Miller (2001), "A wide variety of studies focused on various program models link after-school program participation with improved attitudes toward school, higher expectations of school achievement, better work habits, and higher attendance rates, especially for low-income students." Miller describes three types of after-school programs. School-age child care programs that provide supervision, child care, enrichment, and support for the school curriculum; youth development programs that work proactively to prevent at-risk behaviors and view adolescents as a valuable resource worthy of exposure to museums, mentoring, sports, and libraries; and educational after-school programs that combine the traditional extracurricular clubs with sports, homework help, tutoring, and activities to enhance achievement. In addition, service learning is often a component of after-school programs.

For many high school students, extracurricular clubs and athletic activities tie loyalty and school pride to camaraderie among students and to the success of various activities. Often, a student's self-concept is nourished by a supporting drama teacher, journalism advisor, or track coach who has worked with the student for two or three years. The high school marching band may have a national reputation. The seniors in the band, already suffering from "senioritis," recognize that they will not be able to attend practice if they arrive too late or miss school altogether. Loyalty to team members and the band director become important factors. Also, extracurricular activities offer leadership opportunities. Captain of the debate team, editor of the school newspaper, and student council representative are all responsible positions and good experiences for career development. The possibilities of after-school options are almost limitless. However, a lot depends on funding at the local level. State and federal grants and philanthropic funds have been a boost to programs in recent years. Activities can range from service clubs (e.g., peer support, National Honor Society, the environmental club), to publications (e.g., the school newspaper), fine and performing arts clubs (e.g., jazz band, drama club, art club), and athletics (e.g., soccer, cross-country, swimming, basketball).

Service learning is growing as a club activity in many schools. At the Geraldine Palmer Elementary School in Pharr, Texas, elementary school students are involved in a service learning activity. Most of the students are from impoverished neighborhoods about 11 miles from the Mexican border. The elementary school students

> give back to their community while inspiring a sense of caring and compassion. When students brainstormed ideas for community projects, they found that many of their fellow students needed food and clothing. Many students did not have enough money to purchase school uniforms, so students organized a clothing drive. . . . To complete the project, students practiced math, communication, and decision-making skills as they interacted with community members and documented their progress on computers. (Castillo & Winchester, 2001)

Crisis Management: Balancing Teaming with Decisiveness

"A crisis or emergency is a situation that occurs unpredictably, requires immediate action and poses a threat of injury, loss of life, or significant damage to property" (Shoop & Dunklee, 2002). Emergencies that schools need to prepare for include earthquakes, drug emergencies, bomb threats, chemical spills, kidnappings, traffic accidents, deaths or suicides, fires, hostage taking, terrorist attacks, medical emergencies, severe weather emergencies, shootings or stabbings, sexual assaults, and unwanted intruders. Too often during the past few years, leadership has been tested during crisis situations. The tragic events of September 11, 2001, tested the emergency readiness of many schools and in particular, those 8,000 students in the vicinity of the World Trade Center. Because of the courageous behavior of fire fighters, police officers, emergency service workers, teachers, administrators, students, and parents, not one student was seriously injured.

Reflecting a few days after September 11, many of the top executives in the New York area were asked to give advice concerning how to cope with such an overwhelming tragedy. "Their wisdom, distilled, came down to four basic truisms: be calm, tell the truth, put people before business, then get back to business as soon as possible" (Wayne & Kaufman, 2001). We cannot overstate the importance of this advice. Aspiring and new principals need to know that during a crisis the staff will look to them for action, direction, support, security, composure, and hope. Whether a leader can offer those qualities can only be known during a crisis. What school leaders can do, however , is make sure a written crisis plan is in effect for emergency situations.

GUIDELINES FOR CRISIS MANAGEMENT PLANS

The following crisis management plan ideas are based on the work of Dwyer and colleagues (1998), Warner (2000), National School Public Relations Association (1996), and Shoop and Dunklee (2002). The crisis management plan should include

• An introductory section explaining the rationale, scope, and organization of the manual;

• An organizational chart delineating responsibilities and members of the crisis team, including spokespersons during an emergency and contact telephone numbers for central office personnel and all fire, medical, police, and other emergency services personnel;

- Descriptions of types of crises covered, clearly marked and separated in the manual with specific procedures for each crisis;

- Communication procedures and a phone tree of all faculty and staff;

- Communication procedures for contacting parents and the media;

- A list of faculty and staff with emergency medical training;

- A list of crisis code signals;

- Sites of potential emergencies;

- A checklist of immediate steps to follow during the first 30 minutes of the crisis;

- Maps delineating evacuation procedures and directing individuals to the crisis control center; and

- Procedures for the aftermath of the tragedy relating to counseling and psychological services.

During a crisis everyone needs support. Although the school principal and the leadership team will be expected to handle the situation professionally, emotions will run high. Consequently, select the members of the crisis management team prudently. You want people on the team who can provide important information and are trained to handle a crisis, and whom you believe will use common sense and remain calm during the crisis. Remember, the lives of students and adults are at stake. Although a crisis ends, it is never forgotten. And the people involved always remember how individuals behaved during the difficult period.

Success Story

The high school counselor seemed too quiet, introspective, and a little tentative. He was new to the school, but he was hired because of outstanding recommendations from his previous schools. The high school principal, also new to the school, was a little worried. The principal knew that the counseling department in the school was very important. This was a large, high-profile school with four counselors and an excellent reputation for getting students into the best universities. The counselors played an important role in the university admissions process, helping students complete their applications, remaining firm with students about deadlines, providing advice about "reach universities" and schools that were "safe" choices for admission, writing recommendations, using their personal contacts in the college admissions offices, and meeting with students and parents individually and in groups about the college process. The principal wondered if the counselor could be assertive and dynamic enough to manage the situation. Also, the principal had noticed that the school did not have a peer counseling program and hoped that the counselors would get together and organize the program. The new principal thought that a peer counseling program would add a nice service component to the school with students assisting each other in a variety of personal, academic, and social areas.

The principal met with the counseling team every two weeks. He had decided that once the first-week glitches in the student schedules were resolved and the new students were placed successfully in classes, he would talk to the counselors about the peer counseling program. At the counseling meeting in late September, the peer counseling issue was raised, but not by the principal. The new counselor mentioned that he had coordinated a peer counseling program in his previous school and would like to give it a try here. He was diplomatic about raising the issue. It was obvious that he was surprised that the school, known for its service to the community and excellent academic reputation, had overlooked using in-house talent to support the students. After the peer counseling issue was raised, another counselor said, "Hey, if you want to take this on, fine, but it is going to get pretty hectic once the college application process gets cranked up." The new counselor seemed delighted that others had not suggested tabling his idea.

During October the new counselor visited with the principal once in a while about student issues and progress with the peer counseling program. At the meetings, the principal observed that each time the counselor spoke, he was sincere, thoughtful, and to the point. If a meeting was requested, it was important. Either the counselor wanted to inform the principal about a situation, or he was seeking advice and a little brainstorming about a counseling issue. The principal noticed that although the counselor was introspective and soft-spoken, he never wavered about going back to a student, parent, or teacher to resolve a difficult issue. The counselor seemed to have an uncanny ability to use his time and energy just right. The principal realized that initially he had misjudged the new colleague. He had confused a thoughtful and introspective demeanor with tentativeness and indecision. The principal recognized that he was viewing and judging others through a very personal lens colored by his own personality and style of leadership. He realized that the counselor was a superb addition to the staff, and, as a new principal, he was going to learn a lot from this colleague.

The college counseling process was very successful. All four counselors worked well together, sharing the stage during presentations to parents and students, and handling the student load successfully. During the period when the counseling office was usually frantic with college admissions issues, the new counselor provided calm leadership. The peer counseling program started slowly the first year, with few students involved. However, in May more than 50 students expressed an interest in serving as peer counselors for the following year. The counselor planned a one-day retreat for the new peer counselors to be held two weeks before the next school year.

 **Activity** ———————————————————————————

Is Your School Ready for a Crisis?

Early Warning, Timely Response (Dwyer et al., 1998) provides an excellent "Crisis Procedure Checklist" that can be used to judge your school's crisis preparedness (Figure 10.2). For this activity, meet with a couple of members of your school's crisis management team to review each checklist item. Before reviewing the items, decide on two or three possible crisis scenarios such as an earthquake, drug overdose, or fire. As you examine each item, based on the scenario, discuss the appropriate action and whether there is any confusion concerning what needs to occur. For example, assume that the scenario involves a fire in a science lab. Consider the first item on the checklist, "Assess life and safety issues immediately." Discuss the appropriate action based on that item with the team members you have gathered for this scenario. Take notes as you examine each of the checklist items. If necessary, fine-tune your crisis management plan based on the team review of the checklist.

Figure 10.2

Crisis Procedure Checklist

___ Assess life and safety issues immediately.

___ Provide immediate emergency medical care.

___ Call 911 and notify police and rescue first. Call the superintendent second.

___ Convene the crisis team to assess the situation and implement the crisis response procedures.

___ Evaluate available and needed resources.

___ Alert school staff to the situation.

___ Activate the crisis communication procedure and system of verification.

___ Secure all areas.

___ Implement evacuation and other procedures to protect students and staff from harm.

___ Avoid dismissing students to unknown caregivers.

___ Adjust the bell schedule to ensure safety during the crisis.

___ Alert persons in charge of various information systems to prevent confusion and misinformation. Notify parents.

___ Contact appropriate community agencies and the school district's public information office, if appropriate.

___ Implement postcrisis procedures.

Source: Adapted from Dwyer, Osher, and Warger, 1998.

Reflective Field Notes ————————————

Please use this space to jot down notes that are important for your personal leadership journey. You may do this in a structured way—by responding to questions—or in an unstructured way. Use the approach that works for you.

- Examine the section of your school's student policy manual that reviews student rights and responsibilities. Reflecting on your school culture, what is the balance in your school between student rights and responsibilities?

- How is your school handling bullying, harassment, and intimidation? Do the victims of bullies know that they can expect the support of the administration and teachers if and when they report an incident? Are the bullies receiving attention, discipline, and counseling?

- Review the list of counseling responsibilities with a counselor in your school. How do they view their job description? Do they think that the list is inclusive? What has been omitted based on the contextual needs of your school?

- Examine your school's crisis policy manual. Is it user friendly? Are there parts of the manual that are confusing?

- What insights or new questions do you have as a result of reflecting on the issues raised in this chapter?

11

The Schoolhouse and Central Office Working Together

The superintendent reflected, "Principals need to appreciate what the central office can do for them. They should not be afraid to ask for help. Heck, the principalship can be very lonely, it can be even more lonely if principals do not reach out." New and experienced principals sometimes fail to use an excellent source that is right there for the taking: central office personnel and material resources. Why do some principals, especially new principals, fail to take advantage of this resource? There are several reasons:

- Principals may feel that asking for help will be perceived as a sign of weakness.

- Principals don't know what is available or whom to contact. This is especially true if a principal is hired from outside the district or straight out of the classroom.

- There is a perception that the central office bureaucracy is so overwhelming that it's a waste of time to ask for help. The battles just aren't worth fighting.

- There is competition between the central office and the schoolhouse, and principals prefer to succeed on their own.

Concerning this last reason, Schlechty (2001) advises the principal:

> Learn to see yourself as a member of the district-level team as well as the head of your own team at the building level. Recognize that your school is not the only system you need to consider; it is part of a larger system. Other schools and other principals are not—or should not be—your competition. They are your allies and coinventors . . . Too many recent reform efforts encourage principals to see their schools as fiefdoms or feudal baronies that exist largely apart from the larger school system and the community whose support is needed if a school is to survive in the long run. Instead, principals will be more effective when they learn to use the district and the community, just as district level officials will be more effective once they learn to be more responsive to the needs of principals.

Deal and Peterson (1994) also note the tension between a principal and central office and suggest that by acting as a "bifocal principal," a school leader can follow the "central office directives [yet] be creatively insubordinate." One superintendent expressed the thought that "some principals think that folks in the central office just don't work as hard. There needs to be professional respect across the board. Everyone is working hard. Everyone works hard at every level. It is a matter of attitude." Another superintendent articulated a similar thought, "Principals sometimes think they are the main show. But the budget person is also important. So is the curriculum person. So are the classified staff and we have to treat them as professionals. Principals should realize that the central office folks could get them out of a lot of jams. Central office can help with curriculum, personnel and budgetary issues."

Celebrating the Mission with Internal Constituencies

Grove (2002), in an insightful article in *Educational Leadership*, maintains that, "Central office leaders are effective, in part, precisely because they are invisible, much as the skeleton in the body is invisible. Vitally important, central office staff members provide the support and consistency necessary for a high-quality instructional program." A subtle message in the Grove article is that all staff want to be part of the school success story, even if they are not in high-profile positions—central office wants to assist and celebrate student success just as much as teachers and principals in the schoolhouse. If the central office seems invisible, so be it, just as long as the personnel are making a difference for children and adults. Grove (2002) outlines the broad variety of services provided by the central office:

- Conduct the textbook adoption process.
- Order new textbooks.
- Evaluate supplementary materials.
- Develop programs of studies.
- [Assist with] formal observations of teachers.
- Assist teachers having difficulties.
- Design and conduct staff development.
- Facilitate teacher attendance at professional conferences.
- Organize countywide activities, such as art exhibits and science fairs.
- Organize informational meetings for parents.
- Meet with citizen committees on each instructional area.
- Analyze achievement data.
- Apply for and manage grant-funded projects.
- Complete required state and federal reports.

Additional services noted by Grove and others include assisting new teachers, helping principals with budgetary issues, assisting with personal concerns and, at times, serving as a buffer between the principals and the school board. New principals should take advantage of these services.

Of course, for newcomers, succeeding in the schoolhouse is a top priority. As noted in Chapter 3, the socialization process does not occur overnight. Part of learning the ropes is figuring out which central office contacts are critical. Central office personnel certainly need to reach out to new principals, letting them know about available resources. Whether this occurs through a formal mentoring program or informally by trial and error does not matter, as long as it happens. It is vital to share expertise and exchange ideas. And, as noted at the beginning of this chapter and in Chapter 3, the loneliness of the principalship is a fact of life. Interacting with central office personnel can help to mitigate the isolation that principals sometimes feel.

School districts that engage in professional development activities in which the central office personnel interact with the principals and vice principals can certainly help to create a bond among school leaders. A successful and relatively easy activity is to have the whole administration team engage in a book club with an outside or inside facilitator. As noted in Chapter 5, Central Valley School District, near Spokane, Washington, is engaged in such an activity involving more than 50 administrators. Cheney School District, also near Spokane, has engaged in a similar activity for four years. The activity gives the administrators an opportunity to interact with one another, exemplifying and celebrating lifetime learning.

Tips for Inviting New Principals and Central Office Personnel to the Same Party

New and aspiring principals should take advantage of the human and material resources available at the central office. The following suggestions solicited from central office personnel and school principals can help strengthen the relationship between the schoolhouse and central office. (The authors thank Washington State school superintendents Dr. Wally Stanley of the Central Valley School District and Dr. Phil Snowdon of the Cheney School District for their help with this section.)

• Principals should invite central office personnel to the schoolhouse for assemblies and special programs or to visit classes, and especially to those activities that central office personnel helped initiate.

• Principals should keep central office personnel informed about activities with a formal calendar of events. The superintendent or other individuals in the central office should not learn about a worthwhile scheduled activity after it occurs.

• Consider that the words we use have a powerful effect on people. Constantly using phrases like "classified staff" and "certificated staff" or "noncertificated staff" can have a negative impact on support personnel in the schoolhouse and central office. Inclusive terms such as "staff" can help build relationships. An invisible line between two groups does not contribute to positive morale. And remember, the classified staff are more likely to live in the district—and, as the saying goes, they are "local, vocal, and vote."

• Everyone working for the school district is making a major contribution. If there is a flood in the classroom, the plumber becomes more important than the superintendent!

• New principals should stop by the central office once in a while simply to drop off instructional materials and interact with colleagues whom they only hear on the phone or communicate with by e-mail. When relationships are formed in advance, it is easier to work together on a challenging project.

• Successful innovation will not occur without mutual support: "individual schools can become highly innovative for a short period of time without the district, but they cannot stay innovative without district action to establish the conditions for continuous and long-term improvement" (Fullan & Stiegelbauer, 1991).

• Central office should display student work from various schools during the year. Working with principals and teachers, central office personnel could assign different parts of the central office buildings to specific schools or classes.

• Principals should realize that central office wants to help, and they should not be shy about asking. Ethical alignment includes modeling collegiality throughout the organization. Superintendents, assistant superintendents, principals, and teachers should expect a positive response when requesting assistance.

- If a mentoring program is not in place for new principals, a systematic tour of the central office facility is recommended, including a detailed review of individual responsibilities with *practical examples* of how central office personnel can assist the schoolhouse.

- Principals should keep central office administrators informed concerning potential problems. Superintendents and their assistants can be very helpful if they get a heads up on an issue. However, superintendents do not want to be surprised by a problem that should have been addressed a month ago.

 Success Story ────────────────────────

Two school bus drivers walked into the fast-food restaurant a little before noon. They saw the superintendent sitting down and eating lunch with a colleague. One of the bus drivers noticed a lanyard with the school colors around the superintendent's neck and the school's nickname, "Sioux," inscribed on the lanyard. The bus driver was a little hesitant to talk with the superintendent, but did so and mentioned that he hadn't seen that lanyard before and that he really liked the way it looked. The superintendent responded and said it was a sample and that he just had a few. The bus driver then indicated that he would love to have one because he was a big supporter of the high school athletic program. The superintendent gave the bus driver the lanyard and could tell that the driver was pleased. The driver also mentioned that his barn is painted the school colors, red and black. As the bus driver left the restaurant, he looked back at the superintendent and stated, "Yep, we are big Sioux fans." A few days later the superintendent received a call from someone else who saw a Sioux lanyard and wanted to purchase one. It was clear that this was going to be a popular item. The superintendent reflected back to the moment when the bus driver asked for the lanyard and realized the importance of symbolism, pride, and loyalty. It was a good reminder for the superintendent about the importance of district cultural norms. The bus-driving farmer really represented the spirit of the school district. The superintendent was glad he had eaten lunch at the fast-food restaurant on that particular day. Who knows, he reflected, what good will might have been generated by this brief interaction. The bus driver spends a lot of time in the community. The story of what happened in the restaurant is likely to be told several times.

Activity

A Journey to the Central Office

Figure 11.1 lists the typical official positions of the top personnel working in the central office of a midsize school district. Take a trip to your central office and meet with colleagues who are available. Modify the left-hand column of the table to match the official positions, and inquire about the specific duties and practical responsibilities of each individual you meet. The objective is to use the table to learn how central office personnel and resources can assist the schoolhouse.

Figure 11.1

Central Office Roles

Central Office Position	Specific Responsibilities with Practical Examples	How can this colleague and the resources he or she manages make a difference for the students and faculty in the schoolhouse?
Superintendent		
Executive Secretary to the Superintendent		
Public Information Specialist		

(continued)

── **Figure 11.1** ──

Central Office Roles *(continued)*

Supervisor: Support Services		
Human Resource Director		
Curriculum Director		
Elementary Education Director		
Assistant Superintendent and Mid-level Education Director		
Assistant Superintendent and Secondary Director		
Business Operations Director		
Auxiliary Services Director		
Director of Planning, Research, and Development		
Educational Technology Director		

Reflective Field Notes

Please use this space to jot down notes that are important for your personal leadership journey. You may do this in a structured way—by responding to questions—or in an unstructured way. Use the approach that works for you.

• What is your perception of the effectiveness of your school's central office?

• In what ways does the central office currently interact with and provide support to the school?

• What is the major task that you would like central office to assist with in your school?

• What insights or new questions do you have as a result of reflecting on the issues raised in this chapter?

12

Parents and the Greater Community: Partnering for Student Success

The importance of schools partnering with parents and the greater community is an important theme in today's literature on successful schools. The research on successful schools and individual student success often cite parent involvement as a major contributing factor. Standard Six of the National Association of Elementary School Principals' Standards (NAESP, 2002) is "effective principals actively engage the community to create shared responsibility for students and school success." The Interstate School Leaders Licensure Consortium (Green, 2001) lists Standard Four as "a school administrator is an educational leader who promotes the success of all students by collaborating with families and community members, responding to diverse community interests and needs, and mobilizing community resources." Many politicians and members of the business community are concerned about the performance and direction of the public schools. This has led to the school choice movement and the accompanying interest in vouchers, charter schools, and marketing for-profit schools. And the taxpayers can, and do, say "no" to schools by defeating levy and bond initiatives. This competition and need for taxpayer assistance makes it important to reach out to the parent community and gain its support for the local school. Finally, the changing family with millions of children left alone after school, and the poor or homeless, necessitate strengthening home–school ties. Children cannot succeed alone.

New principals trying to concentrate on succeeding in the schoolhouse can easily forget the important stakeholders outside the school who contribute to school success. These stakeholders have a vital interest in schools. They want the children in their community to succeed and will support new principals. Parents are the most important of these external stakeholders. Their children are in school, and they want the best for them. A lot of parents are paraprofessionals, support staff, or volunteers in schools. The point is that some parents are very involved in school and can be a powerful force in the direction a school takes. Other stakeholders include politicians, political interest groups, members of business and industry, law enforcement agencies, the medical community, social service agencies, community-based organizations, unions, government agencies, clubs (e.g., sporting organizations, arts and museum councils), senior citizens, and former students. Each one of these groups can play an important role in a school's success. For example, a senior citizen can serve as an after-school mentor or tutor and make a difference in the life of a child who otherwise would go home to an empty house.

Parents Supporting Schools: Beyond the Bake Sale

According to Joyce Epstein (2002), families may be involved in schools *six* different ways. Note that the involvement is often two-way, with both the school and family benefiting:

1. *Parenting*: Help families with parenting and adolescent development information. Families help schools understand the family.

2. *Communicating*: Share information with families about school activities and student progress, welcoming family feedback.

3. *Volunteering*: Welcome parents to the school for training as tutors and volunteers and to serve as an audience for student work and performances.

4. *Learning at Home*: Support parent involvement in homework and other school activities.

5. *Decision Making*: Welcome families on school counsels, PTA, and other committees as participants in school decision making.

6. *Collaborating with the Community*: Work with the community by coordinating services and resources to help students and families through involvement with agencies, businesses, and other service providers (Epstein, cited in NAESP Standards, 2002).

Epstein's fifth point includes site-based management (SBM). As noted in Chapter 5, SBM has been an important decision-making strategy to expand school leadership teams to include those who have a major stake in the success of schools. Teachers, parents, and community stakeholders play a major role on site counsels. New principals need to view their own role on these committees as that of facilitators, welcoming parents and other stakeholders into the picture to help with program, policy, budgetary, and instructional decisions. A particularly valuable skill for principals to succeed in the SBM world is the "ability to shift traditional lines of authority to take advantage of the unique skills and perspectives this leadership team brings to the learning community" (NAESP, 2002).

Communicating with parents in a positive manner is so important. Some parents are hesitant to visit a school, possibly because of their own experience with school, their child's unsatisfactory progress, or even embarrassment about not having decent clothes for the occasion. Thus, when parent conferences occur, principals and teachers need to help parents feel welcome as soon as they enter the school. As a school principal, Harvey Alvy (author) posted the following popular adage over the high school office to welcome parents and students: "People don't care what you know, until they know that you care." To prepare for the scheduled parent afternoon or evening conferences, Harvey, with the help of the faculty, developed the following suggestions. Principals should feel free to modify these suggestions to meet the needs of their schools.

SUGGESTIONS TO TEACHERS FOR SUCCESSFUL PARENT CONFERENCES

1. *Parents should feel welcome as soon as they enter your classroom.* Consider greeting them at the door and thanking the parents for coming to the meeting. Even if their child has been experiencing a difficult year, parents should not feel like "they are in trouble." Parents should enjoy meeting you as an individual.

2. *Have a positive thing to say about every child.* Consider opening the meeting with a positive comment.

3. *Student work should be available for the conference.* Try to have samples that show a range of the student's work. Use the work to provide specific suggestions so the parent feels like the meeting was a success. If you involve students in the conferences and ask them to display their portfolio of work, you will need to decide between a "showcase portfolio" and a "working portfolio." The showcase portfolio samples only the student's best work, while the working portfolio portrays a broad range of the student's work.

4. *A key part of the conference should be listening to the parent.* Parents can provide insights into their child's successes and problems that we simply cannot pick up at school.

5. *As good listeners, we need to read body language.* Use your body language to help parents feel comfortable (e.g., smile, make eye contact).

6. *Try to avoid situations that may become confrontational or may lead to an argument.* Parents simply have difficulty being objective about their own children (ask my mother).

7. *Determine if the parent has already seen the report card.* If the answer is yes, avoid reviewing it again; the conference is an opportunity to add the human element.

8. *Avoid educational jargon.* Use everyday language when speaking with parents.

9. *Avoid derogatory phrases when describing a child.* Avoid phrases such as "He is slow."

10. *Use good judgment and consider confidentiality when discussing children.* It is important not to mention names of other children in the class when discussing a child. For example, it is not a good idea to say, "Billy received the third highest grade on this test, with Andrea and Steve the only students in the class with higher grades."

One school district recognized that many parents were not able to attend parent–teacher conferences because of work commitments. Several of these parents worked in a poultry processing plant. Hence, principals asked the employer to support the employees by providing conferencing space at the plant, and allowing teachers and parents to meet during working hours for a brief conference. This collaborative effort created a powerful bridge among the business, parents, and the local schools.

Partnering the Community, Workplace, and the School

"Research during the past 12 years supports what many parents, teachers, and other adults who spend time with young people already know: Community-based programs and organizations make significant contributions to young people's learning and development" (McLaughlin, 2001). McLaughlin's years of research with poor children and children of color indicated that the children involved with community-based organizations (CBOs) gained both academic and life skills that continued into adulthood. Furthermore, the relationship of students with the organizations benefited both parties, with students involved in service projects such as renovating homes. McLaughlin maintains, however, that schools could do more to strengthen the partnerships; that is, "we did not see many *institutional* collaborations between schools and community-based organizations that went beyond shared space" (italics in original document). To strengthen the relationship between schools and CBOs, McLaughlin recommends the following strategies for schools:

- Share space and facilities.
- Set up institutional collaborations.
- Connect mutual goals.
- Integrate school and community resources for teaching and learning by codeveloping curricula.
- Support teachers' involvement in community-based organizations.
- Develop meaningful measures of youth development. (McLaughlin, 2001)

The Variety and Benefits of CBOs

Community-based organizations (CBOs) include community organizations and clubs; professional associations; and local, state, and federal agencies. New principals should view these organizations as an extension of the school program to enrich the social, academic, physical, and emotional lives of children. These organizations, devoted to social service assistance, can help shoulder the *social work* role that many schools have accepted as full-service institutions to meet the needs of children. Morrison (2003), referring to the work of Hardiman, Curcio, and Fortune, cites the following school-linked services as most frequently used (in priority order) by school districts: substance abuse services, psychological services, education services, health services, social services, job training, teen pregnancy, child welfare, juvenile probation, family welfare, and housing services. Some specific community-based support efforts include the following:

- Food banks
- Clothing banks
- Salvation Army Family Emergency Centers
- Sexual assault crisis lines
- Temporary shelters
- Child care services
- Hospitals and health clinics, including dental care
- YWCA therapeutic child development programs
- Libraries
- Disability resource centers
- Alcoholics Anonymous
- Community colleges
- U.S. Armed Forces
- U.S. Postal Services
- U.S. Forest Service
- Social Security Administration
- Parks and Recreation Departments
- Volunteer lawyer programs
- Merchant associations
- Teachers' union
- 4-H Youth Development
- Boy and Girl Scouts
- Youth sports organizations
- Fire, police, and emergency service personnel

- Habitat for Humanity

- Museums and art organizations

- Zoos

- Neighborhood associations

- Newspapers, television networks, and radio stations

- Religious organizations

Many of the CBOs, businesses, and industrial organizations partner with school–career education programs often referred to as school-to-work (STW) programs. These programs link classrooms with authentic work environments. High school students might engage in STW programs during the school day or after school. A student might work in a traditional job setting, such as a bank, or take on social service responsibilities, such as tutoring a child in a homeless shelter. Some states and school districts have highly developed STW programs. For example, every high school in Wisconsin "is required to implement a technical training program with one of the state's 16 technical colleges. A statewide apprenticeship program offers work-based learning. Students can attend institutions of higher education while in high school and can receive both high school and college credit" (Morrison, 2003).

Suggestions for Bringing Families and the Business Community to School

The following suggestions are all successful strategies used by schools to strengthen the relationship with families and the greater community. New principals, after spending some time assessing the school culture, should select activities that they judge to be least risky—that is, an activity that will likely succeed!

- Hold meaningful Open House celebrations for families, businesses, fire, police, and emergency workers, CBOs, and the media to showcase the school (e.g., displays of student work, interactive work from students to parents, music, drama and art presentations, video presentations, portfolios of student work).

- Invite community businesses and senior citizens, in addition to parents, to math, science, and technology exhibitions.

- Plant a garden around the school with community help.

- Invite the community to view school-organized displays of photographs and artifacts of the school's history.

- Ask the community elders to visit school as informal counselors, tutors, and mentors.

- Reach out to the community to create career and expertise database resources for career days, class presentations, and STW programs.

- Hold picnics to reach out to the community, and have meetings in the neighborhood.

- Ask bilingual individuals to be available for meetings and conferences, and establish a bilingual hotline.

- Recruit parents, grandparents, and community partners to read with children and help with classroom projects.

- Conduct "Saturday Morning Parent Institutes" (e.g., helping children with homework or the college admissions process, exploring pathways for high school seniors, giving community service presentations, discussing conflict resolution at home, raising your teenager, exploring what educators mean by learning styles).

- Hold evening sessions for parents (e.g., videos on child care, parenting skills).

- Create a Community/CBO/Business Partnership/Parent Volunteer "Thank You" Luncheon.

- Sponsor a Grandparents' Day celebration with special programs and samples of student work to share with grandparents.

- Invite the community to view a display of projects made by students during service or STW activities.

As noted in the list, new principals should try to implement activities that will likely yield success, depending on the school culture, the resources available, the complexity of the program, and the expected level of cooperation. Checking with veteran principals in the district and the central office should give the rookie a barometer to measure the prospects for success. Also, trust your "gut." If you have a good feeling about an activity—go for it!

Crisis Management and the Community

In Chapter 10 we discussed crisis management in detail. However, there are a few points to consider relating to the community. Depending on the type of crisis, a school will depend on fire fighters, police officers, emergency medical service personnel, the media, parents, social service agencies, and the business and legal communities. Individuals associated with these organizations should not have to wait for a crisis before they visit the school. One of the great revelations of the September 11th disaster was that many people realized that they took for granted the daily risks emergency service workers take for us. We need to invite fire fighters and police officers to schools and celebrate with them the wonderful accomplishments of our children. Also, these individuals, along with armed forces personnel and medical personnel, should be invited to participate during career days and other activities in which students learn to appreciate the accomplishments of these specialists. At the same time, the visits will give students an opportunity to consider careers serving others.

When preparing for a possible crisis, schools often invite fire, police, and medical personnel to look over the school. In addition, legal counsel should be sought when developing a crisis plan. Shoop and Dunklee (2002) note, "Leadership in the education enterprise must be coupled with leadership in preventive law.

Effective educational leadership sometimes involves taking calculated risks [during a crisis] when complicated situations warrant decisive action; however, such risks must be legal and must demonstrate a common sense commitment to preventive law."

 ## Success Story

He was a veteran high school principal, but new to this school. During an administrative conference a few months earlier, he sat in on a workshop about school-sponsored parent reading groups. The presenter indicated that the workshops were a wonderful way to bring parents into a school for a very positive activity that would be intellectually engaging, while building esprit de corps among the parents and the school personnel involved in the project. While participating in the workshop, the principal thought this would be a good activity to help connect positively with the school community. Also, the principal strongly believed that a school leader should model lifetime learning. The parent reading group idea might be a perfect opportunity to do so.

During the summer the principal reviewed a few books that might work for the parent reading group. He was interested in emotional intelligence, so he reviewed Goleman's (1995) book, *Emotional Intelligence*. He reviewed several other books, including *Reviving Ophelia*, by Mary Pipher (1994) about adolescent girls, and *Real Boys*, by William Pollack (1998) about adolescent boys. These books seemed like good possibilities. He also reviewed other books with a strong educational message, but discounted them as possibilities because they seemed to be filled with jargon that only an educator would appreciate.

When the principal arrived at the new school, he reviewed the beginning-of-the-year activities file with the secretary. He noticed that the school had a tradition of holding parent coffees for each grade level, beginning about the third week of school. He told the secretary about his parent reading group idea and asked if she perceived any problems with the idea. The secretary said, "It sounds okay. It has never been done. You know you are going to be very busy." The principal appreciated her comments and agreed that he would be very busy; but the book group idea was appealing. The principal then asked the secretary if she could recommend anyone who might want to partner with him for the group. She smiled and said, "Ask the librarian. I think he would enjoy the project." The principal thought to himself, "It sure makes sense, the librarian. When the teachers arrive at school in a couple of weeks, I'll check with him."

The librarian was thrilled with the idea and even suggested that he would bring in additional resources relevant to the topic and share useful Web sites and books with the parents. The principal mentioned the parent reading group idea during each weekly parent coffee. Several parents expressed an interest, and a list was kept in the high school office to sign up folks. The letter shown in Figure 12.1 (pp. 251–252) was sent to parents.

The reading groups were a success, and the interaction helped the principal to establish relationships with the parents. The PTA became very active in supporting the activity, by using its newsletter to encourage parents to attend the reading groups and supplying refreshments for the book club meetings. The parents did have a couple of requests for the following year. They asked if some of the sessions could be held in the evening so more working parents could attend. They also suggested beginning the book club meetings earlier in the year and avoiding a December session. There was just too much to do around the holiday season. The principal was beginning to consider books for the following year. He had heard that *A Tribe Apart*, by Patricia Hersch (1998), was an excellent and insightful book about the life of teenagers. He planned to read it during the summer.

Figure 12.1

PARENT READING GROUP

"In a very real sense we have two minds,
one that thinks and one that feels."

Emotional Intelligence: Why It Matters More Than IQ
Daniel Goleman

Dear Reading Group Parents,

Both Don Marker and I were pleased with the number of parents who expressed an interest in joining the high school parent reading group during our recent coffees. We've received the first order of 50 books from local bookstores. The cost of the book, *Emotional Intelligence: Why It Matters More than IQ,* by Daniel Goleman is $16.95. Please make out a check to Liberty High School or pay cash for the book at the high school office. We have the books in the office and the secretaries will distribute the books to you.

Because of the number of parents that signed up for the reading group, we will offer two session dates each month, so parents have the option of attending either session. By offering this option, *we will be able to keep the groups relatively small to facilitate a lively discussion.* Choose the session that is best for your schedule. For next month parents can attend a session on Monday, November 15th, or Thursday, November 18th. For December, sessions will be on Monday, December 6th, or Thursday, December 9th. All sessions will be held in H-307 and begin at 9:30 am and end at 11:00 am. The PTA has kindly offered to supply refreshments for the reading group. During the December session we will set up future dates for reading *Reviving Ophelia* by Mary Pipher and *Real Boys* by William Pollack.

We will divide the readings into two main sections. For the November sessions we'll read Parts I, II, and III, from pages 3–212. (During the November session we will also review part of a video with Goleman titled, "Optimizing Intelligences: Thinking, Emotions and Creativity.") In December we will finish the book by reading Parts IV and V, pp. 215–330.

(continued)

Figure 12.1

PARENT READING GROUP *(continued)*

We'd like everyone to consider three initial questions for the November session:

(1) What is emotional intelligence? (2) Do you believe there is a case for emotional intelligence? (3) Are we "programmed" for life, or can we change our emotional reactions? Also, bring questions that you would like to share during the session.

As noted during the parent coffees, the reading group is a low-key activity that should be fun. Goals of the reading group include intellectual stimulation, strengthening relationships among the adults in the group, understanding our children, and engaging in lively discussion. As with all reading groups, it is important for us to be supportive of comments made by others, stay relevant regarding the text, and develop questions and responses based primarily on our interpretation of the book. Additionally, the reading group will give all of us an opportunity to work on our listening skills as we gain insights from group members.

Don and I are looking forward to taking this journey with all of you during these next few months. I know that we will all develop new perspectives and ideas to share with one another.

Sincerely,

Bill Mays
High School Principal

 **Activity**

Do Parents Feel Welcome in the Schoolhouse?

Review the Checklist for Improving Parental Involvement (Figure 12.2, p. 254) to assess how your school measures up in involving parents. You might want to examine the list alone, with members of your administrative team, or with several teachers and counselors. It might be a little risky as a new principal, but after reviewing the list, consider meeting with your site-based management team or a few parents to explore their views on the checklist items. As you gauge each item, write down your thoughts concerning whether you are satisfied with the school's parental involvement strategies. If you believe the involvement area needs to be fine-tuned, brainstorm possibilities with valued stakeholders.

———————————— **Figure 12.2** ————————————

Checklist for Improving Parental Involvement

__ Families are a priority in the school.

__ Parents are comfortable in the building.

__ There is an informal place for parents to gather.

__ The reception and office areas are pleasant and welcoming.

__ The faculty and staff consider parents an asset.

__ The principal holds routine meetings with parent groups.

__ Activities are held to recognize and celebrate parent involvement.

__ The culturally diverse parent community feels welcome.

__ The faculty and staff work with parents to overcome cultural and language barriers.

__ Parent or guardian and teacher communication is effective.

__ "Red tape" and a bureaucratic maze do not stand in the way of parents.

__ Policies relating to parental involvement are clear.

__ Staff development has included parent involvement strategies.

__ Workshops for parents are available on a timely basis.

__ Parents feel like they make important decisions in the school.

__ Community businesses are involved in the school.

__ When people walk in the school, they see evidence of community involvement.

__ Parents are consulted about their child's academic and social issues.

__ Parents volunteer in classrooms to help with student activities.

__ Prompt parental notification is made when a child experiences substantial difficulty.

This checklist was adapted from the Florida Department of Education and the work of E. Flaxman and M. Inger in *Developing the Effective Principal* (Office of School Improvement of the Florida Department of Education, 2002).

Reflective Field Notes ————————————

Please use this space to jot down notes that are important for your personal leadership journey. You may do this in a structured way—by responding to questions—or in an unstructured way. Use the approach that works for you.

• Consider the stakeholders in your school community. With whom do you need to spend more time?

• Some educators and other stakeholders believe that schools are taking on too much of a social welfare function. What do you think? Considering the social welfare issue, how should schools interact with community-based organizations?

• What is the most successful parent involvement activity in your school? Why do you think it is a success?

• How can your school recognize and celebrate the role of the fire, police, medical, and other emergency service personnel in your community?

• What insights or new questions do you have as a result of reflecting on the issues raised in this chapter?

13

Working with the Media

Aspiring or new principals should recognize that the media is a major force to be reckoned with, one that can be an ally or enemy. If a principal and school district work proactively with the media, then an alliance can be forged to benefit the children of the district. It is hard work, however. "One school district in Washington State conducted a news audit and found out that during a 180-day school year, 105 articles were printed about the district in the local papers—only three articles were negative!" (Robbins & Alvy, 2003). Although a district is unlikely to achieve that kind of a track record with the news media each year, there are behaviors and strategies that rookie principals can follow that will lead to success in most situations.

To begin, always be honest with the media. If you are trying to dance around an issue, experienced newspaper and television reporters will detect your dishonesty and question everything you have to say. Further, establishing a relationship based on trust will be very difficult following an insincere beginning. Remember, reporters are also trying to make a living. It is their job to report honest stories. Collaborating *with* a reporter will make the job easier for them and will likely work for you, the district, and the students. Working with the media means honoring deadlines, providing accurate news releases, facilitating media visits to the school or district office, and giving the media a "heads up" on a story that will certainly make news. When a crisis occurs, the media will likely play a major role distributing information to the community. Thus, building a trusting, honest, and personal relationship with the media, in advance of an incident, can go a long way in minimizing communication problems when rapid decisions need to be made.

As a school leader, every time you interact with the media, focus on the school mission, teaching and learning, and student safety. Stay on track. Even if an issue raised seems unrelated to teaching and learning, redirect the issue toward teaching, learning, and student safety. For example, if a weekend fire damages two science classes, a reporter is likely to ask about safety issues and how long it will take to repair the damage. Whether the school principal, district public information officer, or the superintendent responds, the basic response should be the same: (1) We are trying to find out what caused the fire to ensure that the school is safe; (2) We have already set up alternative teaching venues, with the cooperation of other staff; (3) We will restore the damaged areas as soon as we can reasonably do so without interfering with the normal school program; (4) We will keep you informed of our progress, so the information can be shared with the public.

Working effectively with the media means proactively seizing opportunities to showcase student work and performances. In small towns or mid-size cities, newspapers routinely publish information about local schools and the success of students, especially if national achievements are involved. Larger cities have zone editions or newspaper supplements that focus on particular neighborhoods or sections of the city. Student or school successes are usually routinely included in the zone edition paper.

A good strategy to break the ice with the media is to tell them that you welcome serving as a resource on educational issues. For example, a reporter might have questions about a curriculum approach such as *Understanding by Design* (Wiggins & McTighe, 1998) because she heard that all the teachers in the district were required to train with the model. Explaining terms like "essential questions" and "backward design" would be helpful to the reporter. Also, principals will endear themselves with reporters by avoiding the use of educational jargon.

Honesty and trust building will be crucial relationship elements when negative stories occur. Snowden and Gorton (2002) insightfully note that when innovations are newly implemented, the media immediately want to know if the innovation is succeeding. Telling reporters that major educational change usually takes about two to five years is not going to help when they want to report on progress during the evening news hour. Just imagine telling a reporter, "Listen, come back in two years and I'll give you an update on the $100,000 grant the school received for after-school programs." Snowden and Gorton (2002) note,

> Consequently, the media spotlight is on the innovation early and tends to focus on the problems it is encountering, resulting in "bad press." There is no easy answer to this problem, given the nature of the press and the process of introducing change. The media are generally more interested in problems because they are newsworthy, and the period just after the innovation has been implemented is frequently the time when many problems arise. The administrator can, however, attempt to develop a positive relationship with the news reporters in the community and try to develop an understanding on their part (before the innovation is introduced) about the types of problems likely to occur because of the innovation's novelty as well as the school's contingency plans for addressing these problems.

School Communication as a Reflection of Proactive Leadership

Part of leadership is understanding your constituencies and working with them for the sake of children. If a school leader believes in capacity building, then this should extend to media relationships. The following guidelines are intended to help both principals and reporters succeed. New principals should consider posting these guidelines in their office.

GENERAL GUIDELINES FOR SCHOOL LEADERS FOR SUCCESS WITH THE MEDIA

- Tie all interaction with the media to the school mission and your responsibility to the students, teachers, and greater community.

- Honesty *is* the best policy; when answering questions, be specific, don't speculate.

- Be proactive with the media: It is your duty to share school news, good and bad.

- Invite the media to special events on a routine basis.

- If photos are going to be published, obtain permission from relevant parties.

- Keep the media informed about new programs.

- Remember, it is only news if the media say so.

- Recognize the differences among newspapers, television, and radio media.

- Know the media deadlines and the format expectations.

- Develop relationships with the players in the media.

- Partner with the media personalities; invite them to your schools to speak to classes and teacher and parent groups.

- Prepare and practice for interviews.

- Always assume that what you have to say is "on the record."

- To assess your school or district news coverage, conduct a newspaper, television, and radio audit to discern positive and negative coverage, coverage accuracy, and capability to get a story out.

- If you are dissatisfied with a story, do not contact a reporter or consult the senior editor while you are angry. After you calm down, write a letter expressing your view, and try to have a personal meeting with the appropriate reporter.

- In a large district, a public information officer should be the point person for receiving and sending information. In a small district, the point person may be the superintendent.

- Always respect the legal and moral privacy of your students and teachers.

- Keep in mind that every item released from your school to the media should be a first-rate product—*appearance counts.*

As noted in the list, it is only news if the media say so. Three factors that increase your chances of having a story published are (1) *Local interest*—a story based on the community, a local activity, or a local individual; (2) *Widespread appeal*—a current topic that involves most of the community, such as getting ready for the new school year; and (3) *A local angle to a national story*—such as a shuttle astronaut growing up in your community (U.S. Department of Education, 2002).

When new principals develop relationships with reporters, they can direct a newsworthy story to the right source. Notice bylines, and examine the writing style and content of the reporters; you'll get a feel for the type of story they prefer. "[F]ind out if there are particular newspaper, television, and radio reporters who cover the education beat. Identify the influential editors and producers. Keep this information easily accessible in a Rolodex or personal digital assistant for future use. Meet these important contacts for lunch, invite them on a tour of your school, and prepare a 'press kit' for them with essential and lively information about your school (include sample news release forms in the kit)" (Robbins & Alvy, 2003). It is also important that the principal does not show favoritism toward, or bias against, a particular reporter, station, newspaper, or media format. Fair treatment entails promptly returning calls, meeting deadlines, and displaying the same courtesy toward all media representatives.

Partner with the media by inviting them into your school. English classes, journalism classes, television and radio production classes, and career days all present opportunities for media partnerships. Parent meetings and special event nights are also possibilities. For example, reporters who are specialists on a topic, such as the Middle East or the local environment, should be invited to school. Elementary school classes and science classes are wonderful forums for the local television weather reporters.

New principals in larger districts should spend time in the central office with the public information specialist. The public information specialist can provide insights into the community that will be especially valuable to a principal hired from outside the district. Of particular value will be information concerning internal and external developments that affect the district, information about local opinion leaders and key organizations (e.g., business people, news editors, heads of civic organizations, parent group leaders), public support concerning levies and bond issues, how to respond to particular media and alert the media, and how to publicize events such as The Martin Luther King Commemoration and Open House events.

Creating Partnerships with an Array of Media

Warner (2000) makes the following suggestions for working with the various media:

- *Newspapers:*

  – Learn the deadlines for special sections.

  – If the paper has an education column, offer to write an editorial.

  – Determine the paper's policy for main and zone editions.

  – Strictly follow the parameters of the press release (discussed later).

- *Television:*

  – A 30-minute local news show includes only 11 minutes of news, so very few stories are actually broadcast.

  – Television is visual, so the proposed story must have a visual angle.

  – Different stations may have different lead times for a major story; precisely follow the station's suggestions.

  – If only a cameraperson shows for a story, make sure that he or she gets a copy of your news release.

  – Take advantage of public service and community announcements.

  – Invite television personalities to your school.

  – Investigate local cable stations because they often provide opportunities for local school stories.

  – During television interviews, be concise and avoid jargon; begin with what is most important; the tape will edit out the "silent moments," so think first, then respond; discuss only what you know, don't speculate; remember to relax and smile if appropriate.

- *Radio*:

  – Because radio broadcasts 24 hour a day, story timing is critical—seek "a prime spot" when people listen.

  – Remember, this moment's news is old news the next moment.

  – Keep in mind that the format is perfect for immediate news such as school closures.

  – Many radio shows are tailored for specific audiences, so take advantage of the format and explore community service opportunities.

  – Speak clearly and distinctly (appearance is moot; your voice and content count) (Warner, 2000).

THE NEWS RELEASE

The news release should "use simple and easy-to-understand language. Don't let the news release get bogged down with a lot of educational terms and jargon. The superintendent may know what AASA is, but John Q Public does not. Include the most important information in the first paragraph. The submitted story most likely will have to be edited, and it is important to get the school's point across" (Hughes & Hooper, 2000, p. 135). The news release needs to arouse the interest of the editor, so an "angle" or novelty aspect of a story is helpful. Keep the release to one page, and answer the reporter's stock questions: who, what, when, where, how, and why. At the end of the page, write "END" or "###." If you do have additional information that might be helpful, write "more" at the page bottom. Let the newspaper know the date the school released the story (the date line), the contact person at the school if additional information or clarification is needed (contact line) and the date the story can be released to the public (the release line). Try to get your news release to the paper at least five days in advance. Consider attaching a personal note to the release, thanking the reporters for their interest in the school and for considering the article.

Schools in diverse communities have a responsibility to communicate with radio, television, and newspapers that reach the limited or non-English-speaking community. Efforts to work with the non-English-speaking community are critical to send the message that each student and parent affiliated with the school is important. Bilingual parent volunteers, community partners, bilingual students, and teachers of foreign languages can all play a major role assisting the school in communicating with the media. It is particularly important to get out public service announcements related to the opening of school, parent nights, holiday programs, and emergency school closures. Schools cannot overlook this avenue.

In addition to traditional news sources, most schools have set up Web sites to provide background information on the school, important current events, and specific information regarding contacting the administration, faculty, or staff. Technology teachers, students, and the business community can help a school set up a first-rate Web page. The Web page should include links to student activities and photographs that celebrate the school's successes, especially student achievements. Web pages can also offer information about homework, emergency numbers, and links to the school newspaper. This is an excellent source for people who might want information at 5:00 a.m. or 11:00 p.m.

Crisis Management and the Media

When a crisis occurs, television, radio, and newspapers become vital links to events that may affect the rest of our lives. As noted in Chapter 10, crises test leadership. Working effectively with the media is a real test during a crisis. All proactive planning is tested, sometimes within the first 30 minutes of the crisis. Although not all crises are catastrophic events (there may be a crisis concerning poor test results or a major cheating scandal), school leaders need to be prepared to communicate information concerning a crisis almost immediately, to prevent rumors or panic. Shoop and Dunklee (2002) provide excellent suggestions for communicating with the media during a crisis based on guidelines from the Fairfax County, Va., Public Schools' Office of Security and Risk Management Services and the Office of Community Relations. The media guidelines are as follows:

> • Although schools are public buildings, administrators do not have to allow the media on campus. Administrators must grant access to members of the press.
> • Police answer questions regarding criminal investigations. Administrators should focus on what the school is doing to secure student safety and maintain student welfare.
> • Identify one school spokesperson.
> • Identify and maintain a media staging area.
> • Don't let reporters wander.
> • Provide factual written statements for the press and provide updates in cooperation with the police and community relations personnel.

- Be certain that every member of the media receives the same information.
- Be accurate. If you don't know the answer to a question, don't speculate.
- Set limits for the time reporters may be on campus and the areas they visit.
- Don't say, "No comment." If you don't know an answer, offer to get information and to get back to the reporters. Don't speak off the record.
- Ensure that reporters respect the sensitivities of those who are touched by the crisis.
- Obtain staff members' consent before agreeing to let them be interviewed.
- Students under the age of 18 may not be interviewed on campus without parental permission. However, yearbook and school newspaper photographs are public documents and you must provide access to them. (Shoop & Dunklee, 2002, p. 32)

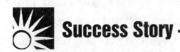

Success Story

Morale in the school district was low. Teachers in the union felt unappreciated because of the animosity created during the year concerning salary, benefits, and working conditions. The faculty, administration, and public were unsure how to restore a professional climate and recognize teachers for their daily dedication to students. After brainstorming with some colleagues, an elementary school teacher in the district approached the local university about sponsoring a "Teacher of the Month" program, partnering the university with regional radio and television broadcast stations and local businesses. The vision was to have K–12 students nominate teachers each month who would be recognized by a local television station in a surprise ceremony at the school. Teachers would be selected from all over the region in a two-state area.

Although there was some initial concern that the Teacher of the Month program might be perceived as competitive, the university, television stations, businesses, and regional school districts supported the idea. A mission statement was developed: "To recognize and honor those outstanding educators who exhibit a personal care and interest in their students' lives; and to enhance public awareness of the positive contributions made by educators to the community." The biggest television station in the region agreed to provide the publicity for the monthly program as a public service, and local furniture stores agreed to pay for the expenses involved. The university rotated a three-member selection committee each month, reviewing the letters from students and selecting the teacher who "in the judgment of the selection committee, best represents the special ideas, and qualities of an exceptional educator, one who has inspired and touched the life of his or her students." Award recipients were showcased on television, received a plaque and sweatshirt from the university, and free tuition and fees for up to four university graduate credits. When receiving the recognition, teachers usually were surprised and gratified, and upon hearing the applause of their colleagues and students, invariably, they would say, "Any of my colleagues could have received the award."

Since the Teacher of the Month program was instituted, more than 150 teachers in the region have been honored. Two years ago the university held a symposium, inviting more than 100 of the recipients to give workshops and answer questions from students in the undergraduate education program. Videotapes were made of all the workshop sessions. It is good to know that others will gain from the library of knowledge of these dedicated teachers.

 **Activity** ————————————————————

Assessing Your Communication Skills

In real estate the mantra is "location, location, location." In the principalship it is "communication, communication, communication." The leader who communicates effectively takes a giant step toward success. Each of us is stronger in some communication areas than in others. We forget sometimes that communication is a two-way process, and that active listening is as important, if not more important than speaking. The Communication Skills Checklist shown in Figure 13.1 will give you an opportunity to consider a wide range of communication issues. As you review the list, select two or three skill areas that you would like to strengthen. Congratulate yourself for the areas that you know are strengths.

Figure 13.1

Communication Skills Checklist

__ Are you an active listener? Can you patiently listen to someone else without considering your response while they are still speaking?

__ Do you write clear and concise memos?

__ How are your skills writing long reports?

__ Do you write effective articles for the school newsletters?

__ How are your skills, and are you comfortable speaking to large groups?

__ How are your skills, and are you comfortable speaking to small groups?

__ How are your skills, and are you comfortable speaking one-on-one?

__ Do you have a preference speaking to student, parent, or teacher groups? Why?

__ Are you effective at facilitating a group?

__ Are you able to synthesize the ideas of a group?

__ How are your skills and are you comfortable communicating via e-mail?

__ Are you skilled and are you comfortable communicating via the telephone?

__ Are you skilled and are you comfortable communicating via the school public address system?

__ Do you communicate effectively with the media, via radio and television?

__ Are you comfortable during school-related social functions?

__ How are your nonverbal skills? Does your body language match your intended message?

__ How are your skills reading the nonverbal messages of others?

__ What other communication issues need to be considered?

Reflective Field Notes ⸺⸺⸺⸺⸺⸺⸺⸺⸺

Please use this space to jot down notes that are important for your personal leadership journey. You may do this in a structured way—by responding to questions—or in an unstructured way. Use the approach that works for you.

- How important is the media in your community?

- Is the television, radio, or newspaper the dominant media force in your community? Explain.

- Review the "General Guidelines for School Leaders for Success with the Media." Which guidelines do you think are particularly important? Why?

- What insights or new questions do you have as a result of reflecting on the issues raised in this chapter?

14

Balancing Professional and Personal Lives: Keeping Fit for the Journey

It's 9:30 p.m., and the lights are on in Stephanie Gonzalas's office. At her desk covered with paperwork, she reflects, "It seems I'm here most evenings until at least 10:00 p.m. How do veteran principals ever get the job done and find time for family, exercise, and life in general? I love the principalship. It's the position I've always wanted. But how do principals find a way to have balance in their lives?"

One of the challenges the newcomer to the principalship often mentions is about how to be an effective, compassionate, productive, learning leader and still have a life. Kent Peterson, professor of Educational Administration at the University of Wisconsin, Madison, studied the principalship for many years. Speaking to a group of newcomers, he described the principal's work life:

The principalship is characterized by brevity, fragmentation, and variety. Brevity—because 85 percent of the tasks you do last 9 minutes or less, and those that last longer rarely last more than 30 minutes. Fragmentation—because you're often interrupted by individuals or events (like a fire alarm being pulled) over which you have no control. Variety—because the tasks in which the principal engages and the corresponding responses require a spectrum of emotions. You may encounter a teacher who is elated because she was just notified that she passed National Board Certification, and in the next moment, receive a call that one of your students was in an automobile accident on the way to school. It's a roller coaster of emotions on a daily basis.

The hectic pace of this complex role makes reflection time scarce—except in the early hours before school or after school. Many newcomers have found that keeping a journal is advantageous because it gives them time to replay events and their responses, as well as reflect on how they have reacted in specific situations over time. Although there are no recipes for finding balance in the role, a principals' support group, created by six principals "to end the 'loneliness' of the role, learn from and support one another" suggested the following advice:

- *Schedule time for yourself on your calendar.* If you don't, something else will consume the time. Make time for the relationships in your life that are precious to you.

- *Create time for physical exercise.* If you are fit, you will have more energy to serve well the organization and its members. Especially on those days when your time is limited, make a commitment to walk the campus and converse with students and staff.

- *Eat well.* Consult books such as *Managing Your Mind and Mood Through Food* (Wurtman, 1986) to learn about which foods will help you to function at maximum potential. Avoid simple sugars. Keep healthy snacks in your office so you aren't tempted to raid the candy jar on the secretary's desk! Try to eat a good breakfast with protein and complex carbohydrates. Take time for lunch. Make it a time to connect and share a meal with staff members, parent–teacher organization members, students, or community members. Try to avoid eating dinners at a late hour. If you must stay late, bring something to munch on while you work, such as a salad, a sandwich, or a well-balanced frozen meal that you can heat in the microwave.

• *Strive to get at least seven to eight hours of sleep.* Although school events often make this goal impossible, when you can, try to bank those Z's. Sleep deprivation affects thinking, decision making, reaction time, creativity, and wellness.

• *Make time for professional reading and learning.* Doing this models being a learning leader and increases the resources available to support staff in serving students. One effective strategy is to find quotes in professional journals you are reading that you wish to share with staff. Collect them in an electronic file and give them out as an opening activity in a faculty meeting. Ask staff members to select a quote, read it, and meet with a colleague to share quotes.

• *Spend time with hobbies or activities you relish at least once a week.* Playing sports, cooking, gardening, volunteering, and a variety of other pastimes help keep one vibrant!

• *Spend time with students and staff.* Cultivating significant connections with individuals in the schoolhouse is a great way to build a nurturing learning environment in which to spend time.

• *Continually seek to learn about and refine one's practice.* This helps you keep sight of your personal vision of what's important.

• *Set a personal example for others to observe and emulate.* When adults in the schoolhouse stay fit, their capacity to serve students well will be enhanced.

Another way to think about staying fit for the journey is to imagine a bicycle wheel with six spokes (see Figure 14.1). Each spoke represents an important dimension of one's life. If any one of these spokes is not addressed, your bicycle ride will be a bumpy one.

Figure 14.1

Wellness Wheel

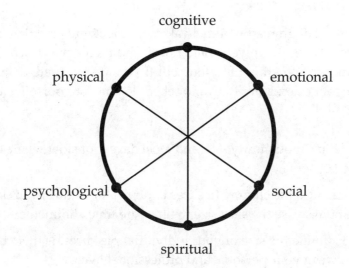

 **Activity** ———————————————

Comparing Pies

All right! Enough reading time! Take a moment and complete the next activity, jot down your field notes, and then—put down this book and do something for yourself! If you are too tired, at least get out your calendar or PDA and schedule time for yourself in the future.

• Think about how you spend most days. Consider where the time goes.

• Create a pie chart with slices to depict how you spend time on most days. Use the slice size to illustrate time allotments.

• Examine the size of your individual pie slices. Is there balance between your personal and professional lives?

Now . . .

• Create a pie chart to depict how you would like to spend your time, ideally.

• Compare your reality with the ideal. Note the discrepancies.

• Decide on an action plan to move toward your ideal.

Reflective Field Notes ―――――――――

Please use this space to jot down notes that are important for your personal leadership journey. You may do this in a structured way—by responding to questions—or an unstructured way. Use the approach that works for you.

- What were the ideas in the chapter that resonated with you?

- How do you currently balance your personal and professional lives?

- What next steps might you take to stay fit for the leadership journey?

15

The Crucial First Steps on the Road to Success

In this final chapter we are going to share first steps to help aspiring and new principals reflect on the values and vision they will develop on the leadership journey. We offer these ideas for you to consider as you formulate your vision. However, at the end of the day, your vision for the children and adults in schools will be conceived as a very personal act. During quiet moments alone in a car or while reading at home, you will begin to shape ideas that will crystallize into a personal leadership vision—a vision that will enable you to be decisive when considering the interests of students and staff. We cannot tell you what your vision should be. However, we offer the following first steps to help you formulate your vision. At the end of the chapter we have included an activity with the National Council for the Accreditation of Teacher Education/Interstate School Leaders Licensure Consortium (NCATE/ ISLLC) standards that should help you with the vision-building journey. Good luck!

Know Thyself

"Our companies can never be anything we do not want ourselves to be." (DePree, 1989, p. 49). A school, more than any other institution, should be a learning community. But it does not happen automatically. If the educators in a school do not encourage community, caring, risk taking, and emotional safety, then a school can be an intimidating institution. Principals and teachers need to be creators and inventors who support students on their educational journey. But, you will find it difficult to advise others confidently about taking a journey unless you have self-confidence and self-knowledge. Writing about the life of Gandhi, Nair (1997) states that Gandhi was successful because he knew his mission, and his compass direction was evident to millions of Indians. "Leaders have the greatest responsibility. Without the compass of absolute values, what instrument do they have to guide others? . . . Gandhi formulated two absolute values: truth and nonviolence." School leaders must formulate their absolute values. These values may go beyond standards or clean formulas. One must decide: Do I want to serve students and adults in schools? If yes, how should I serve the students and adults?

Celebrate What Is Best for Students and Adults in the Schoolhouse

We should celebrate what we honor. In schools that are communities of learners, we honor the following:

- A shared purpose;
- Collaboration;
- High expectations for all students;
- Students engaged in meaningful work;
- Teachers who know they can make a difference;
- Parents as part of the solution and not the problem;

- Leadership that supports adult and student collaboration; and

- Student and staff learning.

With each opportunity, school leaders must celebrate success. Aspiring and new principals need to know that as school leaders, opportunities will surface each day to celebrate student and staff successes. For example, when the principal hears from a counselor that Judy, a 3rd grade student, is doing better in math after a slow start, the principal can celebrate by visiting the cafeteria during lunch and congratulating Judy for her progress. At the end of the school day, when Ms. Bensky, Judy's teacher, is leaving, the principal can congratulate Ms. Bensky on her success. New principals should not underestimate the power of an oral compliment, or a brief note written to a teacher complimenting him or her about a classroom event. It is not unusual to walk into a classroom and see that note proudly posted near the teacher's desk. Even the most veteran teacher appreciates recognition. Principals should take advantage of each large gathering to remind teachers, parents, students, classified staff, and community stakeholders of the school's successes and what is valued. An assembly program with high school students, the moment in the morning when elementary students line up just before the bells ring, faculty meetings, and a parent meeting are all opportunities to talk about success. In one high school a solemn moment occurs during graduation when the teachers walk into the large hall and sit together. After the student procession, the principal begins the graduation with a few words about the dedication of the teachers, stressing that some of the students in the hall would not be graduating without the effort of particular teachers.

Celebration occurs, also, with each sacred story that is part of a school's treasure: stories about a child who overcame every imaginable obstacle and succeeded or stories about a teacher, way beyond retirement age, who is still serving as a senior high school English teacher. Why? Because each year the juniors and their parents beg the English teacher to remain and teach literature. One parent pleaded with an English teacher, "You have to remain next year, my two older children love poetry because of you. I want Danielle to love poetry, too."

Communicate, Communicate, Communicate

Throughout this book we have tried to drive home the importance of communication. We have stressed that communication is a two-way process. Leaders must seek information from faculty, staff, students, and parents to find out how the organization is performing. Throughout history we can find numerous examples of leaders who failed because they were isolated or were fed only what their subordinates thought they wanted to hear. The principalship is no different. Unless you ask good questions and have a trusting relationship with staff, you may not really find out what is taking place. As Bennis and Nanus (1985) discovered in their classic work on leadership, "Successful leaders, we have found, *are great askers*, and they do pay attention" (italics in original). Soder (2001) warns that subordinates are "likely to tell you what they think you want to hear, and the likelihood poses dangers for the leader."

The leader has to aggressively seek information throughout the organization. New principals should not expect totally accurate feedback from colleagues during their first few months on the job. Until the principal enters the *insider stage* (see Chapter 3), staff members may be a little cautious with their remarks, regardless of what the principal says during faculty meetings about appreciating their honesty.

Reaching out appropriately to various constituencies is critical. Principals must ask themselves: What mode of communication should be used? For example, to invite parents to an Open House, should a newsletter announcement be used? Should a flyer be sent out? Should the PTA be asked to call all parents? Should we try to make a public service broadcast about the Open House? It is also important to assess one's communication strengths and areas needing improvement. The various modes of communication addressed in the Chapter 13 activity give you an opportunity to reflect on your strengths as a communicator. Finally, in this day of electronic communication, we need to consider the pros and cons of e-mail and other recent communication innovations. A poignant moment occurred during the February 4, 2003, memorial service for the Columbia Shuttle astronauts when a colleague of astronaut Laurel Clark mentioned, "Laurel never sent an e-mail or used the phone when she could meet with you in person."

Remember That Leadership Is Based on Human Relations

There is no theme in this book related to leadership that is more important than human relations—the forging of quality relationships. Leadership *is* based on human relations. While serving as the conductor of the Los Angeles Philharmonic, Carlo Maria Giulini stated, "The great mystery of music making requires real friendship among those who work together. Every member of the orchestra knows I am with him and her in my heart" (Bennis & Nanus, 1985, p. 55).

Human relations is more than sharing a conversation in a schoolhouse. It is combining the head and heart when working with students and colleagues. As DePree (1989) reflected, "Leadership is much more an art, a belief, a condition of the heart, than a set of things to do. The visible signs of artful leadership are expressed, ultimately, in its practice." A professional looking organizational chart may convince some that the school structure is effective, but unless the individuals represented by each box in the chart want to work with you, and are passionate about the mission, then excellence will not occur. Insightfully and with simplicity DePree addresses this issue:

> Understand that relationships count more than structure. Every educational institution goes through periodic evaluation by some sort of accreditation committee. A small college with which I have been

associated went through such an evaluation recently. The committee's report noted an especially high level of trust between the president, who was to retire soon, and the faculty. To create this trust with the next president, the committee recommended that the college make the necessary changes in their "structure." *The president was justifiably amused. Structures do not have anything to do with trust. People build trust.* (italics added)

Promoting Teacher Leadership

As noted in chapters 5 and 12, site-based management (SBM) and school improvement teams have structurally altered schools and given teachers, parents, and community stakeholders a greater decision-making role. But teacher leadership is more than SBM. Teacher leadership must extend into the fabric of the school and profession so that teachers are no longer isolated from one another. Teachers must work collaboratively and at the same time make independent teaching decisions based on their professional expertise. Teacher leadership also includes pursuing differentiated growth options that meet each teacher's unique professional needs. Evaluation and professional growth models that enable teachers to pursue customized options will increase capacity building and growth.

It is a principal's moral responsibility to facilitate the leadership capacity of teachers. James MacGregor Burns (1978) articulated this moral leadership component initially as *transformational leadership* in his seminal book, *Leadership*. Describing the concept of transformational leadership, Burns stated,

> Such leadership occurs when one or more persons *engage* with others in such a way that leaders and followers raise one another to higher levels of motivation and morality . . . transforming leadership ultimately becomes *moral* in that it raises the level of human conduct and ethical aspirations of both leader and led, and thus it has a transforming affect on both. Perhaps the best modern example is Gandhi, who aroused and elevated the hopes and demands of millions of Indians and whose life and personality were enhanced in the process. (italics in original)

Maintaining a Personal Vision of Teaching and Learning

In Chapter 5 we reviewed Schlechty's 10 critical qualities of student work. The essence of his message is that students should be engaged in meaningful and quality work. Teachers can enhance or impair meaningful work. As leaders, creators, and inventors, working collaboratively as professionals who believe in continuous growth, teachers will most likely succeed. Personally, we envision students in classes pursuing high standards, in a risk-free environment, in which students work collaboratively on authentic and meaningful tasks of their choice within the parameters of the school's goals. We see, also, teachers with a common mission, pursuing professional development opportunities that are intended to help them achieve that mission. The school administration should be actively involved in the professional growth of the staff. And, we envision teachers taking pride in their principal because, instead of leaving immediately after introducing the speaker, the principal remains and learns along with the staff.

Helping All School Personnel Be the Best They Can Be

When discussing the relationship between the central office and the schoolhouse we noted that language is sometimes problematic (e.g., certificated and noncertificated). One superintendent handles this issue by referring to all employees in the district as "staff." We do not have a solution to this issue. However, we do believe that treating each employee in the school with respect can narrow the invisible line between "professional" and "classified" staff. If an organization is aligned ethically, then respect will be honored *throughout* the organization. Principals can set the standard in their own schools by treating everyone with respect—the paraprofessionals, teachers, custodians, students, bus drivers, parents, cafeteria workers, secretaries, clerks, security personnel, and visitors. As noted earlier, leadership is the art of human relations. Treat others the way you want to be treated.

By displaying respect, the coworker will more likely strive to improve. It is just human nature. As part of relationship building, the principal should also look for opportunities to help classified staff raise their job levels, especially for paraprofessionals, who may be considering becoming teachers. If the paraprofessional enjoys children and has the skills, then the individual should be encouraged to pursue further education.

Instructional Leaders Keep the Lights Working

An important theme in this book is the relationship between leadership and management. We view management as an essential leadership tool. Management supports instructional leadership. Instructional leaders *do* make sure that the lights are working so that students and teachers can see what they are reading! Clean hallways, sparkling windows, clean bathrooms, and graffiti-free schools enable teachers and students to feel good about their schools. Not surprisingly, this theme has been noted in other situations. Former New York City Mayor Rudolph Giuliani (2002) noted that the reduction in crime in the city could be attributed, to some extent, to a very simple idea, "'Sweat the small stuff' is the essence of the Broken Window theory that I embraced to fight crime. The theory holds that a seemingly minor matter like broken windows in abandoned buildings leads directly to a more serious deterioration of the neighborhood."

Recognize the Significance of Visibility

Leading and Learning By Wandering Around (LLBWA), purposefully, is a critical principalship strategy to stay in touch with the school culture and to celebrate what is right about the school.

The strategy also enables you to observe areas in the school or situations that need to be improved.

Advice for new principals: Don't become too enamored with your office. The office is not the center of the school, although a lot of people think it is. Symbolism is very powerful. When a principal decides to spend time in a particular area, that area becomes important. For example, if the principal is always visiting English classes, and rarely math classes, it tells the faculty that all is right with English, or all is wrong. Either way, it is noticed. A principal's attendance at an IEP meeting, the junior varsity volleyball match, the rehearsal of a school play, or visit to the nurse's office to say "Hi" all carry symbolic importance. Again, the LLBWA should be carried out purposefully—the goals of the school should be evident as the staff observes the principal around the school.

Remaining Healthy

Quite simply, it is very difficult to help others if you are not healthy. An appropriate analogy is the airline review of emergency procedures before a plane takes off. Parents are directed to place their oxygen masks on, before taking care of their children. As a principal, if you lack oxygen, you cannot help children or adults. Also, setting a personal example of a balanced life is important for the staff to see. Often, first-time principals are also raising young families. There is a lot of pressure with the job and family responsibilities. It is important, however, not to neglect your family. How can you tell other parents or teachers to spend more time with their kids, with any credibility, if you never take the time to watch your own child in a school play?

It is important for your mental and physical health to exercise and eat properly. The principalship can be very stressful. Unless you take time from the job to actively engage in relaxing and fun activities, then the job will get to you sooner or later. Being a workaholic does no one any good, especially not your own family. Remember, when you are 80 years old, in frail health, and thinking about your children, you are unlikely to say, "I should have spent more time at the office."

Continually Seeking to Learn and Refine One's Practice

If the schoolhouse is an authentic learning community, then each of us, as members of that community, should celebrate our membership by continuing to grow professionally and personally. Through reading, conversation, observation, writing, and reflecting, we improve our practice. As former Mayor Giuliani (2002) notes, "Leadership does not simply happen. It can be taught, learned, developed." But leadership is very complicated. A refreshing aspect of refining one's leadership practice is that it can give one an opportunity to converse and interact with other professionals. For example, we strongly recommend attending state and national conferences to hear others talk about leadership, the principalship, curriculum, instruction, assessment, and other topics of interest. Do not let the principalship get too lonely!

On a practical note, your staff will appreciate your involvement in professional development activities. Teachers take pride in their principal when they believe the principal is knowledgeable. When you "sharpen the saw" (Covey, 1989), you will also be much more valuable to your own community of learners, because your insights and new ideas will lead to conversations that will help others grow.

 **Success Story** ————————————————————

It is time to write your own success story!

 **Activity** ————————————————————

Formulating Your Vision Statement Using the ISLLC Standards

In 2000, several organizations, including ASCD, assisted NCATE and ISLLC in the development of standards documents that reflect the expected knowledge and skill level of educational administration students who have completed graduate programs (Jackson & Kelley, 2002). Review the seven standards that follow. After reviewing each standard, consider how that standard could contribute to your *personal leadership vision*, jotting down a few notes as you reflect on each standard. After examining and taking notes on the standards, find some time during the next couple of weeks to formulate a personal vision statement. After writing the statement, compare it to the seven ISLLC standards. Is there a match between your document and the standards? If there is not a match, consider why that is the case. Have you included an important idea that ISLLC omitted? Or, have you omitted an idea that you should have included? Continue to work on your vision statement until you are satisfied.

THE ISLLC STANDARDS

Candidates who complete the program are educational leaders who have the knowledge and ability to promote success of all students by

1. Facilitating the development, articulation, implementation, and stewardship of a school or district vision of learning supported by the school community;

2. Promoting a positive school culture, providing an effective instructional program, applying best practices to student learning, and designing comprehensive professional growth plans for staff;

3. Managing the organization, operations, and resources in a way that promotes a safe, efficient, and effective learning environment;

4. Collaborating with families and community members, responding to diverse community interests and needs, and mobilizing community resources;

5. Acting with integrity and fairness, and in an ethical manner;

6. Understanding, responding to, and influencing the larger political, social, economic, legal, and cultural context; and

7. Completing the internship. (Jackson & Kelley, 2002)

Reflective Field Notes ——————

Please use this space to jot down notes that are important for your personal leadership journey. You may do this in a structured way—by responding to questions—or in an unstructured way. Use the approach that works for you.

- Select two or three of the first steps that you believe are particularly important. Reflect on why you selected these ideas.

- What additional steps have been omitted that you would include?

- Review all of the chapter headings in the table of contents. Identify topics you want to explore further.

- What insights or new questions do you have as a result of reflecting on the issues raised in this chapter?

A Final Thought

May your journey be inspiring and serve as an inspiration to others. Best of luck to you on the leadership path.

References

ABC News Nightline (1997, April 16). Featuring Ray McNulty.

Allen, R. (2003, Winter). Civic virtue in the schools. *Curriculum Update,* 2–3, 6.

Alvy, H. (1983). *The problems of new principals.* Doctoral dissertation, University of Montana.

Alvy, H. (1997, Spring–Summer). Interns offer insights into principalship. *The Principal News* (Association of Washington School Principals), 11–13.

Alvy, H., & Coladarci, T. (1985). Problems of the novice principal. *Research in Rural Education, 3*(1), 39–47.

Alvy, H., & Robbins, P. (1998). *If I only knew: Success strategies for navigating the principalship.* Thousand Oaks, CA: Corwin Press.

Aquila, R., & Petzke, J. (1994). *Education law.* Santa Monica, CA: Casenotes Publishing.

Archer, J. (2002, May 29). Novice principals put huge strains on New York City schools. *Education Week, 1,* 15.

Barth, R. (2001). *Learning by heart.* San Francisco: Jossey-Bass.

Barth, R. (2001, February). Making happen what you believe in. *Phi Delta Kappan, 82*(2), 446.

Barth, R. (2002, May). The culture builder. *Educational Leadership, 59*(8), 6–11.

Bennis, W., & Nanus, B. (1985). *Leaders . . . the strategies for taking charge.* New York: Harper and Row.

Berman, P., & McLaughlin, M. (1978). *Federal programs supporting educational change: Vol. 8. Implementing and sustaining innovations.* Santa Monica, CA: RAND.

Boris-Schacter, S., & Langer, S. (2002, February 6). Caught between nostalgia and utopia. *Education Week,* 35–36.

Boyer, E. (1995). *The basic school: A community for learning.* The Carnegie Foundation for the Advancement of Teaching. Princeton, NJ.

Bridges, E. M. (1976, March). Administrative preparation: A critical appraisal. *Thrust,* 3–8.

Bryk, A., & Schneider, B. (2003, March). Trust in school: A core resource for school reform. *Educational Leadership, 60*(6), 40–44.

Burns, J. (1978). *Leadership.* New York: Harper and Row.

Caine, R., & Caine, G. (1991). *Making connections: Teaching and the human brain*. Alexandria, VA: ASCD.

Castillo, Y., & Winchester, M. (2001, April). After school in a colonia. *Educational Leadership, 58*(7), 67–70.

Cheney, WA, School District (2002–2003). *Summary of student rights and responsibilities*. Cheney, WA.

Cogan, M. (1973). *Clinical supervision*. Boston: Houghton Mifflin.

Costa, A., & Garmston, R. (1991, April). *Cognitive coaching action lab workshop*. ASCD Annual Conference, San Francisco.

Covey, S. (1989). *The seven habits of highly effective people*. New York: Simon & Schuster.

Cubbage, R. (1995). *Assessing the impact of individual and organizational variables on a school district's implementation of a division-wide writing program*. Doctoral dissertation presented to the Faculty of the Curry School of Education, University of Virginia.

Danielson, C. (1996). *Enhancing professional practice: A framework for teaching*. Alexandria, VA: ASCD.

Danielson, C., & McGreal, T. (2000). *Teacher evaluation*. Alexandria, VA: ASCD & Princeton, NJ: Educational Testing Service.

Deal, T., & Peterson, K. (1994). *The leadership paradox*. San Francisco: Jossey-Bass.

Deal, T., & Peterson, K. (1999). *Shaping school culture: The heart of leadership*. San Francisco: Jossey-Bass.

DePree, Max. (1989). *Leadership is an art*. New York: Doubleday.

Duke, D., Isaacson, N., Sagor, R., & Schmuck, R. (1984). *Transition to leadership*. Portland, OR: Lewis and Clark College, Educational Administration Program.

Dunne, D. (2001). Environmental problems blamed for making kids sick. [online] *Education World*, http://www.education-world.com.

Dwyer, K., Osher, D., & Warger, C. (1998). *Early warning, timely response: A guide to safe schools*. Washington DC: U. S. Department of Education. Retrieved April 28, 2002, from the World Wide Web. Available: http://cecp.air.org/guide/guidetext.html.

Elias, M. (2002). Address at ASCD Annual Conference, San Antonio, TX.

Epstein, J. (2002). Six types of parent involvement, in *Leading learning communities: Standards for what principals should know and be able to do* (p. 73). Alexandria, VA: NAESP.

Fullan, M. (1990). Implementing instructional innovations [Workshop]. Professional Development Institute, Jan. 30–Feb. 1. At ASCD, Alexandria, VA.

Fullan, M. (2001). *Leading in a culture of change*. San Francisco: Jossey-Bass.

Fullan, M. (2002, May). The change leader. *Educational Leadership, 59*(8), 16–20.

Fullan, M., & Stiegelbauer, S. (1991). *The new meaning of educational change*. New York: Teachers College Press.

Gardner, H. (1995, Nov.). Reflections on multiple intelligences: Myths and messages. *Phi Delta Kappan, 76*(3), 200–203, 206–209.

Garet, M., Porter, A. C., Desmone, L., Birman, B. F., & Yoon, K. S. (2001). What makes professional development effective? Results from a national sample of teachers. *American Educational Research Journal, 38*(4), 115–145.

Gewertz, C. (2003, February 12). Bathroom blues. *Education Week,* 36–37.

Giuliani, R. (2002). *Leadership.* New York: Talk Miramax Books.

Given, B. (2002). *Teaching to the brain's natural learning systems.* Alexandria, VA: ASCD.

Gladwell, M. (2002). *The tipping point.* Boston: Little Brown and Company.

Glickman, C., Gordon, S., & Ross-Gordon, J. (2001). *Supervision and instructional leadership* (5th ed.). Boston: Allyn and Bacon.

Goleman, D. (1995). *Emotional intelligence.* New York: Bantam Books.

Goleman, D. (1998, November–December). What makes a leader? *Harvard Business Review, 76*(6), 92–102.

Goleman, D., Boyatzis, R., & McKee, A. (2002). *Primal leadership.* Boston, MA: Harvard Business School Press.

Gordon, D. (2002, August). Fuel for reform: The importance of trust in changing schools. *Harvard Education Letter, 18*(4).

Green, R. (2001). *Practicing the art of leadership: A problem-based approach to implementing the ISLLC standards.* Upper Saddle River, New Jersey: Merrill, Prentice-Hall.

Grove, K. (2002, May). The invisible role of the central office. *Educational Leadership, 59*(8), 45–47.

Hall, G., & Mani, M. (1992). Entry strategies: Where do I begin? In F. Parkay & G. Hall (Eds.), *Becoming a principal* (chap. 2). Boston: Allyn and Bacon.

Halverson, C. (2002). *Indoor environmental quality.* Unpublished Manuscript, Eastern Washington University, Cheney, WA.

Hargreaves, A., & Dawe, R. (1989). *Coaching as unreflective practice.* Paper presented at the American Educational Research Association Meeting, San Francisco.

Harris, S., & Petrie, G. (2002, December). A study of bullying in the middle school. *NASSP Bulletin, 86*(633), 42–53.

Hart, A. (1993). *Principal succession.* Albany: State University of New York Press.

Hartzell, G., Williams, R., & Nelson, K. (1995). *New voices in the field.* Thousand Oaks, CA: Corwin.

Hersch, P. (1998). *A tribe apart.* Fawcett Columbine: New York.

Hirsh, S. (1996, September). Seeing and creating the future. *School Team Innovator.* National Staff Development Council.

Hord, S., Rutherford, W., Huling-Austin, L., & Hall, G. (1987). *Taking charge of change.* Alexandria, VA: ASCD.

Hughes, L., & Hooper, D. (2000). *Public relations for school leaders.* Boston: Allyn and Bacon.

Iller, R. (1996). *Can you be liable for injures to a student?* Unpublished manuscript. Whitworth College, Spokane, WA.

Jackson, B., & Kelley, C. (2002). Exceptional and innovative programs in educational administration. *Educational Administrative Quarterly, 38*(2), 192–212.

Kaiser, J. (1995). *The 21st century principal.* Mequon, WI: Stylex.

Kanter, R. (1997). *On the frontiers of management.* Boston: Harvard Business School Press.

Kidder, R., & Born, P. (1998–1999, December/January). Resolving ethical dilemmas in the classroom. *Educational Leadership, 56*(4), 38–41.

Kohn, A. (1996). *Beyond discipline: From compliance to community.* Alexandria, VA: ASCD.

Koppich, J., & Kerchner, C. (2003, February 12). Negotiating what matters most. *Education Week, 41*, 56.

LeDoux, J. (1996). *The emotional brain.* New York: Simon & Schuster.

Louis, M. (1980, June). Surprise and sense making: What newcomers experience in entering unfamiliar organizational settings. *Administrative Science Quarterly, 25*, 226–251.

Lyman, L., Eskildsen, L., Frank, J., Nunn, C., O'Day, D., & O'Donnell, S. (1993). Female principals: Change credibility and gender, *Planning and Change, 24*(1,2), 30–40.

Marzano, R. (2003). *What works in schools.* Alexandria, VA: ASCD.

Marzano, R., Pickering, D., & Pollock, J. (2001). *Classroom instruction that works.* Alexandria, VA: ASCD.

McLaughlin, M. (2001, April). Community counts. *Educational Leadership, 58*(7), 14–18.

Meier, D. (1995). *The power of their ideas: Lessons for America from a small school in Harlem.* Boston: Beacon Press.

Merriam-Webster. (2000). *Collegiate dictionary* (10th ed.). Springfield, MA: Merriam-Webster Incorporated.

Miller, B. (2001, April). The promise of after-school programs. *Educational Leadership, 58*(7), 6–12.

Mondale, S., & Patton, S. (2001). *School: The story of American public education.* Boston: Beacon Press.

Morrison, G. (2003). *Teaching in America* (3rd ed.). Boston: Allyn and Bacon.

Murphy, J. (2002). Reculturing the profession of educational leadership: New blueprints. *Educational Administration Quarterly, 38*(2), 176–191.

Nair, K. (1997). *A higher standard of leadership; Lessons from the life of Gandhi.* San Francisco: Berrett-Koehler.

National Association of Elementary School Principals (NAESP) and the Council for Exceptional Children. (2001). *Implementing IDEA: A guide for principals.* Arlington, VA: NAESP and the Council for Exceptional Children.

National Association of Elementary School Principals (NAESP). (2002). *Leading learning communities: Standards for what principals should know and be able to do.* Alexandria, VA: NAESP.

National School Public Relations Association. (1996). The complete crisis communication management manual for schools (excerpt in) *Practical PR for principals: A handbook to help you build support for your school.* Arlington, VA: National School Public Relations Association.

National Staff Development Council (2001*). National standards for staff development.* Oxford, OH.

Newmann, F., & Wehlage, G. (1995). *Successful school restructuring.* Madison, WI: University of Wisconsin.

Newmann, F., & Wehlage, G. (1996). *Authentic achievement: Restructuring schools for intellectual quality.* San Francisco: Jossey-Bass.

O'Neill, J., & Conzemius, A. (2002, Spring). Four keys to a smooth flight. *Journal of Staff Development, 23*(2), 14–18.

Office of School Improvement of the Florida Department of Education. (2002). *Developing the effective principal.* Gaithersburg, MD: Aspen Publications.

Parkay, F., & Hall, G. (1992). *Becoming a principal.* Boston: Allyn and Bacon.

Peterson, K. (1982). Making sense of principals' work. *Australian Administrator, 3*(3), 1–4.

Peterson, K., & Deal, T. (2002). *The shaping school culture fieldbook.* San Francisco: Jossey-Bass.

Pipher, M. (1994). *Reviving Ophelia.* New York: Grosset/Putman.

Pollack, W. (1998). *Real Boys.* New York: Henry Holt and Company.

Robbins, P. (1991). *How to plan and implement a peer coaching program.* Alexandria, VA: ASCD.

Robbins, P., & Alvy, H. (2003). *The principal's companion* (2nd ed.). Thousand Oaks, CA: Corwin Press.

Rooney, J. (2003, March). Principals who care: A personal reflection. *Educational Leadership, 60*(6), pp. 76–78.

Sack, J. (2002, May 1). EPA pushing improved air quality for schools. *Education Week, 21*(33), 1, 12.

Saphier, J., & King, M. (1985, March). Good seeds grow in strong cultures. *Educational Leadership, 42*(6), 67–74.

Sarason, S. (1982). *The culture of the school and the problem of change* (2nd ed.). Boston: Allyn and Bacon.

Schaps, E. (2003, March). Creating a school community. *Educational Leadership, 60*(6), 31–33.

Schein, E. (1974). Organizational socialization and the profession of management. In D. Kolb, I. Rubin, & J. McIntyre (Eds.), *Organizational psychology* (pp. 1–26). Englewood Cliffs, NJ: Prentice-Hall.

Schlechty, P. (2001). *Shaking up the schoolhouse: How to support and sustain educational innovation.* San Francisco: Jossey-Bass.

Shakeshaft, C. (1995). The cup half full: A gender critique of the knowledge base in educational administration. In R. Donmoyer, M. Imber, & J. Scheurich (Eds.), *The knowledge base in educational administration* (139–157). Albany, NY: State University of New York Press.

Shoop, R., & Dunklee (2002, December). Risk management. *Principal Leadership, 3*(4), 28–32.

Snowden, P., & Gorton, R. (2002). *School leadership and administration* (6th ed.). New York: McGraw-Hill.

Soder, R. (2001). *The language of leadership.* San Francisco: Jossey-Bass.

Solomon, D., Baltistich, V., Watson, M., Schaps, E., & Lewis, C. (2000). A six district study of educational change: Direct and mediated effects of the child development project. *Social Psychology of Education, 4,* 3–51.

Sparks, D. (2002, Winter). In search of heroes. *Journal of Staff Development, 23*(1) 49–50.

Spring, J. (2001). *The American school: 1642–2000.* New York: McGraw-Hill.

Stronge, J. (2002). *Qualities of effective teachers.* Alexandria, VA: ASCD.

Sylwester, R. (1995). *A celebration of neurons: An educator's guide to the brain.* Alexandria, VA: ASCD.

U.S. Department of Education. (2002). *Developing the effective principal.* Gaithersburg, MD: Aspen Publishers.

Viadero, D. (2003, January, 15). Tormentors. *Education Week,* 24–27.

Warner, C. (2000). *Promoting your school: Going beyond P. R.* (2nd ed.). Thousand Oaks, CA: Corwin Press.

Wayne, L., & Kaufman, L. (September 16, 2001). Leadership, put to a new test. *The New York Times (Money & Business Section 3),* 1, 4.

Weissberg, R., Resnik, H., Payton, J., & Utne O'Brien, M. (2003, March). Evaluating social and emotional learning programs. *Educational Leadership, 60*(6), 46–50.

Wiggins, G., & McTighe, J. (1998). *Understanding by design.* Alexandra, VA: ASCD.

Wolfe, P. (2001). *Brain matters: Translating research into classroom practice.* Alexandria, VA: ASCD.

Wurtman, J. (1986). *Managing your mind and mood through food.* New York: Harper & Row.

Young, M., Petersen, G., & Short, P. (2002). The complexity of substantive reform: A call for interdependence among key stakeholders. *Educational Administration Quarterly, 38*(2), 137–175.

Zemelman, S., Daniels, H., & Hyde, A. (1998). *Best practice.* Portsmouth, NH: Heinemann.

Zirkel, P. (December, 2001– January, 2002). Decisions that have shaped U. S. education. *Educational Leadership, 59*(4), 6–12.

Index

Page numbers followed by an *f* indicate reference to a figure.

About the Authors

Pam Robbins is an independent consultant who works with school systems, universities, professional organizations, and corporate clients across the United States and in Europe, Great Britain, South America, and the Far East. Her professional background includes work as a special and regular education teacher, a high school basketball coach, Director of Staff Development and Special Projects for Napa County Office of Education, and Director of Training for the North Bay California School Leadership Academy. She has designed and delivered training for leadership academies throughout the United States and internationally for the Department of Defense Education Equity Division. She has also presented at ASCD's Professional Development Institutes. Her publications include *How to Develop and Implement a Peer Coaching Program* (ASCD, 1991), *A Professional Inquiry Kit on Emotional Intelligence* (with Jane Scott; ASCD, 1997), *The Principal's Companion* (with Harvey Alvy; 2nd edition, 2003), *If I Only Knew* (with Harvey Alvy; 1998), and *Thinking Inside the Block Schedule* (with Gayle Gregory and Lynne Herndon; 2000).

Robbins earned her doctorate in Educational Administration from the University of California, Berkeley, where she focused on the development of professional learning communities. Currently, she conducts workshops on the topics of leadership, supervision, school culture, professional learning communities, the brain research and implications for quality teaching, mentoring, peer coaching, and presentation skills.

She can be reached at 1251 Windsor Lane, Mt. Crawford, VA 22841; by phone: (540) 828-0107; by fax: (540) 828-2326; by e-mail: probbins@shentel.net; or at her Web site: http://user.shentel.net/probbins.

Harvey Alvy's teaching career began as an inner-city elementary school teacher in 1968. He later taught in middle and high schools, and his experience in multicultural, international schools is extensive. His international experiences have taken him to the American School in Kinshasa, Zaire; the American International School in Israel;  the American Embassy School in New Delhi, India; and Singapore American School. Alvy also has served in the principalship for more than a decade in both elementary and secondary schools. In 1991, the National Association of Elementary School Principals selected him as a National Distinguished Principal for American Overseas Schools. Alvy is a founding member of the Principals' Training Center for International Schools.

In 1983, Harvey earned his doctorate in Educational Administration from the University of Montana, focusing on the problems of new principals. He has conducted seminars, workshops, and presentations, both nationally and internationally, on the newcomer to the principalship, supervision and evaluation, ethical leadership, curriculum alignment, enhancing teacher growth, assisting new teachers, characteristics of great teachers, and shaping school cultures. With Pam Robbins, he cowrote *The Principal's Companion* (2nd edition, 2003) and *If I Only Knew...Success Strategies for Navigating the Principalship* (1998).

Harvey is a professor at Eastern Washington University specializing in leadership and foundations. He can be reached at 312 Williamson Hall, Department of Education, Eastern Washington University, Cheney, WA 99004; by phone: (509) 359-6093; or by e-mail: harvey.alvy@mail.ewu.edu.

Related ASCD Resources: Principals

At the time of publication, the following ASCD resources were available; for the most up-to-date information about ASCD resources, go to www.ascd.org. ASCD stock numbers are noted in parentheses.

Audiotapes

First-Year Principals: Support Them or Watch Them Struggle by Ronnie Williams and Thomas Wilson (#203166) **Also on CD!**

Instructional Leadership: A Catalyst to Student Success by Karen Dyer (#203339) **Also on CD!**

Mentoring the Assistant Principal by Pam Robbins (2 audiotapes) (#203078)

The Principal's Role in Building a Professional Learning Community by Richard DuFour (#200259)

Multimedia

Guide for Instructional Leaders, Guide 1: An ASCD Action Tool by Roland Barth, Bobb Darnell, Laura Lipton, and Bruce Wellman (#702110)

Guide for Instructional Leaders, Guide 2: An ASCD Action Tool by Grant Wiggins, John L. Brown, and Ken O'Connor (#703105)

Networks

Visit the ASCD Web site (www.ascd.org) and search for "networks" to find information.

Online Resources

Visit ASCD's Web site (www.ascd.org) for professional development opportunities, including *Ask Now, Not Later: How to Evaluate Professional Development* and *Effective Leadership, (for a small fee; password protected)*.

Print Products

Educational Leadership "Beyond Instructional Leadership" (May 2002) (#102278)

Finding Your Leadership Style: A Guide for Educators by Jeffrey Glanz (#102115)

The First Amendment in Schools by C. Haynes, S. Chaltain, and others (#103054) **NEW!**

School Money Matters: A Handbook for Principals (with CD-ROM) by Davida W. Mutter and Pam J. Parker (#103057) **NEW!**

Staffing the Principalship: Finding, Coaching, and Mentoring School Leaders by Suzette Lovely (#104010) **NEW!**

Videos

The Principal Series Tapes 1–7 (with 2 facilitator's guides) Educational consultants: Richard DuFour and Karen Dyer (#499242)

For more information, visit us on the World Wide Web (http://www. ascd. org), send an e-mail message to member@ascd.org, call the ASCD Service Center (1-800-933-ASCD or 703-578-9600, then press 2), send a fax to 703-575-5400, or write to Information Services, ASCD, 1703 N. Beauregard St., Alexandria, VA 22311-1714 USA.

DATE DUE

1/2/07			
JUN 0 4 2008			
GAYLORD			PRINTED IN U.S.A.